COMMONWEALTH

vs.

SACCO

and

VANZETTI

Edited by

ROBERT P. WEEKS
University of Michigan

Englewood Cliffs, N.J.
PRENTICE-HALL, INC.

FIRST PRINTING .... MARCH, 1958
SECOND PRINTING .... JANUARY, 1959
THIRD PRINTING .... JUNE, 1959

PRINTED IN THE UNITED STATES OF AMERICA

15281

FOREWORD

More has been written about the Sacco-Vanzetti case than any other criminal case in the history of the United States. It has been described, analyzed, and argued not only in English but in Italian, French, German, Spanish, Russian, and Dutch. Probably the chief reason for its strong and universal appeal is that it raised so many doubts, many of which have not yet been, and probably never will be, resolved. Why were these two conscientious objectors carrying revolvers at the time of their arrest? Why did they tell numerous lies to arresting officers? If these two frugal, hardworking Italian immigrants stole a $16,000 payroll, why was there no evidence of the money when they were arrested three weeks later? Which experts are we to believe: those who swore Sacco's .32 Colt fired the bullet found in the body of the dead guard, or those who swore it did not? Which witnesses are we to believe: those who swore they saw the two men taking part in the holdup, or those who swore they saw them many miles away while the holdup was taking place? The Sacco-Vanzetti case was not a simple miscarriage of justice. If the conviction of the fish peddler and the shoemaker for a 1920 holdup murder was the result of a frame-up, which is the opinion of many responsible laymen and legal experts, it was a highly subtle, complex, far-reaching frame-up that wove together factory hands, policemen, and the presidents of Harvard and M.I.T.

A second reason for this case's wide appeal was the defendants themselves. To millions, Sacco and Vanzetti, irrespective of their being anarchists, draft dodgers, and convicted murderers, were saintly, dignified men—martyrs to social prejudice. Vanzetti in particular became a hero to a whole generation of liberal intellectuals, who memorized phrases from his unidiomatic but powerful speeches and letters. And to millions of others the two men just as dramatically embodied all that threatened the American way of life; to them the two immigrants were symbols of opposition to God, country, and property.

A third source of interest in the case is somewhat less partisan. Lawyers have been drawn to the lengthy record of the case as a source of sustained and searching insight into the operation of our system of securing justice. The more than 6,000-page record of the Sacco-Vanzetti case raises with particular force such questions as: "Is our adversary system of justice (the arrangement of pitting the prosecutor against the defense counsel with the judge sitting as umpire) a fair system?" "Do we give a convicted person adequate opportunity to appeal for a new trial?" "Is the testimony of experts handled wisely in our courts?" "Are there adequate safeguards against judges' abuse of their power?"

The millions of words written about the Sacco-Vanzetti case in editorials, speeches, news stories, handbills, poems, plays, and novels, and articles in periodicals as varied as *The Harvard Law Review* and *True Detective Mysteries*, all testify to the remarkable strength and universality of its appeal, but they should not be allowed to eclipse the case itself—the jolting stimulus that provoked this amazing reaction. Some outstanding specimens of this reaction appear in the latter pages of this book, but most of the material assembled here is from the official record of the trial.

The first chapter, "Setting the Stage: 1919-1920," may seem inconsistent with the intention to focus on the case itself, for it includes newspaper articles that appeared before the trial began. These are in a real sense part of the case, however, for Sacco and Vanzetti were tried at a time in our national history when fear of radicals, especially those of foreign birth, was intense. The newspaper materials are a primary record of these fears and as such are useful in weighing the argument of the defense that the "consciousness of guilt" displayed by the defendants at the time of their arrest resulted not from their having committed murder but from their being active radicals.

In the succeeding chapters, the greater part of the material is excerpted from the official record of the trial, *The Sacco-Vanzetti Case: Transcript of the Record of the Trial of Nicola Sacco and Bartolomeo Vanzetti in the Courts of Massachusetts and Subsequent Proceedings* (New York: Holt, 1928-29). The publication of the transcript was sponsored by a group of ten prominent men, including Elihu Root, John W. Davis, and John D. Rockefeller, Jr., who donated sets of the six volumes to the chief libraries of the country. The limited availability of these volumes and their great bulk (they average 1,000 pages each) were regarded as sufficient justification to create a shorter, more accessible version of the trial record. But this book attempts to be more than that. In addition to the materials in Chapter 1, there are other items which are not a part of the official record but are contemporaneous with it and add to its meaning. These include letters written from jail by Sacco and Vanzetti, as well as journalistic and literary responses to the case.

Although this collection is intended to combine a close, firsthand view of the Sacco-Vanzetti case with a coverage of all its major phases, it is in no sense complete. One of its largest omissions is the so-called Bridgewater case involving Vanzetti. After his arrest with Sacco, but before he and Sacco were indicted, Vanzetti was indicted, tried, and convicted of taking part in an attempted payroll robbery in Bridgewater, Mass., on Dec. 24, 1919. The prosecutor and judge were the same as in the later trial at Dedham. Although the Bridgewater trial obviously has some bearing on the Dedham trial, it was felt that its omission would not significantly alter one's understanding or judgment of the trial of both men at Dedham.

Because the pagination of the *Transcript of the Record* is consecutive, references to it in this book give the number of the page but not the number of the volume. To find volume numbers, the following list can be used: (The volume number is followed by the first page in that volume.) I, 1; II, 1093; III, 2267; IV, 3479; V, 4360. Volume VI, a supplement dealing with the Bridgewater case, has independent pagination.

To give this collection of source materials some coherence, I have in many instances filled in the gap between two selections with a brief explanatory note. Many of these notes account for the time intervening between selections or provide facts that make the selection that follows more meaningful. In addition, all such notes contain full bibliographical data on the item they introduce. To keep these notes distinctly apart from the primary materials, they have been set in smaller type, and they begin and end with a rule. Although these notes are secondary sources, students may find it useful to cite them in their writing on the case.

The choice of the selections that make up this collection is, of course, mine. While reading and re-reading the 6,000-page *Transcript of the Record*, I pieced together those segments of it that I thought gave the most responsible and readable account of the trial and subsequent legal proceedings. As I went through the trial record, I read the newspaper and magazine coverage of it from 1920 to 1927 in a variety of periodicals including *The New York Times*, *The Boston Evening Transcript*, *The New York Daily Worker*, *The Literary Digest*, *Time*, *The New Republic*, and *The Nation*. From these sources I selected a few of the articles that I felt were most illuminating, most provocative—or both. Although space prevented my making much use of literary materials, I found that the plays and novels in particular provided a valuable insight into the case.

In making my selections from the *Transcript of the Record*, and from the books, pamphlets, and periodical materials that I consulted, I was greatly helped by two superb studies of the case: Osmond K. Fraenkel's *The Sacco Vanzetti Case* and G. Louis Joughin's and Edmund M. Morgan's *The Legacy of Sacco and Vanzetti*. I am indebted also to John Dos Passos who brought certain useful materials to my attention. To Professor Henry W. Sams of the University of Chicago I owe a double debt. Certain pages of his *New Problems in Reading and Writing* introduced me to the controlled materials method of teaching the research paper. I am also indebted to him, and to Ruth Schelkun and my wife, Frances Weeks, for reading and commenting on the manuscript. Finally, I am grateful to Donald R. Hammonds of Prentice-Hall, Inc., for his encouragement and advice from the conception of the book to its publication.

ROBERT P. WEEKS

CONTENTS

CHRONOLOGY

1920

April 15	Parmenter and Berardelli murdered at So. Braintree
April 25	Vanzetti goes to New York City
April 29	Vanzetti returns
May 2	Boston meeting attended by Sacco and Vanzetti
May 3	Andrea Salsedo falls to his death in New York
May 5	Sacco, Vanzetti, Boda, and Orciana visit Johnson house; later Sacco and Vanzetti arrested
May 6	District Attorney Katzmann interviews Sacco and Vanzetti
June 11 to August 16	Indictment, trial, conviction, and sentencing of Vanzetti for Dec. 24, 1919, attempted holdup in Bridgewater
September 11	Sacco and Vanzetti indicted for So. Braintree murders

1921

May 31 to July 14	Trial of Sacco and Vanzetti at Dedham
July 14	Sacco and Vanzetti found guilty of 1st degree murder
November 5	Motion for new trial on the weight of the evidence
November 8	1st Supplementary motion (Ripley) filed
December 24	Motion for new trial on weight of evidence denied

1922

May 4	2d Supplementary motion (Gould) filed

1923

October 1	Supplement to 1st motion (Daly) filed
November 5	5th Supplementary motion (Proctor) filed

1924

October 1	Judge Thayer denies all motions

1925

November 18	Medeiros sends confession to Sacco in Dedham jail

1926

May 12	Supreme Judicial Court of Massachusetts affirms conviction of Sacco and Vanzetti and denial of 1st, 2d, and 5th Supplementary motions
May 26	7th Supplementary motion (Medeiros) filed
October 23	Judge Thayer denies Medeiros motion

1927

April 5	Supreme Judicial Court affirms denial of Medeiros motion
April 9	Judge Thayer sentences Sacco and Vanzetti to death
May 3	Sacco and Vanzetti petition Gov. Fuller for clemency
June 1	Gov. Fuller appoints Advisory Committee
August 3	Gov. Fuller denies clemency
August 6	Motion for new trial based on judge's prejudice filed
August 8	Judge Thayer denies motion
August 10	Justice Holmes of U.S. Supreme Court denies petition for writ of *habeas corpus*
August 20	Justice Holmes denies petition for writ of *certiorari*
August 22	Justice Stone of U.S. Supreme Court denies petition for writ of *certiorari*
August 23	Sacco and Vanzetti executed

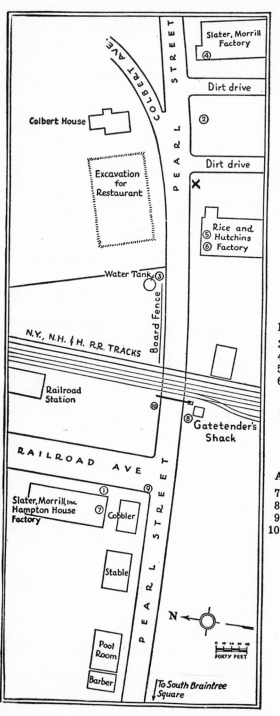

THE NEIGHBORHOOD
OF THE CRIME

BEFORE THE SHOOTING:

1. Neal
2. Andrews
   Campbell

DURING THE SHOOTING:

3. Bostock
4. Carter
5. Pelser
6. Liscomb

AFTER THE SHOOTING:

7. Splaine
8. Levangie
9. Burke
10. Gould

1

SETTING THE STAGE: 1919–1921

Sources used in this chapter: *The New York Times, The Boston Evening Transcript, The Christian Science Monitor,* and *The Federal Reporter.*

————IN 1919 Attorney General A. Mitchell Palmer warned that there were 60,000 dangerous alien radicals in the United States seeking to bring the Red revolution to America by bombs, bullets, and other, less violent, means of subversion. For evidence Palmer could point to the scores of bombs mailed in April of that year to judges, cabinet members and other public officials; or to the midnight bombings on June 3, 1919, of government officials' homes in eight cities, including Palmer's own house in Washington.

Unable to track down a single person responsible for the bombs, the Justice Department laid plans for a nation-wide raid in which federal agents assisted by local police would in one night round up thousands of what were variously described as "communists," "anarchists," "Bolsheviki," "reds," or simply "radicals." After several small-scale practice raids, the time finally agreed on was the night of January 2, 1920. Justice Department undercover agents in the Communist Party of America, the Communist Labor Party, the Socialist Party, and other leftist organizations succeeded in scheduling meetings of those organizations for the night of January 2. That night in 33 cities and towns across the country, police swept down on meetings in homes, offices, lodge halls, union headquarters, and churches to gather in approximately 3,000 men and women, most of them aliens, believed to be guilty of trying to overthrow the United States government.

This raid and the smaller ones that came before and after it were praised by some for making America safe for Americans and damned by others as hysterical and undemocratic. The raids went on for nearly a year; from July, 1919, to June, 1920, warrants were issued for 6,000 alien radicals, 4,000 were arrested but fewer than 1,000 were deported.[1]

[1] Louis F. Post, *The Deportations Delirium of Nineteen-Twenty* (Chicago, 1923), p. 167.

1

SETTING THE STAGE

On April 15, 1920, while the "deportations delirium" still raged, five men staged a brutal payroll robbery in South Braintree, Mass. Seemingly, the robbery had no connection with alien radicals. A paymaster and his guard were shot down in the street and robbed of nearly $16,000 by bandits who fled in a large touring car. However, because the bandits were described as "foreign looking," all garage proprietors in the metropolitan area south of Boston were asked to notify police if any foreigners tried to obtain an automobile, especially if their conduct was suspicious. One night three weeks after the holdup, Nicola Sacco and Bartolomeo Vanzetti with two Italian friends, Mike Boda and Ricardo Orciana, appeared at the Bridgewater home of garage owner Simon Johnson. They wanted Boda's 1914 Overland, which had been stored in Johnson's garage. Mrs. Johnson, her suspicions aroused, went to a neighbor's house and telephoned the police that some foreigners were at her house trying to get a car. Shortly afterward Sacco and Vanzetti were arrested.

Both men carried revolvers at the time of their arrest and lied to police about various matters including their activities on the night of their arrest. Five months later the men were indicted for the Braintree slaying. During the trial, counsel for the defense suggested that Sacco and Vanzetti had been indicted not because they were robbers or murderers but because they were foreigners and radicals. This claim was made more insistently by the men and their lawyers during the six years in which they sought a new trial. The district attorney repeatedly denied that radicalism had anything to do with the arrest, indictment, or conviction of Sacco and Vanzetti. The jury apparently agreed. The judge said after the trial that Sacco and Vanzetti had been convicted because the lies they told shortly after their arrest, along with certain other acts, demonstrated consciousness of guilt.

Did Sacco and Vanzetti show consciousness of guilt after their arrest because of their participation in the South Braintree crime or because they knew they were guilty of being radicals and draft dodgers? In other words, did they lie to avoid the penalty for murder, or to protect their friends and themselves from the mistreatment and deportation they expected to receive as anarchists and slackers?

To answer such questions is at best extremely difficult. But it is nearly impossible to frame a convincing answer to them, no matter which side one is on, without some understanding of the public opinion toward alien radicals and the official treatment of them by police, federal officials, and the courts during the year or so prior to the arrest of Sacco and Vanzetti. The materials in this chapter were selected to contribute to this understanding.

"All the News That's Fit to Print."

The New York Times.

THE WEATHER

VOL. LXVIII...NO. 22,410. **** NEW YORK, TUESDAY, JUNE 3, 1919. TWENTY-EIGHT PAGES. TWO CENTS

MIDNIGHT BOMBS FOR OFFICIALS IN 8 CITIES;
BOMBERS DIE AT ATTORNEY GENERAL'S HOUSE;
TWO VICTIMS AT JUDGE NOTT'S HOUSE HERE;
BOMBS IN BOSTON, CLEVELAND, PITTSBURGH

WRECK JUDGE NOTT'S HOME

Man and Woman Killed May Have Been Bomb Setters.

MRS. NOTT IN THE HOUSE

She and Caretaker's Family Escape, Though Front of Building Was Shattered.

JUDGE NOTT IN THE COUNTRY

Police Rush Guards to Homes of Officials and Judges Throughout the City.

ATTACKS IN 6 OTHER CITIES

House of Boston Justice Who Sentenced Reds Is Shattered.

BOMB TO PITTSBURGH JUDGE

Cleveland Mayor's House Damaged—Attempt at Philadelphia Church.

PATERSON SCENE OF ATTACK

House of a Legislator in the Bay State is Badly Wrecked.

TWO BOMBS EXPLODED IN PHILADELPHIA

Attempts to Destroy Catholic Church and Residence in Different Sections.

LEGISLATOR'S HOME DAMAGED BY BOMB

EXPLOSION AT HOME OF CLEVELAND MAYOR

—Police Report Nobody Was Injured

Senator King Demands Removal of F. C. Howe for Having Presided at Soviet Meeting

PALMER AND FAMILY SAFE

On Second Floor When Explosion Wrecked Lower Part of House.

TWO MEN BLOWN TO BITS

Parts of Bodies of Bombers or Passersby Projected Through Windows Across Street.

RED LITERATURE FOUND

Defiance of Authority and Acclaim of the Social Revolution Voiced.

Attorney General A. Mitchell Palmer, Whose House in Washington Was Bombed Last Night.

THE BOMB CONSPIRATORS.

Has the gift of skill and genius in ferreting out criminals been denied to our present-day detectives? It is astonishing that they should fail to identify and apprehend the criminals who have attempted so many assassinations by bombs, when the conspiracy is so widespread, obviously involving so many persons, and when clues appear to be so abundant. Five weeks ago a large number of packages containing explosives were deposited in the Post Office in this city for transmission through the mails to Judges, public officials, and other persons who had incurred the hostility of the conspirators.

  • • •

    So far as is known, none of the conspirators engaged in that early attempt is known to the authorities.

Other assassinations through the use of violent explosives were attempted on Monday night. Again the conspiracy was widespread, for bombs were placed in eight cities, including New York and Washington. The attempt was even more daring than the first, and again the victims selected were for the most part officials who have been identified with proceedings undertaken to bring to account violent agitators and enemies of the Government. It was to be expected that the conspirators would repeat their attempt. Certainty of detection and punishment is the greatest deterrent of crime. In their case this deterrent was quite inoperative. Weeks had passed, all efforts to seek them out and bring them to account had failed; it was natural that they should be emboldened to further bloody endeavors by their success in eluding detection. In their latest plot they attempted to take the life of Attorney General PALMER. When the head of the Department of Justice of the United States is singled out for assassination, it is time for the Federal Government to employ every resource at its command to find out who these venomous miscreants are, to trace them to their hiding places, to destroy them. If the Secret Service men of the Post Office Department, if the police and detectives of the cities where these outrages have been committed, have to confess their inability to run down the authors of them, the effect of their failure upon the public mind will be appalling.

There is public disquietude already, and even alarm, at the large latitude and freedom allowed to Bolshevist and I. W. W. agitators and their aiders and abettors. They have been allowed to preach their doctrines openly. In various parts of the country they have instigated strikes and labor disorders. In speech and in writing, they are trying to persuade those who will listen to them to hate the Government and its flag, to seek the overthrow of the one and to insult the other. They openly assail the Government, they preach the destruction of property and its owners, they demand revolution and the establishment of a rule of their own kind, with such certain consequences as we see in Russia. The sober common sense and solid law-abiding character of the American people reject these disciples of destruction and all their doctrines, but there are certain publications issued in this and other cities of the country by persons presumed to be intelligent which give aid and encouragement to the depraved Bolshevist element by continual praise of their works, by dissemination and approval of their doctrines, and by heated protests against attempts by law or its enforcement to restrain their poisonous activities.

FREE SPEECH DEFENDED

Red Menace Said to Be Greatly Exaggerated

Present Hysteria Called Menace to Democracy

By the Harvard Liberal Club's Speakers

Judge Anderson Denounces Pseudo-Patriots

That there is greater danger to democracy in the United States from the attempts to limit the constitutional right of free speech than there is from the plots of the Reds was the theme upon which numerous speakers enlarged at the meeting of the Harvard Liberal Club at the Boston City Club last evening. Judge George W. Anderson compared the present mental condition of a part of the public regarding Red plots with that which existed at the time of the great agitation over German propaganda and stated that 99 per cent of the so-called German plots did not exist.

Justice Oliver Wendell Holmes of the United States Supreme Court sent a letter in which he said:

"For obvious reasons I should not care to speak upon your subject except as from time to time I have to. I see no impropriety, however, in suggesting the isolated reflection that with effervescing opinions, as with the not yet forgotten champagnes, the quickest way to let them get flat is to let them get exposed to the air."

Joseph Lee presided and in addition to Judge Anderson the speakers were Professor Zachariah Chafee, Jr., of Harvard Law School, Judge Julian Mack of Chicago, Attorney General J. Weston Allen, Dr. Samuel McChord Crothers of Cambridge, J. Randolph Coolidge, Jr., and John Maguire.

Joseph Lee on Free Speech

Joseph Lee, '83, who presided, said in part: "Everybody wants free speech; everybody wants law and order. The question is just where the two conflict and what is the principle which unites them

and by which we draw the line. Democracy is government by public opinion. Free speech is the soil in which public opinion grows. To prevent free speech is to kill democracy, and to leave anarchy or tyranny as the alternative. Free speech must be limited at the point where it interferes with government. This is not the point where it becomes unpopular or tends to bad results. It is not the point where it advocates the overthrow of popular government. It is not even the point where it advocates revolution. Revolution in a democracy is part of the governmental process. To upset a free government is like trying to upset a sphere. Where the right to free speech ceases is the point where it begins to prevent government by free speech from being carried out."

Professor Chafee outlined the difficulty of drawing the line between permissible and unpermissible speech. "The whole essence of American Government," he said, "is that the people elect their rulers, that the people are the masters and the rulers their servants, and that the masters should be able to criticise their servants. The American policy is not to interfere with words until they have broken out or are on the point of breaking out into unlawful action. Is it wise to exclude aliens in view of the reputation of our country as an asylum for the oppressed? Look at it as a matter of international policy. We first try to settle Russia by sending in Admiral Kolchak; now we are trying to settle it by sending Emma Goldman. Are we likely to decrease our discontent by dragging men away from their families? How many of the relatives and friends of these men are likely to remain loyal to our Government?"

Mr. Coolidge blamed some of the newspapers for failure to supply the needed facts and also for failure to keep adequately before the public the distress which exists in the European countries.

Judge Anderson's Protest

"It is fit and proper time for the Harvard Liberal Club—and for liberal organizations of every kind—to consider and discuss freedom of speech and the other great guarantees of liberty," said Judge Anderson. "It is depressing—almost appalling—fact that, as an aftermath of our war to make the world safe for democracy,' real democracy now seems unsafe in America. It is increasingly clear that America's loss of valuable lives and of money in this war was as nothing compared to her loss of moral, social and political values.

NATION-WIDE PLOT TO KILL HIGH OFFICIALS ON RED MAY DAY REVEALED BY PALMER; PLOTTERS ACTING WITH RADICALS ABROAD

MEN ON DEATH LIST WARNED

Federal and State Authorities Are Protecting Them.

GENERAL STRIKE PROPOSED

Workers in Basic Industries Incited to Uprising by Red Emissaries.

PART OF WORLDWIDE PLAN

Communists, Communist Laborites and I. W. W. Said by Attorney General to be in Plot.

Special to The New York Times.

WASHINGTON, April 29.—Many Federal and State officials and other prominent figures in national life have been marked by the Reds for assassination on May Day, according to information gathered by Department of Justice agents, Attorney General Palmer announced this afternoon.

The assassination plot, said the Attorney General, was a part of a general radical demonstration set for May 1.

"A warning has been issued by the department to all those whose names are included in the list of marked men, and the department has taken steps to furnish protection," said Mr. Palmer. "I am hopeful that these measures will be effective."

The Attorney General would not reveal the list of those marked for assassination. He stated, however, that the department had been conferring with the officials of different States to devise adequate safeguards for the men and property threatened.

Members of the Communist Party, the Communist Labor Party and the I. W. W. are said to be planning a May Day uprising in their efforts to force recognition of the Russian Soviet by this Government and the establishment of friendly relations with Lenin and Trotzky. Russian and German agents are alleged to be encouraging the Reds and doing their best to foment trouble among American workingmen.

Plot Nation-Wide.

"The information that comes to us concerning the proposed assassinations is reported from a considerable portion of the country, indicating that the plot is nation-wide," said the Attorney General. "Both as to this and to the proposed general strike, we rely in great measure on wide publicity to frustrate the plans of the plotters, just as such publicity blocked the plans for the general strike called by the agitators for July 4, 1919.

"Red agents were obviously trying to organize the workers in the United States as closely as they appeared to have done in France for the May Day strike" the Attorney General said.

"I feel, however," said he, "that our action in arresting their leaders and deporting numbers of the alien agitators has upset their program to a great extent."

•   •   •

COOLIDGE WARNS REDS

Governor Says Law Will Prevail in Massachusetts

State to Keep Order, No Matter What Happens

Police and Guards Now Are All Ready

Machine Guns on Trucks for Street Work

Special Protection for State House and Jail

Nothing Definite on "Uprising" Here

In Mill Centres Strikes Called For

Tomorrow's programme is not definite. The word "uprising" has been used by the radical elements to describe what in their opinion ought to happen, and strikes have been advocated in numerous circles, but except in certain instances those who hope to shape the May-Day activities of the restlessess have given no specific directions to the "masses." The workman has been told that he should "rise" tomorrow; but he does not know who is to "rise" with him. He has been told to strike, but whether to strike at law and order or merely quit work is a matter of uncertainty with him. He has been keyed up to a nervous tension by the mass of literature thrust into his hands, by the speeches he has heard recently in the labor meetings, and he is depending upon the spontaneous psychology of the day to govern his action.

Whatever happens tomorrow Boston will have in common with the rest of the world, for it has been proclaimed an International Labor Day, but there is likely to be less of it in Massachusetts than elsewhere. Both the State and the city of Boston are prepared to preserve law and order.

Governor Coolidge issued a statement this noon relative to the situation. The Boston police department has made provisions to cope with developments, and the Federal Government has armed itself for eventualities.

Menace Now Harmless

The statement from the governor is as follows:

* * *

"Threats are of no consequence. The life of one man, even though he hold an important official position, is not of supreme consequence. The orderly execution of the law will go on so long as I have any authority over it, and it has been amply demonstrated that Massachusetts will provide for its continuance whatever contingency may arise.

* * *

Extraordinary precautions are being taken by Sheriff Keliher of Suffolk County to protect the court house in Pemberton square and the county jail on Charles street from any possible May Day attack. Believing thousands of supporters of the Soviet form of government will come to Boston tomorrow, Sheriff Keliher has arranged for extra and heavily armed guards for the Charles Street Jail and has ordered all deputy sheriffs and court officers and plain-clothes guards to be on hand at 8.30 tomorrow to protect the court house, which closes early, it being Saturday, when only a few courts sit.

Machine-Guns A-Plenty

Seven machine guns mounted in automobiles will be stationed in various districts of Boston and each police division will have a quota of police officers trained in the use of that weapon and the Winchester riot guns. The special detail for a riot guard numbers 125 policemen.

Superintendent of Police Michael H. Crowley stated that the department does not expect any violence on the part of the Communists, but will be prepared for any emergency.

Judge Hayden's house will be given special protection, as Judge Hayden presided over the trial of the rioters who were arrested in the May Day disturbances last year, as the result of which his house was bombed.

One of the assurances of protection for the general public is that the State Guard will be mustered in the various State armories tomorrow, merely to drill if the day is calm, but ready for action if action is called for.

The Boston Evening Transcript, April 30, 1920, pp. 1-2.

RED'S DEATH PLUNGE, 14 STORIES, BARES LONG BOMB TRAIL

Andrea Salsedo, Informer June Plots, Dashes Through Window.

America, President Grant, and Fitzpatrick Reported Ready to Follow Wake of "Ark."

"REVOLUTION" IS SMASHED

---

500 REDS AT ELLIS ISLAND

Prisoners Taken in Raids Hurried to This Port for Deportation

---

MAY GET AWAY THIS WEEK

BOLSHEVIKI ACTIVE IN GREAT BRITAIN

Authorities Admit a Widely Organized Campaign Is On, but Await Overt Acts.

SOVIETS START IN GLASGOW

BOSTON IS CALM

May Day Tendencies of the Radical Silenced

- - -

rderly Labor Meetings and Quiet Streets

---

spicuous Preparedness by the Police

by Plumbers for More Pay In

STILL HUNTING UNCAUGHT REDS

Federal Raiders Will Serve All of the 4,000 Warrants

Peaceful Celebrations All Over the Country As Result of Precautions by the Government

xpectancy to the contrary, May Day was
ithout disturbance of any kind.
here by all

————SEVERAL HUNDRED of the alleged alien radicals arrested in New England during the nation-wide raid on the night of January 2, 1920, were detained in jail on Deer Island in Boston Harbor. Lawyers representing one Colyer and nineteen others jailed there sought to force the Boston Immigration Commissioner, H. J. Skeffington, to release them on writs of *habeas corpus*. Excerpts from the opinion of Federal Judge George W. Anderson, who was petitioned for the writs, appear below. They are taken from the full decision which appears in *Federal Reporter*, 265 Fed. 17.————————

COLYER et al. v. SKEFFINGTON
(District Court, D. Massachusetts, June 23, 1920.)

These are petitions for *habeas corpus* brought by or in behalf of 20 aliens against the Commissioner of Immigration at Boston. [20]

. . . . .

At the opening of the trial the cases were said by counsel on both sides to be, in many aspects, test cases of the legality of an undertaking of the government to deport several thousand aliens alleged to be "members of or affiliated with any organization that entertains a belief in, teaches, or advocates the overthrow by force or violence of the government of the United States. . . ."

Controlling Legal Principles

. . . . .

Aliens have constitutional rights. The Fourth, Fifth, Sixth and Fourteenth Amendments are not limited in their application to citizens. [24] . . . One of the most fundamental of the "body of liberties" guaranteed the inhabitants of the United States by our Constitution is freedom from unreasonable search and seizure, and from arrest without due process. [25]

. . . Conduct of the Raid in New England

. . . . .

I refrain from any extended comment on the lawlessness of these proceedings by our supposedly law-enforcing officials. The documents and acts speak for themselves. It may, however, fitly be observed that a mob is a mob, whether made up of government officials acting under instructions from the Department of Justice, or of criminals, loafers, and the vicious classes.

. . . . .

There were instances of the arrest of women under conditions involving great hardship. For instance, the witness Mrs. Stanislas Vasiliewska, the mother of 3 children, aged 13, 10, and 8, was arrested in a hall in Chelsea, taken in the police patrol wagon with her eldest girl to the police station, and both put with another woman into one cell. About midnight they took her child and sent her home alone to a remote part of the city. Mrs. Vasiliewska was [43] taken the next day to the wharf, where she was confined for about 6 hours in a dirty toilet room. She was then taken to Deer Island, where she was kept 33 days.

The witness Minnie Federman was arrested at her home at 6 o'clock in the morning. Several men, showing her no warrant, entered her room where she was in bed. She was told to get out of bed and dress, which she did in a closet. Then she was taken in a police wagon to the police station, after they had searched her premises for I.W.W. literature. When they found she was a naturalized citizen, she was allowed to go.

.   .   .   .   .

It was under such terrorizing conditions as these that these aliens were subjected to questionnaires, subsequently used as, and generally constituting an important part of, the evidence adduced against them before immigration inspectors.

.   .   .   .   .

Pains were taken to give spectacular publicity to the raid, and to make it appear that there was great and imminent public danger, against which these activities of the Department of Justice were directed. The arrested aliens, in most instances perfectly quiet and harmless working people, many of them not long ago Russian peasants, were handcuffed in pairs, and then, for purposes of transfer on trains and through the streets of Boston, chained together. The northern New Hampshire contingent were first concentrated in jail at Concord, and then brought to Boston in a special car, thus handcuffed and chained together. On detraining at the North Station, the handcuffed and chained aliens were exposed to newspaper photographers and again exposed at the wharf where they took the boat for Deer Island.

.   .   .   .   .

Private rooms were searched in omnibus fashion; trunks, bureaus, suitcases and boxes were broken open; books and papers seized. I doubt whether a single warrant was obtained or applied for. [44]

.   .   .   .   .

At Deer Island the conditions were unfit and chaotic. No adequate preparation had been made to receive and care for so large a number of people. Some of the steam pipes were burst or disconnected. The place was cold; the weather was severe. The cells were not adequately equipped with sanitary appliances. . . . For several days the arrested aliens were held practically incommunicado. . . . Most of this confusion and resultant hardship to the arrested aliens was probably unintentional. . . . Undoubtedly it did have some additional terrorizing effect upon the aliens. Inevitably the atmosphere of lawless disregard of the rights and feelings of these aliens as human beings affected, consciously or unconsciously, the inspectors who shortly began the hearings [to determine the aliens' rights] . . . to stay in this country.

In the early days of Deer Island one alien committed suicide by throwing himself from the 5th floor and dashing out his brains in the corridor below in the presence of other horrified aliens. One man was committed as insane; others were driven nearly, if not quite, to the verge of insanity. [45]

. . . . . .

[*The Decision*]

I find on all the evidence that the records in these cases are not reliable, and that they originated in proceedings which were unfair and therefore lacking in due process of law. . . . There is no evidence warranting a finding that these aliens, if released on reasonable bail . . . would have endangered in any way the public safety. . . . There is no reasonable explanation offered for fixing bail in sums [from $5,000 to $10,000] which must have been expected to be prohibitive. . . . The aliens, when bailed by this court, had already been held as though under sentence for crime for 3 to 4 months.

Even if the arrests had been lawful and the proceedings been regular throughout, it cannot be the law that an alien shall be held beyond a reasonable time for trial and determination of his right either to go free and earn his living in this country, or to be deported. . . . Their detention under all the unprecedented and extraordinary circumstances of this case, I find and rule was illegal, warranting the issuance of the writs . . . [of *habeas corpus*]. [78]

2

THE TRIAL

Sources used in this chapter: *The Sacco-Vanzetti Case: Transcript of the Record of the Trial of Nicola Sacco and Bartolomeo Vanzetti in the Courts of Massachusetts and Subsequent Proceedings, 1920-27, Volumes I & II.*

A. THE CASE FOR THE COMMONWEALTH

FIRST DAY

COMMONWEALTH OF MASSACHUSETTS

NORFOLK, SS.

SUPERIOR COURT
CRIMINAL SESSION
Thayer, J., and a Jury.

COMMONWEALTH
v.
SACCO

COMMONWEALTH
v.
VANZETTI

APPEARANCES:

Frederick G. Katzmann, Esq., District Attorney; Harold P. Williams, Esq., Assistant District Attorney; Wm. F. Kane, Esq., Assistant District Attorney; George E. Adams, Esq., Assistant District Attorney, for the Commonwealth.

Fred H. Moore, Esq., and Wm. J. Callahan, Esq., for the defendant Sacco.

Jeremiah J. McAnarney, Esq., and Thomas F. McAnarney, Esq., for the defendant Vanzetti.

Dedham, Mass., May 31, 1921.

THE CLERK. Mr. Crier, you will make the opening proclamation.
[*The crier makes opening proclamation.*]

THE CLERK. Mr. Crier, make proclamation to all persons summonsed as jurors to answer to their names.

[*The crier makes proclamation to persons summonsed as jurors.*]

THE COURT. Gentlemen, you have been summonsed as jurors. You will kindly give me your attention while I address you concerning the qualification of jurors. . . . [1]

At the outset I should say to you the cases to be tried are indictments between the Commonwealth of Massachusetts and Nicholas [*sic*] Sacco of Stoughton and Bartolomeo Vanzetti of Plymouth. The charges in the indictment allege the killing by them of one Frederick A. Parmenter and Alessandro Berardelli at Braintree, sometime in April, 1920, by the use of a revolver. The penalty upon conviction of this alleged crime is death.

I now beseech you, gentlemen, to follow me with the greatest possible attention in order that each of you may answer certain questions that will be put to you by the Court not only intelligently, but also truthfully and conscientiously. There are five of these questions. . . .

1. Are you related to either party? That is, to either of the defendants, . . . or to either of the deceased . . . ?

2. Have you any interest in the trial or the result of these indictments?

3. Have you expressed or formed any opinion upon the subject matter alleged in either or both of these indictments?

4. Are you sensible of any bias or prejudice therein?

5. Are your opinions of such a character as to preclude you from finding a defendant guilty of a crime punishable by death? [2]

.   .   .   .   .   .

[L]et me impress upon you as deeply as possible the . . . desirability of resting your answer to [question number five] . . . upon the solid foundation of truth rather than a strong desire to escape jury service. . . .

It is not a sufficient excuse that the service is painful, confining and distressing. It is not a sufficient excuse that a juror has business engagements and other duties more profitable and pleasant that he would rather perform, for you must remember the American soldier had other duties he would rather have performed than those that resulted in his giving up his life upon the battlefields of France, but he with undaunted courage and patriotic devotion that brought honor and glory to humanity and the world rendered the service and made the supreme sacrifice. He answered the call of the Commonwealth.

So, gentlemen, I call upon you to render this service here that you have been summonsed to perform with the same spirit of patriotism, courage and devotion to duty as was exhibited by our soldier boys across the seas, and let no juror decline this call of the Commonwealth excepting in such cases that he can swear in fact and in truth, before man and Almighty God, that his conscience will not permit him to find a defendant guilty of a crime punishable by death.

In this age of freedom of thought and of speech an individual is entitled to have his own private views upon all social, religious, political and economic questions, but he should never bring them with him to the jury room, especially when they might operate in the least possible degree to the prejudice of either party. . . . [3]

.   .   .   .   .

What, gentlemen, in conclusion, does the law seek to accomplish by the use of these questions and by the request and suggestions of the Court? It seeks to select 12 jurors who will stand between these parties, the Commonwealth on the one hand and these defendants on the other, with an unyielding impartiality, with absolute fairness and unflinching courage in order that truth and justice shall prevail. . . . [6]

.   .   .   .   .

————BETWEEN May 31 and June 4, 1921, 700 citizens of Norfolk County were summoned for jury duty before a panel of 12 was obtained. In accordance with Massachusetts law, the judge examined each prospective juror and the prosecution and defense had the privilege of challenging the selection of any juror for cause or peremptorily. Nearly 200 were challenged peremptorily and the others were rejected for such causes as having a previous knowledge of the case or having such strong feelings against capital punishment that in either instance they would not have been able, in the judge's opinion, to reach a true verdict according to the evidence. Finally, at 1:35 A.M., June 4, the last juror was accepted and the jury was sworn in.————

THE CLERK. [*To the Jurors*[1]] You each of you solemnly swear that

---

1 Names and occupations of jurors:

Wallace R. Hersey, real estate dealer	Louis McHardy, mill operative
John E. Ganley, grocer	Harry E. King, shoe worker
Frank R. Waugh, machinist	Alfred Atwood, real estate dealer
Frank B. Marden, mason	Frank McNamara, farmer
Walter R. Ripley, stockkeeper	Seward B. Parker, machinist
John F. Dever, salesman	George A. Gerard, photographer

you shall well and truly try and true deliverance make between the Commonwealth and the prisoners at the bar whom you shall have in charge according to your evidence. So help you God! [48]

. . . . .

[June 6, 1921]

MR. KATZMANN. I call your Honor's attention to the fact that as yet there has not been a foreman appointed on the jury.

THE COURT. Oh, pardon me. [*To a juror*] What is your name?

A JUROR. Ripley.

THE CLERK. Mr. Ripley, the Court has appointed you foreman for the trial of this case. . . . Gentlemen of the jury, harken to the indictment found against the prisoners at the bar by the grand inquest for the body of this County: [49]

"COMMONWEALTH OF MASSACHUSETTS

NORFOLK, SS.

At the Superior Court begun and holden at Dedham within and for the County of Norfolk, on the first Monday of September, in the year of our Lord one thousand, nine hundred and twenty, the jurors for the Commonwealth of Massachusetts on their oath present that Nicola Sacco of Stoughton, in the County of Norfolk, and Bartolomeo Vanzetti, of Plymouth, in the County of Plymouth, on the 15th day of April, in the year of our Lord one thousand, nine hundred and twenty, at Braintree, in the County of Norfolk, did assault and beat Frederick A. Parmenter, with intent to murder him by shooting him in the body with a loaded pistol and by such assault, beating and shooting, did murder Frederick A. Parmenter, against the peace of said Common- [52] wealth and contrary to the form of the Statute in such case made and provided.

A true bill,

JOHN B. WHALEN,
Foreman of the Grand Jury.

FREDERICK G. KATZMANN
    District Attorney.
September 11, 1920.

Returned into said Superior Court by the Grand Jurors and ordered to be filed.

Attest, R. B. Worthington, Clerk."

————The indictment for the murder of Berardelli is identical to the one above.————

To these indictments, the prisoners at the bar have pleaded not guilty, and for trial put themselves upon the country, which country you are. You are sworn to try the issue. If the defendants are guilty, you will say so; if they are not guilty, you will say so and no more. Good men and true, stand together and harken to your evidence. [53]

·　·　·　·　·

[*June 7, 1921*]

THE COURT. Perhaps I might as well say now, gentlemen, [that] [58] . . . an opening statement is merely a statement made with a view to explaining to the jury the issues involved, together with the evidence that the counsel making the statements desires to offer and will later offer. An opening statement is never evidence, and as evidence you will never give it any consideration whatsoever. That is true of every statement made by counsel.

·　·　·　·　·

You must judge these cases according to the evidence which comes from the lips of witnesses who take the witness stand and who testify under oath. That is the evidence that you are to determine, and you are to determine nothing else, and you must allow nothing else to have any weight whatsoever with you. . . . [59]

·　·　·　·　·

Opening Statement by Mr. Williams

We have now cleared away the preliminaries of this case and are prepared to introduce real evidence upon which you will base your verdict. . . .

We have had some evidence introduced, and that evidence is the evidence of your senses that you observed yesterday in a tiresome and dusty route. [*The jury, judge, and counsel for the defendants were given an automobile tour of the scene of the crime by the prosecution.*] Whatever you saw yesterday, gentlemen, connected with this case, is evidence for you to consider. . . .

We now come down to the evidence which is to be presented in court and is to be presented by word of mouth. Let me pause a moment here to speak of what is called circumstantial evidence, because I have used the term "word of mouth." . . . It is all, gentlemen, presented to you by word of mouth. It comes directly from the mouths of the witnesses on the stand. The difference between so-called *direct* and *circumstantial* evidence is that in direct evidence the witness testifies directly to what he has seen, the real point at issue. If it is by stabbing he says, "I saw that man stab." The witness to the circumstantial evidence simply testifies to the circumstances, from which circumstances you, as the judges and jurors, draw the inferences which you would naturally draw from those circumstances. [62]

To use the illustration which I have just used of a stabbing, a man may see a shadow on the window or the window pane of a house with an arm raised, the shadow of struggling men. He may go into the room afterwards and see a knife on the floor. He may see the victim lying wounded or dead upon the floor. Those are circumstances which he may testify to, and when he testifies to them on the stand it is for the jury to say what is the natural and reasonable inference to be drawn from those circumstances, and if the inference from the circumstances that have been described naturally and reasonably—and I may say necessarily—follows, you are just as sure of your judgment as to what happened as if the eye witness himself had been in the room.

Now, gentlemen, before we begin on this case, I want you to appreciate one thing. The sole responsibility does not rest on you. . . . We are starting in on the trial of a case where the lives of two men who are now in the court room may be involved. Nothing could more impress us with the seriousness of what we are about to do. And the attorneys for the Government are as acutely conscious of the seriousness of this as you can possibly be. It is their duty to present evidence to you, but no pride of profession, gentlemen, no desire to win a case, I assure you, will influence them in presenting the evidence. They realize to the full what they are doing, and what the evidence which they are responsible for in the way of presentation means, and they share with you the burden of trying the case.

His Honor, likewise, in presiding in this trial, shares that, perhaps doubly so, because if there is a conviction it is upon him to pronounce sentence and [he] shares with you the burden of trying the case. We are all here, gentlemen, with one aim in view and one aim alone, with the utmost seriousness to search for the truth in this case, and if we find it to declare it with the greatest courage which we possess.

And gentlemen, this crime, this alleged crime—because until it is proved it is only alleged—took place, as you have been told before, on the 15th day of April, 1920, at about three o'clock in the afternoon. The place was South Braintree, the southerly part of the town of Braintree in Norfolk County. On that day money had been received by Slater & Morrill, shoe manufacturers, occupying that upper factory near the South Braintree Station, for the purpose of making out their pay roll, and paying their employees.

The money came out by express . . . early in the morning, and was received by the local agent of the American Express at the Station shortly after nine o'clock in the morning. . . . The amount involved was some $15,776. . . . The local express agent, a Mr. Neal, . . . received it at the station and took it across to his office. . . . [63]

Naturally, he was accustomed to watch very closely anybody around the building . . . [H]e noticed a large, black automobile, apparently a seven-seater, standing in front of his door or between his door and the Slater & Morrill door, with its engine running, and he observed a man standing on the sidewalk or near the car, a rather slight man with a light hat, emaciated, yellowish face. . . .

Neal went into his office and changed the money and within a few minutes, perhaps ten or twelve minutes, came out again, with the money for Slater & Morrill. At that time the man was still standing there by the car. . . . The man watched him, and as Neal . . . went into [Slater & Morrill] . . . the man got into the machine. The engine, if you recall, was still running, and drove in a northerly direction. . . . And that was about 9:30.

The money was taken into the Slater & Morrill Company. The pay envelopes were made up by the pay mistress. . . . The exact amount was put into the envelopes, and if I am correct, the moneys so allotted were put into two boxes, perhaps two and one-half feet long, a foot and a half deep, a foot wide, something like that. . . .

The acting paymaster at that time . . . was Frederick A. Parmenter. The man employed to accompany him . . . from factory No. 1 up there by the station down the hill to factory No. 2 . . . was Alessandro Berardelli, a man of Italian descent, and at three o'clock, or about then, Mr. Parmenter and Mr. Berardelli left the Slater & Morrill factory with these boxes to make the payments in the lower factory. They were seen leaving [64] the middle entrance of the Slater & Morrill factory, each with a box filled with the money and the pay envelopes. They were seen to proceed across that square there, across the railroad tracks. . . .

The scene shifts from there, gentlemen, because of the passing out of sight of the witnesses in No. 1, and we slip down to the slope leading down from the railroad crossing down the hill back of Rice & Hutchins to the Slater & Morrill factory. Down there . . . were two men leaning against the fence on the right-hand side of the road. They were two short men, perhaps five feet, six or seven, rather stocky, described as perhaps being 140 and 160, in that vicinity; caps, dark clothes, caps somewhat lighter than their clothes, of apparent Italian lineage.

. . . Parmenter and Berardelli stopped and talked with a friend of theirs just after leaving the railroad crossing and after so talking they proceeded down the hill by the Rice & Hutchins factory, Berardelli apparently a little in advance. They came down to where the two men were, . . . and these two men on the fence stepped out and approached them. There is some testimony that one of the men seized hold of Berardelli, shots were fired by these two men, Berardelli fell wounded, Parmenter ran across the street and fell wounded on the other side of the street. [65]

. . . . .

Berardelli fell mortally wounded and died shortly thereafter. Parmenter died the next day. . . . Berardelli had four bullets in him at the autopsy. Parmenter had two. [66]

. . . . .

As Parmenter was shot, he dropped his box and turned and ran towards the excavation over there. One of the bandits followed him across the street and as he ran shot him in the back. . . . Poor Parmenter fell across the street over by a [67] double-horse team which was backed up into the excavation. Berardelli dropped, as he was shot, in the gutter, on the same side of the street where he had been walking. Ten or twelve or fifteen, or perhaps twenty feet, on the crossing side of the lower telegraph pole in the gutter, and as he fell . . . one of the bandits, a fellow who had lost his cap, a short, swarthy man, with his hair brushed back, slightly thin on the temples, was standing in front of Berardelli with a pistol, and fired two shots at the prostrate man. That man, gentlemen, who shot Berardelli as he was on the ground, is described and identified as Nicola Sacco, the defendant on the left.

While this was going on—you have got six shots in the man. There were presumably more, perhaps seven or eight or nine at that time. While that was going on, this big, black car which Neal alleged he saw early in the morning, was down below the Slater & Morrill factory. . . . As Berardelli fell dead—and he died within a few minutes, —a bloody froth from his mouth,—as he fell there, that car approached driven by this light-haired man with an emaciated face. It was a seven-passenger 1920 Buick with a top, that is, the canvas top up, with the back up and with the curtains up on both sides, or at least mostly on one side.

. . . . .

There were two men in the car, the driver and a man we cannot describe, in the back seat. The car crawled up to the scene of the shooting. The two bandits, the man who had shot Berardelli when he was on the ground and the fellow who chased Parmenter when he was across the street, came back [along with a third bandit], took up the two boxes, and piled them into the car.

. . . [T]here then being five men in the car, it proceeded up the street to the crossing. [68]

As it went up the street a man [Pelser] in the Rice & Hutchins factory . . . got the number 49,783 on back. As they went up the street they noticed that the rear window of the back, that isinglass window, perhaps that long [*indicating*], that wide, and so forth, was out, and a gun or the barrel of a rifle or shotgun protruded from the window in back.

As they went over the crossing the gate-tender [Levangie] was at his post in the little shanty on the other side of that track. The gates were up. He had heard the shooting and at the same time he heard an approaching train. . . . And he started to wind his crank to lower that gate. At that time the car was just entering upon the other side of the crossing, and the men in the car hollered at him and intimidated him so that he did not close the gates, and they proceeded up across the crossing. As they came across he noticed on the front seat an Italian with a moustache, I believe with a slouch hat on, whom he identified as the other defendant, Bartolomeo Vanzetti. . . .

By that time the shots below the crossing had, first, attracted a lot of attention. People had come to the window of Slater & Morrill's factory No. 1, men inside the cobbler's shop on the crossing had come to the door, there were others scattered around the street that had been attracted to the shooting, and as the car came up from the crossing going rather slowly—it had not got under its real headway at that time—a man seated or crouched or standing between the right front seat of that car, leaned out under that flapping curtain . . . in the right-hand side of the car, and shot at the crowd until the slugs in his pistol were exhausted.

. . . [U]p in the corner window of Slater & Morrill's factory . . . —Miss Splaine—looked out of the window right down on that car as it went past and [she] will tell you that that man who was leaning out under the curtain with his revolver raised, with his cap off, and shooting at the crowd along the street, was the defendant Nicola Sacco. . . .

The car, gathering headway, finally, of course, reached the corner of Hancock Street by the drug store, turned down Hancock Street to the left. As they turned down, the occupants of the car scattered rubber-headed tacks along the road, a good many of which were picked up. [69]

. . . . .

We next find them at Matfield Crossing. . . . The crossing-tender [Reed] . . . noticed them coming down the grade there towards the crossing at the same time that a train was approaching, and ran across the crossing with his stop signal, that big signal with the "Stop" on it, this big car and these men in it, and they stopped. He held them there until the train got by. And then the man who was on the front seat and whom he describes as Bartolomeo Van- [70] zetti, said, "What to hell are you holding us up for?" . . . They started across the crossing, he in the meantime going back towards his shanty. When they got to the other side and were just straightening out to proceed, Vanzetti again said, "What in hell are you holding us up for?" And they went off. . . .

. . . . .

The shooting was at about five minutes past three. . . . The Matfield Crossing incident took place around 4:10, and there we leave them for the time being. Meanwhile, back in South Braintree, they were taking care of the unfortunates that had been stricken down. Berardelli was practically dead. . . . He was unconscious. There was some froth coming from his mouth, and he shortly died. . . . Parmenter was still alive. . . . He died at . . . five in the morning of the following day, April 16th, after an operation which removed the bullet which remained in his body.

. . . . .

After the bodies had been removed, or probably before they had been removed, a cap was found on the road beside the body of Berardelli. Some empty shells were found on the road. I believe that is all that was discovered other than the bodies of the victims themselves there at the scene.

Before the shooting had occurred and after Shelley Neal had seen this car in the early morning, that car was not unknown to the citizens of South Braintree. You remember at about 9:30 Neal saw it driving off northerly from in front of his office. Sometime after ten o'clock, perhaps half past ten, it was seen coming up Holbrook Avenue and turning into Hancock Street. . . . And the gentleman who was on the front seat of the car at that time or was in [71] the car and was noted to be in the car by an intelligent and reliable witness [Dolbeare] was the defendant Vanzetti.

Now, where had the car been from the time that Neal saw it roll away from in front of his office at 9:30, . . . to where this witness saw it coming up Holbrook Avenue between 10 and 11? Here is where East Braintree comes into this story. . . . There was a gentleman who took the train at Cohasset on that morning at 9:20, who got into the smoker, and it was the South Shore train that came up from Plymouth. Plymouth being the place where the defendant Vanzetti lives, and carries on spasmodically some sort of a fish business. This gentleman from Cohasset [Faulkner] got into the smoker and sat down in the rear seat, on the rear cross seat on the left-hand side of the smoker, and across from him was a little side seat or a smaller seat in front of the men's toilet.

. . . . .

. . . [A]t East Braintree, . . . [a] gentleman . . . got up to go out, . . . and he was an Italian, he had an Italian look, and he had a moustache. He had an Italian accent. . . .

And the gentleman from Cohasset will come into court and tell you that that man who got off at East Braintree station . . . was the defendant Bartolomeo Vanzetti.

Now, what was the significance of Vanzetti arriving at the East Braintree station from Plymouth . . . on that particular morning? You will recall the relation of East Braintree to the South Braintree route, and you will recall, gentlemen, what I have just told you of the witnesses seeing the car coming back up Holbrook Avenue sometime after ten o'clock with Vanzetti in it.

There were two strangers, not in the car, but apart from the car, in around South Braintree that morning. . . . [72]

. . . [T]hey were seen later in the morning, around 11:30. . . . [T]hat car was placed between . . . the Slater & Morrill factory No. 2 and . . . Rice & Hutchins' factory, headed up the hill, and there were two men at that time working around the car, the pale faced, thin faced, emaciated faced driver, and another man, who was fooling around the car, and you will be told by a witness [Andrews] that that second man who was fooling around the engine is the defendant Nicola Sacco or his double. . . .

Where was Sacco supposed to be this day? You naturally ask me, and I have told you that Vanzetti was a fisherman and peddled fish at times in Plymouth. Sacco doesn't come from Plymouth. He comes from South Stoughton, and he is a shoe worker. He works in what is called the "3-K" factory. I have no doubt some of you gentlemen are familiar with it, in South Stoughton.

Early in the week of April 15th—the 15th was Thursday as I recall —Sacco said that he might want to get off some day that week. Finally, he asked to get off on Thursday. He was allowed to get off on Thursday, and Sacco was away from his job in the 3-K factory all day Thursday.

April the 17th . . . two men riding on horseback for pleasure went up that little wood road that we traversed yesterday, and there they found up there . . . with its head away from the street, if I am right, a 1920, seven-passenger, black Buick car with the top up, with no number plates on it, with the rear window, that long window of isinglass in back, out of it, and with a bullet hole in the right-hand side in back, shot from the inside to the outside, and that car . . . [was] identified by the witnesses of the shooting as the car involved in the shooting. . . .

It was stolen . . . on November 23, 1919, and was never traced until the time it was discovered in the woods. The numbers 49,783, which were on the car at the time of the shooting, but which were not on the car at the time it was found, were stolen . . . sometime in the early part of 1920.

We next hear of Sacco on the evening of May 5th. Perhaps it would be well to jump for a moment to the Coacci house. . . . [I]n the early part of 1920 it was inhabited by a family by the name of Coacci, and there lived at that house with the Coaccis a man by the name of Mike Boda. [73]

Mike Boda had . . . an Overland . . . but sometime in the early part of April, the latter part of the winter of 1920, he was observed driving a larger car, . . . of the description of this 1920 Buick. He was seen at one time driving it early in the morning. A large car with four dark complexioned men in it was observed several times driving up to the Coacci house on Sunday evenings and the men getting out there.

After the . . . shooting police officers visited the Coacci . . . shed and they there discovered the remains of curtains which had been nailed over the four windows of the shed. . . .

. . . [O]n May 5th Mrs. Simon Johnson, who first appears in this picture, was awakened by a knock on her door . . .

Mr. Johnson and Mrs. Johnson were at home on May 5, and they heard this knock on the door, and Mrs. Johnson went down, and there she saw Mike Boda [who had left his Overland at Johnson's garage a day or two after the shooting]. She came out of the door of her house, . . . and there was Mike Boda standing beside the telegraph

pole, and down here on the Brockton side was a motor-cycle with a
side car pointing toward Mike Boda, and with the light streaming on
Mike Boda, and beside that motor-cycle and the side car was a man
whose name is Orciana, . . . and as she saw Boda and Orciana standing there, she saw two men come over that bridge by Boda on the
other side of the road from her, and one of those men was Nicola
Sacco, and he had with him his co-defendant, Bartolomeo Vanzetti.

By reason of some pre-arranged plan, which it isn't perhaps compe-
[74] tent for me in this case to speak of, she went over to the Bartlett house, . . . and as she went Sacco and Vanzetti followed alongside of her on the other side of the street . . . She turned into the
Bartlett house and was there for ten minutes, or about that. When she
came out Sacco and Vanzetti were watching opposite the Bartlett
house.

She came out . . . and there was something said in a foreign language, she thought it was Italian, and they followed back with her on
the other side of the street, and when she got back to her house the
motor-cycle had been turned towards Brockton, and as she reached
the house she saw Boda get into the side car of the motor-cycle,
Orciana get onto the motor-cycle and the motor-cycle went off towards Brockton.

Later that evening a street car was proceeding up North Elm Street
towards Brockton . . . Sacco and Vanzetti got aboard the car. . . .

They rode in the car that night of May 5th to Brockton and were
apprehended and arrested when they reached Campello, by Brockton
police officers. They were searched, and on Sacco was found a Colt
automatic pistol, which was found tucked down, as I recall, inside his
trousers. It was fully loaded. If I might say it was a 10-shot pistol, .32
calibre. There were 22 loaded cartridges in his hip or pants' pocket.
Vanzetti had on him a loaded .38 Harrington & Richardson revolver.
There were no extra cartridges for the revolver found on Vanzetti.
They were taken to the Brockton Police Station and booked.

On the next day, . . . various witnesses from South Braintree were
brought to the Brockton Police Station, and several identified Sacco
as the man who had participated in the shooting and was in the aban-
doned car after the shooting. Vanzetti was also identified at that time.
Vanzetti and Sacco had known each other for some period before
this. During the few days immediately preceding the joint arrest, Vanzetti had been at Sacco's house in West Stoughton, and their . . .
reasons, stated to a police officer, for going to West Bridgewater that
night, was [sic] to go down and see a man named Peppy or Poppy

whom Vanzetti thought lived in West Bridgewater, and that they lost their way [75] . . . .

The contention of the Government, gentlemen, is that this crime was committed by five men; that use was made of this stolen Buick car, which for some time, at least, previous to the crime and after its theft . . . had been kept in the curtained shed at the Coacci house in West Bridgewater; that on the morning of the murder or at some time previously before that it was taken from the Coacci house and was driven to South Braintree; that they picked up Vanzetti at the East Braintree station; that the men who guided and drove that car were very familiar with the localities of West Bridgewater and the roads leading to and from that section. . . .

I have mentioned about a cap being found at the scene of the shooting near the body of Berardelli. Sacco was in the habit of wearing a cap, and witnesses [Kelley] who know the kind of cap . . . that Sacco was in the habit of wearing will tell you that the cap found at the scene of the shooting is similar to the cap that Sacco wore.

There were six bullets found in these two men, two in Parmenter and four in Berardelli. The two in Parmenter were fired from a Savage automatic pistol. It is perfectly easy to tell from what type of gun a cartridge is fired by reason of the marks left on the bullet by the rifling of the gun or pistol. They have certain ridges in the pistol which makes depressions in the bullet, and the distances between those depressions or ridges give you a clue as to the kind of gun or to the weapon from which the bullets came. And the bullets in Parmenter's body came from a Savage automatic . . . of .32 calibre.

Three of the bullets in Berardelli's body came from a Savage automatic of .32 calibre, but the bullet, gentlemen, that caused Berardelli's [76] death, the bullet that was fired as he was crouched on the ground or prostrate on the ground, that entered in behind his shoulder and went down through his body and lodged in his intestines, or lower abdomen, was fired from a .32 Colt automatic pistol. And when Sacco was arrested three weeks afterwards he had on his person, tucked down inside his trousers, a fully-loaded Colt automatic pistol of .32 calibre, and he had twenty-two additional bullets for that pistol in his pants' pocket.

Gentlemen, I think I have covered the main facts which the Government will present to you through the witnesses which it will call. As his Honor stated to you the other day, what I have stated to you is not evidence. It is simply stated to you by me, with the utmost good faith, as what we intend to show to you and what we expect to show to you. No man can guarantee what the testimony of witnesses will be. The story in the rough is as I have told you. . . .

You have got to remember—and I say this because this is your first case, and you have not been sitting through a long, criminal term—that the stand, and particularly . . . in an important trial, is a difficult place to put any witness. Any one of you, if you had to go, in a murder case particularly, on that stand and were subjected to cross-examination before a jury and before a judge and before a court room of spectators, would not tell your story the way you would tell it to your wife at home. You would be bound to be embarrassed. You would be oppressed by the responsibility that is put upon you, and, gentlemen, when you listen to the witnesses on both sides in this case, you will bear in mind the difficulties under which the witnesses are laboring and the situation in which they are first put. But you will size up their opportunities of observation and what they apparently have remembered, how they tell it, and from that and from your own instinct you will say whether or not they are telling, or attempting to tell, the truth.

The law in this case is not as complicated as it is in some murder cases. It is apparently a case of first-degree murder . . . [or] nothing. First-degree murder is a killing perpetrated with deliberately premeditated malice aforethought. . . .

.   .   .   .   .

You have got two defendants. The Commonwealth has no evidence of any eye witness that saw Vanzetti fire any gun. They have direct evidence of Sacco shooting at Berardelli, but their evidence connecting Vanzetti with this murder connects him with the gang that perpetrated the murder and puts him in the car. . . .

The law is this, gentlemen. If two or more conspire to kill and do any joint act looking towards the killing and do kill, one is as guilty as the other. . . .

Now, gentlemen, the medical evidence will be called first to give you an idea as to how these men met their death. We will follow it up with the description of the shooting and go down the line as I have now brought it to you. Very likely it will be a long trial. There are a good many witnesses to be heard. We will try to make it as short and concise and as to the point as possible. I ask for your patience in the matter because it is too serious a case to go over lightly. Watch the witnesses carefully and bear in mind as far as you can the general scheme which I have laid out to you, for it embodies the claim of the Commonwealth. . . .

[Mr. Williams is called to the bench by the Court.]

THE COURT. Also the degree of proof required, and also that the defendants are entitled, as a matter of law, to the presumption of innocence [78] until the Commonwealth has established beyond reasonable doubt that the defendants are guilty.

MR. WILLIAMS. His Honor very properly reminds me that I have failed to state to you the position of the defendants at the bar at the present time, an oversight on my part. You must not take into consideration, gentlemen, the fact that either defendant is under arrest. The fact that they have been indicted by a Grand Jury, that has nothing to do with the case. The Grand Jury is simply the grand inquiry body of this County, which investigates one side of a case, and on such investigation where the defendants are not present, where they are not represented by counsel, returns a complaint, on which complaint the defendants are arrested and held in custody.

The defendants are presumed to be innocent. They are just as innocent at the present time as you or I may be. They do not become guilty until evidence is offered before you gentlemen to overcome that presumption of innocence, and such evidence as you will find does overcome that presumption. The evidence must be so strong as to maintain that burden of proof which is upon the Government in a case of this kind. It is not mere preponderance of the evidence in a criminal case. It is what we call proof beyond reasonable doubt, and you must find, before you say that these men are guilty and not innocent, that they have been proved guilty beyond a reasonable doubt. . . . You must remember that you gentlemen are not here to try to find a doubt. You are here to find the truth, but if, in searching for the truth, you do have a reasonable doubt, it is your duty to say so. . . .

I presume, Mr. Foreman and Gentlemen, that there is no such thing in any case tried in court as an absolute certainty. What we are trying to find is what are called moral certainties. . . . If you find to a moral certainty beyond any reasonable doubt, if you as reasonable men in your varied experiences believe that these defendants are guilty, it is your duty to say so. That is, gentlemen, the law that applies to all criminal cases. It is no different in a murder trial than it is in any other. . . . [79]

———AFTER hearing testimony by the doctors who performed the autopsies, the prosecution called several witnesses of the shooting, one of whom was Bostock.———

Mr. James F. Bostock, Sworn

Q. [*By Mr. Williams*] What is your name? A. James F. Bostock. [185]

. . . . .

Q. Now, will you tell the jury what you . . . saw . . . ? [186]

. . . . .

A. . . . I saw Parmenter and Berardelli coming down the street and as I walked towards them Parmenter says to me, "Bostock, . . . go into the other factory and fix the pulley on the motor," and I says to him, "I'm going to get this quarter past three car to Brockton . . . ," and as I started to turn around to leave, I heard two or three shots fired, and as I swung around there were two men shooting at him. [187]

. . . . .

Q. Where was Parmenter and where was the other man you say was doing the shooting? A. Parmenter had left and started across the street in that direction [*indicating*]. When he started to go down, there was a stone and grass place and a stone step, and as he started to fall somebody helped him and lowered him. I could not tell who it was.

Q. Tell us what either of the men you say were doing the shooting did after you had turned around and how many shots, if any, you heard fired. A. Well, I couldn't say. I should say there was probably eight or ten shots.

Q. What did you see this man you saw standing over Berardelli . . . [do] after that? A. Why, he stood there over him. He shot, I should say, he shot at Berardelli probably four or five times. He stood guard over him.

Q. And then what happened? A. I started to walk in the direction towards him. Probably I was away from him 50 or 60 feet, such a matter, and as I turned they swung around and shot at me twice.

Q. What did you do then? A. I started for the railroad crossing.

Q. Now, at the time they shot at you, where was Parmenter and the other shooter? When I say "the other one" the one who was not at that time shooting at Berardelli? A. They stood practically where they were.

Q. Where was the second? If I may call him "bandit" simply for the purposes of questioning, where was the second bandit as to location, with reference to the man who was shooting at Berardelli? A.

Why, he stood, I should not think he was a very few feet away off from Berardelli, and he probably stood away from him five or 10 feet. He stood looking down the road and as he stood looking down the road he made a beckon in that direction.

Q. What happened then? A. The automobile came up the street.

Q. Had you seen that automobile before? A. No, sir. [189]

Q. Where was it when you first saw it? A. It was down beyond the Slate [sic] factory. . . .

.   .   .   .   .   .

Q. How many bandits—using that term again—did you see on the road at any time? A. Four.

Q. During the shooting? A. Three on the road. I saw the two that done the shooting and one other got off the running-board or got out of the auto, I could not positively swear whether he got out of the automobile or whether he was on the running-board, but he got out and helped throw the two cans, or boxes, whatever they were, that had the pay roll in.

Q. Now, take up the story from the time you saw the automobile coming up by Slater's there, tell us what happened, what you saw happen. A. I saw first, I saw the machine come up. I saw this man come up to where the——

Q. When you say "this man" which one do you mean? A. I could not tell you.

Q. You meant the third man you saw? A. The third man, yes. He got up, and when he got to within about probably 10 or 15 feet he came out of that automobile and run to where the other two stood, and he picked up one can and one of the bandits who stood took the other, and the man who was with them got into the back seat of the car, and as I say, as he came towards the railroad crossing he crawled from the back seat to the front seat.

Q. Which side of the automobile were the money boxes put in? A. The left-hand side. [190]

Q. What did you observe as to the car or the inmates of the car, as it came up to the crossing? A. I saw it was a Buick car. As it passed me I went back to where Berardelli was laying, but as it passed me I noticed it, the back end glass was broken out and the covering on one side was flying out and then one of the bandits laid over on the outside of the car, out in about that direction [indicating], firing as he came along all the way up the street.

Q. What part of the car was he firing from? A. From the front [191] end opposite from the,—as he came up the street he was firing right from the front end. He laid out of the car, in about that direction [*indicating*].

Q. From the time the car reached the crossing, as it went up the street, did you hear any shots fired? A. I heard him fire shots until they got to . . . the cobbling shop. Then . . . I went back to where Berardelli was.

Q. Did you see the crossing tender at any time? A. Yes, sir. I hollered to the crossing tender to lower the gate.

. . . . .

Q. Could you tell how many men were in the car, or not? A. No, sir, I could not. I could say there was four, but I could not say there was any more.

Q. Did you notice anything through the back window of the car? A. No, sir.

Q. Was that window in or out? A. That window was out.

Q. After the car passed you, you say you went down the street? A. Yes, sir.

Q. Where was the body of Berardelli lying when you got there? A. He laid, he set, just off the sidewalk, and as I remember him, he wasn't laying clear down. He laid in a kind of crouched position, and I helped to lay him down, and he was [*witness makes puffing movement with lips*], and every time he breathed blood flowed, was coming from his mouth. [192]

. . . . .

Q. Will you now describe, so far as you can, the appearance of the men who were doing the shooting? A. Why, there was two dressed in—— The two that was doing the shooting was dressed in sort of dark clothes, with caps, dark caps. I should say they was fellows of medium build, fellows not quite so heavy as I am.

Q. Can you tell us anything further about their appearance? A. Why, they appeared to be foreigners.

Q. Can you tell us what nationality? A. Well, I should call them Italians.

Q. Notice anything about how their faces looked? A. Why, I told you they resembled, to me—— I have seen Italian fruit peddlers, and as I saw them as I passed them I thought they was Italian fruit peddlers. That is what I thought they was as I passed them. [194]

Q. Can you tell us anything more definitely how their features looked to you? A. They was smooth face, dark complected. One I should call swarthy, dark complected.

Q. Can you describe the appearance of the man you saw leaning out of the car and shooting going over the crossing? *A.* Well, I don't know as I could really describe him.

Q. How far was he from you? I understand you were around the fence at that time. How far was he from you when you saw him leaning out and shooting? *A.* Well, as I was around the fence he was coming towards me, and, as I told you, if I had layed around the corner of the fence I could have almost reach [*sic*] and touch that car as it passed me.

Q. How fast was the car going as it went over the crossing? *A.* He threw his car into high speed as he went over the crossing. He was just getting the car into high speed. The car coming up the hill choked. I thought it was going to stop. Coming up the hill it acted as if it choked, that they gave too much gasoline in it. That car had not really got under speed until they got to the other side of the crossing.

Q. Do you know whether you have ever seen any of these men implicated in the shooting since that time? *A.* Yes—— I don't know as I have seen any of the men implicated in the shooting, no, sir.

Q. Have you been able to identify any of those men? *A.* No, sir.

Q. Were you taken to the Brockton police station at any time? *A.* Yes, sir.

Q. Did you look at the defendants at that time? *A.* Yes, sir.

Q. Could you tell whether or not they were any of the men? *A.* No, sir, I could not tell whether or not they was, no sir. [195]

.   .   .   .   .

——UNDER cross-examination by Mr. Williams, Bostock testified that on the Saturday night previous to the crime Berardelli had shown him his revolver.——————————————————————————

.   .   .   .   .

Q. What kind of a revolver was it, do you know? *A.* No. I couldn't tell you the make of it. I don't know anything about revolvers. It was a .38 calibre revolver, that is all I can tell you. I don't know. I never owned one.

Q. What did it look like? *A.* It was a nickel-plated revolver. [198]

.   .   .   .   .

Mary E. Splaine, Sworn

Q. [*By Mr. Williams*] Were you employed as bookkeeper by Slater & Morrill on April 15th of last year? *A.* Yes, sir.

Q. At that time where was the bookkeeper's office or room where you worked? *A*. It is in the southeast corner of the building, on Railroad Street.

Q. On which floor? *A*. The second floor. [220]

. . . .

Q. After you saw them [Parmenter and Berardelli] go down the street there, what did you next see or hear in reference to the case we are now trying? *A*. I heard some shots, which sounded like back-firing from an auto.

. . . .

Q. After you heard them, what did you do? *A*. I stood up in the middle of the office, and then I walked to the window on the south side.

. . . .

Q. You are pointing to the corner window on the Pearl Street side on the second story? *A*. Yes.

. . . .

Q. How far from that window could you see toward the Rice & Hutchins' building? *A*. You mean the distance? [221]

Q. I do not mean in feet, no, but what objects could you see from that window, going down Pearl Street towards the east? *A*. I could see the wooden factory of Rice & Hutchins, and I could see a portion of the brick factory. That is, the back portion of the brick factory.

Q. Could you see the railroad crossing? *A*. I could see to the,—well, by standing just close to the window you could see to the second track, but if you peered out the window close you could see almost across the entire track.

Q. From that position which I understood you took, what did you see? *A*. I saw an auto as it was approaching about the second track, just about leaving the crossing, come up Pearl Street.

Q. What did you see happen in regard to that auto? *A*. When it was half way between the crossing and the corner of this street here on the corner——

Q. When you say "this street here" what do you mean? *A*. Pearl Street and Railroad Street here on the corner. When it is half way between the crossing and this point here [*indicating*] there was a man appeared on the side of the machine.

Q. Which side? *A*. The right hand side.

Q. That is the side toward you or away from you? *A*. Toward me.

Q. What did you see him do? *A*. The first thing I noticed was a hand was laid on the front side of the auto and then his body from the waist up appeared outside the machine.

Q. What did he do, if anything? *A.* He was looking in the direction of the cobbling shop. [222]

. . . . .

Q. Did you see that man that appeared at that place? *A.* Yes, sir.

Q. Can you describe him to these gentlemen here? *A.* Yes, sir. He was a man that I should say was slightly taller than I am. He weighed possibly from 140 to 145 pounds. He was a muscular,—he was an active looking man. I noticed particularly the left hand was a good sized hand, a hand that denoted strength or a shoulder that——

Q. So that the hand you said you saw where? *A.* The left hand, that was placed on the back of the front seat, on the back of the front seat. He had a gray, what I thought was a shirt,—had a grayish, like navy color, and the face was what we would call clear-cut, clean-cut face. Through here [*indicating*] was a little narrow, just a little narrow. The forehead was high. The hair was brushed back and it was between, I should think, two inches and two and one-half inches in length and had dark eyebrows, but the complexion was a white, peculiar white that looked greenish.

Q. How long was he in your view, do you know? *A.* Now, the distance that it took him to travel from the middle of the street, from the middle of that distance to that corner.

Q. You say "The middle of the distance." You mean what? *A.* The middle of the distance between the railroad track and the corner of Pearl and Railroad streets.

Q. That is practically to the cobbling shop that is on the corner of Pearl and Railroad, isn't it? *A.* Yes.

Q. Did you ever see that man after that? *A.* Yes. [223]

Q. Where did you see him? *A.* I saw him in the police station in Brockton.

Q. When was that? *A.* That was three weeks after the murder.

. . . . .

Q. I want you to look around the courtroom and see if you see in the courtroom the man that you saw that day in the automobile? *A.* Yes, sir, the man sitting nearest to me on this side of over there.

Q. Where? *A.* On this side.

Q. Of what? *A.* What do you call it, a cage?[2]

Q. On the side of the cage? *A.* Yes.

Q. The man with the mustache, or the man without the mustache? *A.* No, sir, the man without the mustache.

---

[2] In Massachusetts the defendant in a criminal case is kept in a cage-like enclosure in the courtroom.

Q. Is that the same man you saw at Brockton? *A.* It is.

Q. Are you sure? *A.* Positive.

. . . . .

Q. Do you know the name of the man you just pointed out to this jury? *A.* Well, I have learned it since.

Q. What is the name you learned? *A.* Nicola Sacco.

Mr. Williams. You may inquire.

Cross-Examination

Q. [*By Mr. Moore*] [224] . . . [Y]ou looked out of the window that gave you a view towards Pearl Street over the cobbler shop to the angle from it. Is that right? *A.* I did not look over the cobbler's shop. I looked down the street. I can see over the corner of the cobbler's shop roof. That is, the lower corner.

Q. That is what we understand. At that time had the automobile passed the gate on the side towards Rice & Hutchins? *A.* Not when I first went to the window.

Q. It was approaching the gate at that time, was it? *A.* Not when I first went to the window.

Q. Where was it when you first looked out of the window? *A.* I did not see it when I first looked out of the window. [225]

. . . . .

Q. Well, now, this man leaning against the forward seat of the car, back of the forward seat of the car, I understand you to say he was not firing anything? *A.* I did not see him fire. He was not leaning against the front seat of the car. He was leaning out of the car. He was steadying himself against the front seat.

Q. That is, with his back to the front seat or side or what? *A.* He was facing out slanting from the car. [230]

Q. Then his both hands were inside of the body of that car, were they? *A.* I saw his right hand,—I mean, his left hand, inside the car. I do not know anything about his right hand.

Q. Do you remember testifying on the preliminary examination in this case as follows, in response to questions asked, I believe, by counsel, by Mr. Adams?

Mr. Katzmann. The page?

Mr. Moore. Page 50. At the bottom of page 50.

"*A.* He stood there with one hand resting on the front seat and the other hand discharging."

A. No, sir, I never said that in Quincy.

Q. What? *A.* No, sir, I never said that.

Q. Well, now, I want to be entirely fair. This is your name, Mary E. Splaine? *A.* Yes.

Q. You were questioned there by Mr. Adams? *A.* Yes, sir.

Q. And this is the official transcript made by Sadie E. Thomas, 1416 Hancock Street, Quincy. [231]

. . . . .

Q. Did you say that you,—do you wish now to say that this report is incorrect? *A.* That report is incorrect so far as my saying I saw his right hand. I never saw it. I never said so.

Q. It is also incorrect on the next page of the same transcript[?] "*Q.* Have you seen this defendant before?"

And you answered, "Yes." And then this question:

"*Q.* Where?"

And you answered,

"*A.* I am almost sure I saw him at Braintree, but I saw him at the Brockton police station afterwards."

Is that incorrect also? *A.* I saw him at South Braintree first.

Q. Did you tell the court below that you were "almost sure"? *A.* I won't say that I did.

Q. You won't say that you did not, either? *A.* I don't remember that.

"*Q.* Your opinion is he bears a striking resemblance to him?

A. I could be mistaken."

You remember so testifying? *A.* Yes, sir.

"*Q.* You are not sure that he is the man? *A.* No."

A. No, I did not say that.

Q. You did not say you weren't sure? *A.* No.

Q. I want to be entirely fair with you, Miss Splaine.

"*Q.* You are not sure he is the man? *A. No.*"

A. I did not make that answer.

Q. You did not make that answer? *A.* No. [232]

. . . . .

Q. At any rate, these matters that I have directed your attention to in your testimony are all matters of error in the record? *A.* Those things to which I have taken exception are errors.

Q. Including this statement:

"*Q.* Do you say this is the man? *A.* I will not swear positively he is the man.

"*Q.* You did not get a sufficient look to say positively this is the man? *A.* I would not swear positively he is the man."

A. I did not answer that question that way.

Q. Do you want to say that this is not a correct transcript of your testimony? *A.* I should say that was an incorrect transcript of that answer.

Q. Have you read your testimony since the preliminary examination? *A.* No, sir, I have not.

Q. Haven't seen it at all? *A.* No, sir.

Q. So that you do not know but what the entire transcript is erroneous? *A.* It might be, for all I know.

Q. The only things, Miss Splaine,—by the way, you did not see anyone, did not see this man that you now claim to identify until some 21 or 22 days thereafter, did you? *A.* Three weeks after.

Q. Three weeks after. And then you were taken to the Brockton [233] police station in the presence of,—taken down there by police officers? *A.* No, sir, I was not brought by any policeman.

Q. Well, you went down there. *A.* Yes, I went.

Q. There you and a number of others were shown the defendant. Is that correct? *A.* I saw him before I was asked to look at him.

Q. Well, I mean you saw him in the Brockton police station? *A.* Yes, I did.

Q. And you knew you were down there for the purposes of identification? *A.* Yes, sir.

Q. And he was the only man that was brought in to you at that time? *A.* He was the second one that was brought in.

Q. The other person being the defendant Vanzetti? *A.* Yes, sir.

Q. Was Vanzetti brought in first? *A.* Yes, sir.

Q. And then the defendant Sacco brought in? *A.* Yes, sir.

Q. And you knew you were down there for the purpose of identifying him? *A.* To see if I ever saw them before.

. . . . .

Q. Did you say at any time on the preliminary examination in this matter, either in fact or in substance, "I will not swear positively he is the man"? *A.* I said that I would——

Q. Answer my question, please, yes or no. *A.* I did not make that remark that way.

. . . . .

Q. [*By Mr. Moore*] Miss Splaine, the nearest point that this automobile was to you at any time, I take it, is the straight line down your street to Pearl Street? *A.* What would be the corner of Railroad Street and Pearl Street, that is the nearest point. [234]

. . . . .

Q. Now, what do you estimate that distance to be? *A.* I should say the distance would not be as far as the back of the court room from me. Not quite as far as that.

Q. Would you say something in the neighborhood of from 80 to 100 feet? *A.* Oh, it wasn't as far as that.

Q. Would you say from 35 to 40 feet? *A.* It would be nearer forty.

Q.. What? *A.* I think it would be nearer the forty.

Q. If you stated 40 feet in the trial below, you would be repeating that statement that you made, 35 or 40 feet in the preliminary? *A.* I don't remember just what I did say.

Q. You said 35 to 40 feet. *A.* I should say it was just about that, 40 feet.

Q. The map reveals, as prepared by the Commonwealth, a minimum distance of 80 feet, based on the distance that you made it, on a straight line——

MR. WILLIAMS. Are you quite correct there in making that statement?

MR. MOORE. I am figuring 20 feet to the inch, and I am figuring from the window here. You can figure it yourself. [235]

. . . . .

Q. Now, all this data that you are giving to the jury relative to the formation of his shoulders, his weight, is all based on what you saw while that car was running some 50 or 60 feet, some 60 or 80 feet away from you and on the ground below your windows? *A.* On the vision I got of him during that time. [236]

. . . . .

Q. [*By Mr. McAnarney*] My question is: Do you feel that you had sufficient opportunity, time of observation and position of observation, that you feel you had opportunity sufficient to say that this is the man? *A.* Yes, sir, I think I did.

Q. I now direct your attention to the official record, at the bottom of page 57. The last question: "You don't feel certain enough of your own position to say he is the man?" That is the question. I will now read to you your answer given in the Quincy court on the 26th day of May, 1920. "I don't think my opportunity afforded me the right to say he is the man." You so testified in the Quincy court on the 26th of May, a year ago? *A.* Yes, sir, I did make that statement. [240]

. . . . .

Q. How far did that automobile travel while it was in your vision? *A.* Well, I should say it was traveling— It was just to the last track, or between the second and last track on this side next to the hotel, and from that it passed out of my direct sight at the corner of the cobbling shop, that constitutes the corner, and from that other window you speak of I could see the back of it disappearing up Pearl Street.

Q. Try and put your mind back there that day, and see if you don't recall that your vision was only while the automobile was traveling half the distance from the railroad track to the corner where the cobbler shop was. A. My vision of the car was from the railroad track to the corner.

Q. I am now reading the last question on page 51 of the record:

"How long an opportunity did you have to make an observation of him and his features? A. The machine traveled about half the distance from the railroad to the sidewalk, a distance as I think would [240] be probably 60 to 70 feet, and half that distance would be 30 to 35 feet."

Did you not so testify May 26th, last year, in the Quincy Court? A. I think I said that was the distance at that time.

Q. You haven't measured it since, have you? A. I walked over it once.

Q. The fact stands out, though, that the machine had traveled half the distance, and your observation was half the distance from the railroad track to the building, and be that distance whatever it may be, it was one-half of that distance, wasn't it? A. That I saw Sacco, yes.

MR. WILLIAMS. She has always said that.

MR. McANARNEY. Pardon me; there is no occasion for interruption. [242]

. . . . .

Q. Now, [one week] after the shooting, you were examined [in Captain Proctor's office]. . . . While you were there you were shown some photographs? A. Yes, sir, pictures.

Q. You picked out a certain photograph? A. There was——— [243]

Q. Pardon; yes or no. A. Yes, sir.

. . . . .

Q. You identified that photograph as the photograph of the man you saw leaning out of the car? A. No, sir, not in detail.

Q. Not in detail? A. No.

Q. Did you not say, "There, I think that is the man that I saw leaning out of the car?" A. He had some of the features, but not all.

Q. Pardon. Can't you answer that question yes or no? A. No.

Q. Did you not say, Madam, in substance, that the features of the man on one of the photographs shown to you were in substance the features of the man that you saw leaning out of the car? A. They were a striking resemblance to the man.

Q. That is what you said? *A.* Yes,—a "striking resemblance."

Q. Later you learned that man [Anthony Palisamo] was in Sing Sing at the time of this [crime]? *A.* I learned the man was not at large.

Q. The man whose photograph you picked out as a striking resemblance to the man leaning out of the car you learned later was in some other jail for some other offence? You learned that, didn't you? *A.* Yes, sir, I did. [244]

． ． ． ． ．

[*Q.*] So, in describing this man whose picture you saw in the Rogue's Gallery, and whom you learned was in jail for some other offence, you said then to these men, Captain Proctor and others, he bore a striking resemblance to the man you saw leaning out of the car? *A.* In some features.

Q. Pardon, you said he bore a striking resemblance to the man you saw leaning out of the car? *A.* In regard to some features.

Q. You said "striking resemblance," didn't you? *A.* That is not the whole answer.

Q. Did you use the words "striking resemblance"? *A.* I said, a striking resemblance in some features. [245]

． ． ． ． ．

Q. When you saw the defendant Sacco he was alone except he was accompanied by an officer? *A.* Yes, sir.

Q. He was not stood with other men, or other Italians, or any other person, from whom you were to pick out any man? He was brought into the room by the officer, and you looked at him. This is what transpired? *A.* Yes, sir. [248]

． ． ． ． ．

Re-Cross-Examination

Q. [*By Mr. McAnarney*] You now say that on reflection you feel sure he is the man? *A.* I feel most certain he is.

Q. You were answering in the lower court from your observation, weren't you? *A.* Yes, sir.

Q. From what you saw? *A.* Yes.

Q. Your answer now is that you feel most certain that he is? *A.* Yes.

Q. That is not the position that you are sure beyond any doubt, is it? You are most certain now, aren't you? *A.* I am positive he is the man, certain he is the man. I admit the possibility of an error, but I am not making a mistake.

Q. Your answer in the lower court was you didn't have opportunity to observe him. What did you mean when you said you didn't have opportunity sufficient, kindly tell us, you didn't have sufficient opportunity to observe him? *A.* Well, he was passing on the street.

Q. He was passing on the street, and you didn't have sufficient opportunity to observe him to enable you to identify him? *A.* That is what I meant.

Q. That is the only opportunity you had? *A.* Yes, sir.

Q. You have had no other opportunity but that one fleeting glance? *A.* The remembrance of that.

Q. Which is half the distance between the railroad track and the cobbler shop 30 or 35 feet with this car going the speed it was? *A.* Yes, sir.

MR. McANARNEY. I think that is all.

Q. [*By Mr. Moore*] Miss Splaine, you went down to Brockton the morning of the sixth of May, didn't you? *A.* Yes, sir. [253]

. . . . .

Q. Now, you saw him four or five times that day, didn't you? *A.* I saw him twice that day,—well, three times including when I first saw him at the doorway coming in, but twice when I looked at him afterwards.

Q. All told, the time you looked him over in these various positions, with his hat on and with his hat off, and walked around him, and so forth, consumed upwards—these various occasions—upwards of a couple of hours, didn't it? *A.* I don't think so. I saw him while he passed through the room, and while he was in the room I don't think I took more than five minutes to look at him.

. . . . .

Q. At any rate, when you took the witness stand at the time of the preliminary, you looked right square at the defendant, didn't you? *A.* Yes, sir.

Q. And you looked at him during the entire period of your twenty-five or thirty pages of testimony? *A.* Yes, sir.

Q. And you haven't seen the defendant from that time since you saw him in the Brockton jail all that you wanted to see him and the time [254] that you saw him on preliminary, you haven't seen him from the day until you saw him in this courtroom, have you? *A.* No, sir, I did not. . . . . .

MR. McANARNEY. Just one question, if your Honor will pardon me.

. . . . .

Q. And that I may have the situation correct, you testified in the Quincy court and then you did not see him until he came in here? *A.* No, sir.

Q. So that you testified and gave the answer which has been given, about not having a sufficient opportunity, and then changed your mind without looking at the man again? A. Not since I saw him in Quincy.

Q. In other words, you changed your mind as to whether he was the man without making any further examination of him, didn't you? A. Yes, sir.

MR. McANARNEY. That is all.

THE COURT. Is that all, Mr. Williams?

MR. WILLIAMS. Yes, sir. [255]

.   .   .   .   .   .

————AFTER Miss Splaine had finished testifying, the prosecution introduced a witness, Louis Pelser, who testified that he saw Sacco shoot down Berardelli.————

[June 10, 1921]

THE COURT. I suppose I might as well make this announcement at this time. I know the jurors must feel very anxious to get back to their business, and on that account I feel we ought to sit part of the day tomorrow, and for that reason a session will be held until one o'clock tomorrow. [291]

Louis Pelser, Sworn

Q. [By Mr. Williams] . . . Where do you work? A. Rice & Hutchins shoe factory.

.   .   .   .   .

Q. What floor were you working on . . . [on April 15, 1920]? A. I would call it the first floor. There is a basement underneath it.

Q. First floor above the basement? A. Yes, sir. . . .

.   .   .   .   .

Q. And what did you first know that day with reference to the shooting, either by hearing something or seeing something?

A. Well, I heard something first, and then I opened the window afterwards.

.   .   .   .   .

Q. And what did you see when you looked out? A. I seen this fellow shoot this fellow. It was the last shot. He put four bullets into him. [292]

Q. You saw this fellow shoot this fellow. Who was the man that was shot? A. Berardelli. [293]

.   .   .   .   .

Q. Will you describe that man that you saw there who was doing the shooting? *A*. Well, he was about two or three feet away, and he stood like that, and put the last bullet in him.

Q. How did he look? Describe his appearance if you will. *A*. Describe the fellow?

Q. Yes, describe his appearance. *A*. He was kind of crouched down.

Q. I don't mean the way he was standing, but the way he looked? *A*. You mean his description?

Q. Yes, that is just what I do mean. *A*. He had a dark green pair of pants and an army shirt tucked up. He had wavy—hair pushed back, very strong hair, wiry hair, very dark.

Q. What complexion? *A*. Dark complexion.

Q. How far were you from him at that time? *A*. Oh, about seven feet away.

. . . . .

Q. Do you see in the courtroom the man you saw shooting Berardelli that day? *A*. Well, I wouldn't say it was him, but he is a dead image of him.

Q. Who is the man you are referring to? *A*. The fellow on the right here.

. . . . .

Q. Well, there are a good many men in this room—— *A*. Right in the cage on the right-hand side. Not the fellow with the mustache. [294]

Q. Do you know what his name is? *A*. Well, I have heard it was Sacco. [295]

Cross-Examination

. . . . .

Q. [*By Mr. Moore.*] Mr. Pelser, on March 26 of this year did a gentleman call on you, Mr. Reid, and talk with you with reference to the facts of this case? . . . *A*. Yes, sir.

Q. And you talked with him at that time, and he told you who he was,—he introduced himself? *A*. Yes, sir.

Q. Told you his name was Mr. Reid, and he had a Miss Bemish [a stenographer] with him, is that correct? *A*. Yes, sir.

Q. And he told you who he was and what he was there for? *A*. Yes, sir.

Q. And you talked with him freely and frankly and fully, did you not? *A*. Yes, sir.

Q. And told him on that day, March 26th, you told him freely and frankly everything that you knew about this case? *A.* Not everything, no, sir.

Q. You didn't? *A.* No, sir.

Q. Why didn't you? *A.* Well, I didn't feel like telling him the whole story.

Q. You didn't talk freely and frankly? *A.* Yes, sir. I told him some, but I didn't tell him the whole story.

Q. In other words, part of the things you told him were true? *A.* Yes, sir. [299]

Q. Other things you told him were not true, is that what you mean to tell the jury? *A.* No, I told him parts of the story, and that is all.

Q. Well, everything you told him was true, was it? *A.* Yes, sir.

. . . . .

Q. Now, I understand you stated, in response to counsel's questions, that when you looked out of the window, raising the window up——— You raised it clear to the top sash, did you? *A.* Yes, sir.

Q. And you stood square in the window? *A.* Yes, sir.

Q. Standing square in the window, you saw a man shooting? *A.* Yes, sir.

. . . . .

Q. [*Reading*] Question: "Did you see any of the shooting?" Answer: "Why, no. I just seen him laying there, that is all." Did you so state to Mr. Reid? *A.* Yes, sir.

Q. Was that a true statement of the fact? *A.* Well, yes, it was.

Q. What? *A.* It was.

Q. It was? This is a correct statement of what you told Mr. Reid? *A.* That I told Mr. Reid, yes, sir.

Q. Now, is it a true statement of what you saw? *A.* No, sir.

Q. Why was it that you didn't tell Mr. Reid the facts? *A.* Because I didn't want to tell my story.

Q. Why? *A.* Because I didn't like to go to court.

. . . . .

Q. Did you tell Mr. Reid a falsehood in order to avoid being called as a witness in this case? *A.* Yes, sir. [300]

. . . . .

Q. [*Reading*] Question: "The shooting was all over by the time you opened the window?" Answer: "Yes." Did you so state to Mr. Reid? *A.* Yes, sir.

Q. Was that the truth? *A.* No, it was not.

. . . . .

Q. [*Reading*] Question: "Did you see the man who did the shooting?" Answer: "No; they were just gone." Did you so state to Mr. Reid? *A.* Yes, sir.

Q. Why did you tell Mr. Reid that, Mr. Pelser? *A.* Because I didn't know him well enough. I didn't know who he was.

Q. He told you that he represented the defendant? *A.* Yes.

Q. He talked with you with entire frankness? *A.* Yes, sir.

Q. You didn't refuse to talk with him? *A.* No, sir.

Q. You told him what you thought about all the facts, didn't you? *A.* Yes, sir.

Q. [*Reading*] Question: "They had just gone?" Answer: "Yes." [*Reading*] Question: "Did you see any [of the bandits] around there?" Answer: "Well, I'll tell you, they were shooting while I was at the window, and I got under the bench and that is all I seen of them." Did you so state to Mr. Reid? *A.* Yes, sir.

Q. Didn't you duck under the bench? *A.* No, sir.

Q. Why did you tell Mr. Reid that you ducked under the bench? Now, Pelser, isn't it the truth that you did duck under the bench? *A.* No, sir.

Q. Didn't you tell counsel for the Commonwealth in direct examination that you got scared? *A.* Yes, sir.

Q. Then you ducked under the bench, didn't you, sir? *A.* Yes, sir.

·   ·   ·   ·   ·

Re-Cross-Examination

Q. [*By Mr. Moore*] . . . [W]on't you tell the jury just exactly what you told the officers on May 6th and 7th when they attempted to get you to go down and you said, "I did not see enough to be able to identify anybody," just exactly as you told Mr. Reid on March 26th? *A.* Yes.

Q. You did tell the officers that, didn't you? *A.* Yes. [322]

·   ·   ·   ·   ·

————ON JUNE 11 Mrs. Andrews, a prosecution witness, began her testimony in the course of which she identified Sacco as one of the bandits.————

Mrs. Lola R. Andrews, Sworn

Q. [*By Mr. Williams*] . . . What time of day did you go to South Braintree? *A.* It would be between half past 11 and somewheres around quarter of 12 that I was there.

. . . . .

Q. From the South Braintree station, where did you go? *A.* . . . [T]o the Slater factory . . . below the Rice & Hutchins factory.

. . . . .

Q. Who was with you? *A.* A lady by the name of [Mrs. Julia] Campbell. [333]   . . . .

Q. How long did you stay in the Slater factory? *A.* . . . 15 minutes, possibly not that.

Q. What were you doing in there? *A.* Inquiring for work.

. . . . .

Q. Where did you go when you came out of the Slater factory? *A.* To the Rice & Hutchins factory.

. . . . .

Q. How long were you in there? *A.* . . . I should say 15 minutes.

. . . . .

Q. And will you tell the jury whom you saw and where you saw them? Under what circumstances? *A.* As I went into the Slater & Morrill factory I saw a car standing by the roadside of the Slater factory, as you go into the factory, and there was a man working on the car, at the front part of it, and there was another man there with him. I passed by them and went into the factory, and as I came back from the factory the same man was standing there at the same place where I first went in. [334]

. . . . .

Q. . . . I want you to place the men when you went into the factory. [335] . . . *A.* As I went into the factory the first man was bending over the front part of the car, which I would call the hood, and the other man was sitting in the back of the car.

Q. Can you describe the appearance of either of those men? *A.* The man that was bending over the hood was a dark complexioned man, and I would say medium height, smooth face.

Q. Can you tell how he was dressed? *A.* In dark clothing.

Q. Could you tell about the man whom you say was inside the car at that time? *A.* He was light, very light.

Q. Could you say anything more about him? *A.* He was thin. . . . His features were fine, emaciated like he was sick, he looked sickly.

. . . . .

Q. You were in there about 15 minutes, you say? *A.* Yes.

Q. Then you came out? *A.* Yes.

Q. Where was the car when you came out? *A.* At the same point as it was when I went in.

Q. Where were the men at that time? *A.* The light man was behind the auto as I came out, standing behind, and the other man was down under the car, like he was fixing something.

Q. Under what part of the car? *A.* Back of the forward wheels, under that part of it.

Q. Did you have any talk with either of those men at that time? *A.* Yes, sir.

Q. Which man? *A.* With the man who was fixing the car.

Q. Was he the light man or the dark man? *A.* No, sir, he was the dark man.

Q. Where was he when you had the talk with him? *A.* When I had the talk with him, he was under the car.

Q. Did he get up at any time? *A.* Yes, sir.

Q. I mean, when you had your talk with him, did he get up? *A.* I spoke to him and he got up, as I spoke to him.

Q. And you had some talk with him? *A.* Yes.

Q. Will you tell the jury what talk you had with him? *A.* I asked him if he would please show me how to get into the factory office, that I did not know how to go.

Q. What did he say? *A.* He told me,—he asked me which factory I wanted, "The Slater?" I said "No, sir, the Rice & Hutchins." [336]

Q. Anything more? *A.* That is all the conversation.

Q. Did he say anything more? *A.* No.

Q. Did he tell you how to get in? *A.* Yes.

.   .   .   .   .

Q. Have you seen the man you talked with that morning since? I am referring to the dark man with whom you talked. *A.* I think I have, yes, sir.

Q. Where did you see him? *A.* I saw him at the Dedham jail, first.

Q. Have you seen him since then? *A.* Yes, sir, I have.

.   .   .   .   .

Q. Do you see him in the court room now? *A.* I think I do, yes, sir.

.   .   .   .   .

Q. Just point to the man you mean. *A.* That man there [*indicating*].
Q. Do you mean——

[*The defendant Sacco stands up in the cage and says:* ". . . I am the man? Do you mean me? Take a good look."]

Q. Then you mean the man who just stood up and made the remark. *A.* Yes, sir.

Q. The man they call Sacco? *A.* Yes, sir. [337]

.   .   .   .   .

Q. Tell the jury what, if anything, he said? *A.* He said to go in the driveway and told me which door to go in, it would lead me to the factory office.

Q. Where did you go then? *A.* After I talked with him?

Q. Yes. *A.* I went into the Rice & Hutchins factory.

Q. Now, this Mrs. Campbell who was with you is a lady of what age, roughly? *A.* I would say she would be 69.

Q. And where is she now, do you know? *A.* At Stockton Springs, Maine. [338]

.   .   .   .   .   .

Cross-Examination

[June 13, 1921]

Q. [*By Mr. Moore*] Why, Mrs. Andrews, did you speak to that man . . . underneath this car, rather than to the other man who was standing doing nothing at a point no farther removed from you than am I at this moment? . . . *A.* Simply because I was standing there talking and I directed my conversation to him to ask him that question, instead of going back.

Q. Talking to whom? *A.* To Mrs. Campbell.

Q. Yet you couldn't see even the face of the man you were directing your question to. *A.* Why, sir, I saw his face when he got up.

Q. You had to call him up before you were able to see his face at all, weren't you? *A.* He was getting up when I spoke, getting up from under the auto.

Q. And you waited there for him to get up rather than to direct any remarks to the man that you had just passed or just seen at a point as far removed as far as I am from you now, is that right? *A.* I waited until he answered my question, yes, sir.

Q. At the time you asked him the question, he was down on the ground under the car? *A.* His head and shoulders was under the car. [375]

.   .   .   .   .   .

————TO ATTACK Mrs. Andrews' credibility, the defense presented three witnesses, Campbell, Fay, and Kurlansky. Actually, they took the witness stand more than two weeks after Mrs. Andrews testified, but in the interests of continuity their testimony is presented here instead of in the case for the defense. The first of these witnesses to testify was Mrs. Julia Campbell.————

Q. [*By Mr. Jeremiah McAnarney*] On the day of April 15th, 1920, did you go to Braintree, or South Braintree, with Mrs. Andrews? *A.* I did. [1308]

. . . . . .

Q. Did you see any man doing anything to the automobile [standing by the Slater & Morrill factory]? *A.* There was a man down underneath the automobile. He never looked up at all.

Q. Did you or Mrs. Andrews speak to that man who was down under the automobile? *A.* We did not. [1309]

. . . . .

————MRS. CAMPBELL testified that she and Mrs. Andrews went into the Slater & Morrill factory and asked a man there for work.————

Q. Tell us what was said by you or Mrs. Andrews or this man inside the factory, anything about the Rice & Hutchins factory? *A.* We asked him if that was the Rice & Hutchins factory, and he said no. . . . We asked him where it was, and he told us right the next building. . . . [H]e pointed up to the Rice & Hutchins building, and then we asked him how to get there and he told us, so we went in at the lower gate and went around right in the door, don't you see?

Q. When you and Mrs. Andrews came out of Rice & Hutchins, did either you or she speak to a man there at the automobile? *A.* We did not.

Q. Slater & Morrill factory? *A.* No, we did not.

Q. Did you hear Mrs. Andrews have any talk with any man who was working around an automobile that morning? *A.* No, sir. [1310]

. . . . .

George W. Fay, Sworn

Q. [*By Mr. Jeremiah McAnarney*] . . . You are a member of the Quincy Police Department? *A.* I am.

. . . . .

Q. Do you know . . . Lola Andrews? *A.* I do.

Q. Was your attention at any time called to her during February last? *A.* It was.

Q. And in what way, please? *A.* In passing the Alhambra Building one night in the middle of February. [1373]

. . . . .

Q. What happened? *A.* I was called in.

. . . . . .

Q. And what did she say? *A.* She said that when she came home she went up into the apartment, went into the toilet [and] . . . as she stepped into the toilet she was grabbed by a man and forced down onto her knees.

. . . . . .

Q. Now, tell us the questions you asked her and the answers she gave. *A.* I asked her if the man who assaulted her, if she thought that [1374] he was one of the men she saw at Braintree on the day of the shooting, and she said that she could not tell because she did not see the faces of the Braintree men. I asked her how he compared in appearance with the men at Braintree that she saw. She said that she could not tell. I asked her if his clothes were like the clothes that any of the men wore in Braintree. She said she could not tell. [1375]

. . . . . .

Harry Kurlansky, Sworn

. . . . . .

Q. [*By Mr. Jeremiah McAnarney*] Do you know Mrs. Lola Andrews? *A.* Yes, sir.

Q. How long have you known her? *A.* I have known Mrs. Lola Andrews for the last seven or eight years.

Q. Sometime in February of this year did you have a talk with her? *A.* Yes. [1377]

. . . . . .

Q. Now, tell us what was said. *A.* As I sat on my door step and as I know her I always spoke to her when she went by. I said to her, "Hello, Lola," and she stopped and she answered me. While she answered me I said, "You look kind of tired." She says, "Yes." She says, "They bothering the life out of me." I says, "What?" She says, "I just come from jail." I says, "What have you done in jail?" She says, "The Government took me down and want me to recognize those men," she says, "and I don't know a thing about them. I have never seen them and I can't recognize them." She says, "Unfortunately I have been down there [the shoe factories] to get a job and I have seen many men that I don't know and I have never paid any attention to any one." [1378]

. . . . . .

THE COURT. Mr. Witness, I would like to ask one question. Did you attempt to find out who this person was who represented the Government who was trying to get her to take and state that which was false?

THE WITNESS. Did I what?

MR. JEREMIAH McANARNEY. What is that question?

¶ THE COURT. Did you try to find out who it was who represented the Government?

THE WITNESS. No.

THE COURT. Why not?

THE WITNESS. Well, it didn't come into my mind. I wasn't sure, you know. It didn't——

THE COURT. Did you think the public interest was served by anybody representing the Government to try to get a woman——

THE WITNESS. I don't think of anything——

THE COURT. ——to identify somebody?

THE WITNESS. I don't think of anything at all. [1383]

. . . . .

——AFTER the prosecution had presented witnesses who identified Sacco as having been in So. Braintree before, during, and after the shooting—Andrews, Pelser and Splaine—it turned to the task of identifying Vanzetti as one of the bandits. No one identified Vanzetti as having been present at the shooting, but four witnesses testified they had seen him shortly before or after it in or near So. Braintree. The first of these was a commuter, Faulkner.——

John W. Faulkner, Sworn

Q. [By Mr. Williams] . . . What time did you leave your home in the morning [of April 15, 1920]? A. Why, I got the 9:23 train, I think it is. 9:20 or 9:23.

Q. From what station? A. Cohasset.

Q. A train going in what direction? A. To Boston.

. . . . .

Q. Do you remember what car of that train you got into? A. I always ride in the smoking car.

. . . . .

Q. And where in the smoker did you sit? A. Second seat on the left hand side.

Q. From which end? A. At the baggage end. [425]

. . . . .

Q. Was that one of those half-and-half smokers, with part for a baggage car in that end? A. Baggage, with a toilet on the right hand side.

. . . . .

Q. Now, at any time as you were traveling going towards Boston from Cohasset, was your attention directed to any conversation across the way? *A.* Why, yes. As we come in East Weymouth, the fellow on my right asked me if this was East Braintree. I said no. He said, "The man behind me wants to know if it is East Braintree."

Q. Did you look at the man behind? *A.* Yes, I took a look at the man behind.

Q. Where was he sitting? *A.* In the single seat next to the toilet.

. . . . .

Q. What kind of a looking man was that? *A.* Why, he looked like a foreigner, with a black mustache, and cheek bones. [426]

. . . . .

Q. Do you see that man that you saw in the train that day, and which you subsequently saw in the Plymouth jail, in the court house here? *A.* Yes, sir.

Q. Where do you see him? *A.* Sitting right over there [*indicating Vanzetti*].

. . . . .

[*June 28, 1921*]

Mr. JEREMIAH McANARNEY. By agreement of counsel it is agreed that this letter may be read into the records and its contents as given received as evidence. . . . [*Reads letter from N.Y., N.H. & H. R.R. addressed to him dated 27 June.*]

"Your inquiry of even date regarding make-up of Train 5108, Plymouth to Boston, April 15, 1920: According to our records this train consisted of the following equipment: Type; baggage and mail, number 2741. . . . Smoker number 1183; . . .

. . . . .

"Train was handled by engine 323. Smoker 1183 is a full length wooden vestibule smoker. . . ." [1350]

. . . . .

Cross-Examination

Q. [*By Mr. Moore*] Mr. Faulkner, there wasn't anything about this occurrence on the train that was extraordinary? Simply, a man asking for information, that is all that I understand that you said? *A.* Why, yes.

Q. You ride that train every day, do you? . . .

. . . . .

A. At that time I was.

Q. Did you see anybody on that train that you knew? *A.* Not that I remember of, no, sir.

. . . . .

Q. How about the man in front, that you say was sitting in front of him and right opposite you, who was that man? *A.* I don't know. He said he was a stranger.

. . . . .

Q. What kind of a looking man was he? *A.* I didn't notice him.

. . . . .

Q. Was he an oldish looking man? *A.* I don't remember.

Q. Or a youngish looking man? *A.* I don't remember.

Q. Was he a large man, or a small man? *A.* I don't remember that. [434]

. . . . .

————THE NEXT witness, Dolbeare, was a prospective juror who, upon seeing Vanzetti in the courtroom when the jury was being impanelled, disqualified himself for jury duty because he believed he had seen Vanzetti in a car in So. Braintree between 10 A.M. and noon, April 15, 1920.————

Harry E. Dolbeare, Sworn

Q. [*By Mr. Williams*] Did you see a car with a number of men in it? *A.* I did. [488]

. . . . .

Q. Did you see anybody . . . that you could describe. . . ? *A.* I did.

Q. And where did you see anybody that you now refer to? *A.* In the back part of the car.

Q. Will you describe him to the jury? . . . *A.* He looked like a foreigner, and he had a very heavy mustache, quite dark. . . .

. . . . .

Q. Do you see him now? *A.* I do.

. . . . .

Q. The one known as Bartolomeo Vanzetti? *A.* Yes, sir.

Q. Did you recognize him when you saw him in the court room that day? *A.* I did. I had the same view of him that day in the court room as I had in the car, a profile view.

Q. Is there any doubt in your mind he is the man you saw that day in South Braintree? *A.* Not a particle. [490]

. . . . .

Cross-Examination

Q. [*By Mr. McAnarney*] You were on Washington Street? *A.* I was. [491]

.   .   .   .   .

Q. About how fast should you say that car was going? *A.* I shouldn't say it was going over ten to twelve miles an hour.

.   .   .   .   .

Q. Then there was nothing to attract your attention to this man until the car was about directly opposite you? *A.* Yes, there was.

Q. What was it? *A.* The appearance of the whole five attracted my attention.

Q. . . . How did the whole five appear? *A.* They appeared strange to me, as strangers to the town, as a carload of foreigners. [495]

.   .   .   .   .

Q. Some time in your life you have seen an automobile with five people in it whom you didn't know? *A.* Yes, sir.

Q. And you have seen many an automobile with foreigners in it haven't you? *A.* Yes, sir.

Q. So the fact that they were not known to you, and they were foreigners, did that stand out to make a tremendous impression on your mind? *A.* It did.

Q. You have seen the automobiles coming up from the Fore River district, 5-passenger, 7-passenger, and all kinds and number of men in them? *A.* Yes, sir.

Q. And most of them appeared like foreigners, didn't they? *A.* No, I can't say they do.

Q. Haven't you ever been over and watched that crowd come out of Fore River? *A.* I have.

Q. There are a large number of foreigners working there? *A.* Yes.

Q. And it is nothing unusual to see an automobile with three or five or seven foreigners in it, is it? *A.* No.

Q. And those automobiles go through Holbrook, to Randolph, and all through that district from the Fore River with those workmen, don't they? *A.* Yes, sir.

Q. Well, give me some kind of a description of the men who were on that front seat? *A.* That I can't do. [496]

.   .   .   .   .

————MICHAEL LEVANGIE, the gate tender at the Pearl St. crossing of the N.Y., N.H., & H. R.R., said his gates were lowered when the bandits' car approached the crossing.————

Q. [*By Mr. Williams*] Now go ahead and tell us everything that happened from that point on. *A.* It came right up the hill as far as the gate. Of course, I had my gates down, and the first thing I knew, there was a revolver pointed like that at my head. I looked back at the train to see if I had a chance enough to let them go. I saw there was chance to let them go, and I let them, and I put my gates back again where they belonged. [415]

.   .   .   .   .

Q. Did you see anybody in that machine? *A.* I saw one man.

Q. Whereabouts did you see him? *A.* Driving the machine.

Q. Will you describe the man that you saw as it came across the crossing? *A.* Dark complected man, with cheek bones sticking out, black hair, heavy brown mustache, slouch hat, and army coat.

.   .   .   .   .

Q. How near were you to that man at any time—what was the closest? *A.* I didn't measure it, but I should say it was about 10 or 12 feet.

Q. Have you ever seen that man since? *A.* Yes, sir.

Q. Where have you seen him since that time? *A.* Brockton police station.

Q. Have you seen him since then? *A.* Yes [*indicates Vanzetti*]. [417]

Cross-Examination

Q. [*By Mr. McAnarney*] About two weeks ago, one afternoon I was up at your crossing, wasn't I? You talked with me two or three weeks ago, didn't you? *A.* I believe I did.

Q. What is that? *A.* I think I did.

Q. You know you did, don't you? Any doubt about that? Come, any doubt about that, Mr. Levangie? *A.* I don't know.

Q. You don't know whether you are in doubt about it, or not? I didn't have any revolver, did I,—nothing shiny in my hand? *A.* No, no.

Q. Was I there talking to you? *A.* Possibly you was. [421]

.   .   .   .   .

Q. Do you remember telling me about the man on the front seat? *A.* No, sir.

Q. Did you tell me anything? *A.* I don't know.

.   .   .   .   .

Q. Can't you remember asking—inviting me back to sit beside that shanty, that man getting up and me taking a seat there, and you talking to me? *A.* I don't remember.

Q. Can't you remember . . . telling me that my brother had acted for you in a case? *A.* I don't remember that.

. . . . . .

Q. Do you remember telling me that all the view you got of the man in the car was when the car was coming towards you, and you looked through the windshield, and could not see as he went by you on account of the curtains? Didn't you so tell me, Mr. Witness? *A.* I don't remember. [422]

. . . . . .

————ON JULY 11, nearly a month after Levangie testified, the defense presented Henry McCarthy, a locomotive fireman, who testified that he had talked to Levangie less than an hour after the shooting.————

Q. [By Mr. Jeremiah McAnarney] Now, will you please tell us what was said by Levangie or you . . . *A.* Levangie . . . was at the gate. The gates were up. He says, "There was a shooting affair going on." I says, "Someone shot?" I says, "Who?" "Someone, a fellow got murdered." I said, "Who did it?" He said he did not know. He said there was some fellows went by in an automobile and he heard the shots, and he started to put down the gates . . . one of them pointed a gun at him and he . . . ducked in the shanty. I asked him if he knew them. He said, no, he did not. I asked him if he would know them again if he saw them. He said, "No." He said all he could see was the gun and he ducked. [2000]

. . . . . .

————THE crossing tender at the Matfield crossing, Austin Reed, said he had seen a car coming from W. Bridgewater at 4:15 P.M., April 15, 1920, just as he was signalling the approach of a train.————

[June 15, 1921]

Q. [By Mr. Williams] What happened as you stood there with your sign at the side of the track? *A.* . . . I had my sign in my hand, and as they approached they did not seem to want to stop then.

Q. Yes. *A.* And one of them in the automobile asked me, "What to hell are you holding us up for?" He pointed his finger at me, and they were talking amongst themselves, and seemed quite anxious to get by. [595]

. . . . . .

Q. The train went by? *A.* Yes.

Q. Then what did you see? *A.* This automobile came by, and they swung up aside of the shanty, and he pointed his finger at me again.

Q. Who? *A.* And he says, "What to hell did you hold us up for?" And they beat it down the street and went down Matfield Street.

Q. Was it the same man who had spoken to you before, or a different man? *A.* This is the same man.

Q. How near was he to you when he made that second remark to you by your shanty? *A.* Within about four feet of the doorway.

Q. Was the machine standing still or was it moving? *A.* It was moving. [596]

. . . . . .

Q. Will you describe the appearance . . . of that man who spoke to you those two times? *A.* He was a dark complected man, kind of hollow cheeks, with high cheek bones, had a stubbed mustache . . . bushy. His hair was black.

Q. Do you remember how he was dressed? *A.* He had a slouch hat on, dark, dark slouch hat, and a dark suit.

Q. Have you ever seen that man since that day? *A.* Yes, sir.

Q. Where did you see him after that time? *A.* Brockton police station.

Q. When did you see him there? *A.* About three weeks after he was arrested.

Q. Do you see that man in the court room now? *A.* Yes, sir [*indicates Vanzetti*]. [597]

. . . . . .

Cross-Examination

Q. [*By Mr. McAnarney*] Now, when was it that you were brought to see any man, to see if you could identify him as the man who was in that automobile? When was it? *A.* Along the first of May.

. . . . . .

Q. Well, where? *A.* The Brockton police station.

. . . . . .

Q. You were sent for? . . . *A.* No, sir. [605]

. . . . . .

Q. You thought you would do a little detective work of your own. Is that right? *A.* [*Witness hesitates.*]

Q. That is right, isn't it? *A.* [*Witness hesitates.*] Yes.

. . . . . .

Q. Well, what did you do first? *A.* Why, I asked to see the two defendants that were there.

Q. Where did you have to go to see the defendants after you made that request? *A.* I was told to go into a room. They brought the two men into the room.

. . . . . .

————ON JUNE 16, the fourteenth day of the trial, the prosecution turned from identification to a new strategy, one not even announced in Mr. Williams' opening statement. Using the testimony of Mr. & Mrs. Simon Johnson and the police officers who arrested the defendants, the prosecution sought to show that the defendants exhibited a "consciousness of guilt" that proved their involvement in the So. Braintree crime. So important was this testimony in the eyes of the judge that he wrote in 1924, "The evidence that convicted these defendants was circumstantial . . . evidence . . . known in the law as 'consciousness of guilt.'" [3514] Johnson owned a garage in which Mike Boda, a friend of Sacco and Vanzetti, had stored his 1914 Overland. After the So. Braintree robbery, the police in surrounding communities asked garage owners to report any suspicious attempt of foreigners to obtain a car. Thus, when the four Italians, Boda, Sacco, Vanzetti and one Orciana, appeared at the Johnson's house at 9:20 P.M., May 5, to ask about Boda's car, Mrs. Johnson, on the pretext of going to borrow some milk, walked to a neighbor's house to telephone the police.————

Q. [*By Mr. Williams*] Now will you tell us what happened from that time on? *A.* [*By Mrs. Johnson*] Well, I stepped out of the door, and I started toward Brockton. These two men seemed to come right along with me, only on the other side of the street. I was on the left-hand side, and they were on the right-hand side. Then I went [175 feet] over to the next house. [677]

. . . . . .

Q. Where were those men that you spoke of? *A.* They walked right along with me.

Q. How far away from you were they, Mrs. Johnson? *A.* About three yards and a half.

Q. You were walking along the road? *A.* Yes. [679]

. . . . . .

Q. Now, after you came out, Mrs. Johnson, what did you do? *A.* I walked down the driveway, and as I got to the end of the driveway two men walked alongside of me.

Q. What two men? *A.* The same that followed me up.

Q. Where were they when you got down to the end of the drive-way? *A.* They seemed to walk right along with me.

• • • •

Q. And as you walked along on the same side going back, what did you notice about the two men? *A.* I could see them plain. They were on the car track.

Q. What were they doing? *A.* Just walking along as I did. [680]

• • • •

Q. Now, what happened as you went along there going back to the house? *A.* As I got up to the motorcycle [on which Boda and Orciana had ridden] I heard it was running. Then I saw the two men stop.

Q. Stop where? *A.* At the motorcycle. [681]

• • • •

Q. Now, do you see that man you saw on North Elm Street with the motorcycle, and you later saw in the Brockton police station, here in court today? *A.* Yes.

Q. And where do you see him? *A.* Right there [*pointing to Sacco*].

• • • •

Cross-Examination

Q. [*By Mr. McAnarney*] Now, Boda came there to get his car, didn't he? *A.* [*By Mr. Johnson*] Yes.

Q. There were no 1920 number plates on it? *A.* No.

Q. You advised him not to take the car and run it without the 1920 plates, didn't you? *A.* Yes.

Q. And he accepted your view? *A.* He seemed to.

Q. He seemed to. And after some conversation went away? *A.* Yes. [715]

• • • •

————SHORTLY after they left the Johnsons', Sacco and Vanzetti boarded a streetcar for Brockton. They were arrested on the streetcar by a policeman, Michael J. Connolly, responding to Mrs. Johnson's telephone call.————

Q. [*By Mr. Williams*] Will you tell the jury what you did after boarding the car. . . ? *A.* [*By Mr. Connolly*] . . . I got up where the motorman stands—one of them closed cars—I looked the length of the car to see if I could see two foreigners, which the telephone had said had tried to steal or take an automobile in Bridgewater.

Mr. Jeremiah McAnarney. I ask that be struck out.

The Court. That may be stricken out.

. . . . . .

Q. What was said to you is not competent. What you saw and what you did is all I am asking about. *A.* That is what I am doing now.

Q. Well, you looked down the car, and what did you see and do? *A.* I seen Sacco and Vanzetti sitting on the end seat, the left-hand end seat. [751]

. . . . . .

Q. I went down through the car and when I got opposite to the seat I stopped and I asked them where they came from. [751] They said "Bridgewater." I said, "What was you doing in Bridgewater?" They said, "We went down to see a friend of mine." I said, "Who is your friend?" He said, "A man by the—they call him 'Poppy.'" "Well," I said, "I want you, you are under arrest." Vanzetti was sitting on the inside of the seat. . . . Toward the window. The inside of the car; and he went, put his hand in his hip pocket and I says, "Keep your hands out on your lap, or you will be sorry."

The Defendant Vanzetti. You are a liar!

The Witness. They wanted to know what they were arrested for. I says, "Suspicious characters." We went,—oh, it was maybe about three minutes' ride where the automobile met the car coming from the central station. Officer Vaughn got on just before, and when he got on I told him to stand up, and I told Officer Vaughn to fish Vanzetti; and I just gave Sacco a slight going over, just felt him over, did not go into his pockets, and we led them out the front way of the car.

Q. Now, just a minute, please. Was anything found on either man at that time? *A.* There was a revolver found on Vanzetti.

. . . . . .

Q. Go ahead, then. *A.* I put Sacco and Vanzetti in the back seat of our light machine, and Officer Snow got in the back seat with them. I took the front seat with the driver, . . . turned around and faced Sacco and Vanzetti.

Q. All right. *A.* I told them when we started that the first false move I would put a bullet in them. On the way up to the station Sacco reached his hand to put under his overcoat and I told him to keep his hands outside of his clothes and on his lap. [752]

. . . . . .

A. I says to him, "Have you got a gun there?" He says, "No." He says, "I ain't got no gun." "Well," I says, "keep your hands outside of your clothes." We went along a little further and he done the same thing. I gets up on my knees on the front seat and I reaches over and I puts my hand under his coat but I did not see any gun. "Now," I says, "Mister, if you put your hand in there again you are going to get into trouble." He says, "I don't want no trouble." We reached the station, brought them up to the office, searched them. [753]

. . . . .

Q. [By Mr. Williams] Will you describe to the jury what you did in respect to Sacco, where you did it and what you found, if anything, upon him? A. [By Officer Merle Speare.] At the desk in the central police station they were brought and searched, and I first,—we took a number of automatic cartridges from his right hip pocket. I took an automatic revolver.

THE COURT. How many, did you say?

THE WITNESS. Later counted twenty-three. From in his waist I took an automatic .32 Colt revolver. [781]

————AT THE Brockton police station, Police Chief Michael Stewart questioned the defendants. The prosecutor read a transcript of interrogation to the jury.————

. . . . .

THE COURT. I suppose it is agreed that the testimony should have exactly the same effect as evidence as though the witness himself testified to it on the witness stand?

MR. McANARNEY. That is correct.

. . . . .

MR. KATZMANN. [Reading]

"I am going to ask you [Vanzetti] some questions. You are under arrest for crime. You are not obliged to answer them unless you see fit, and if you do, what you say may be later used against you.

"Q. What is your nationality? A. Italian.

"Q. What is your name? A. Bartolomeo Vanzetti.

. . . . .

"Q. What is your business? A. Am fish peddler. [842]

"Q. Were you in West Bridgewater tonight? A. I think so. I am not sure. I am not acquainted.

"Q. Who was with you? A. My friend.

"Q. Who is he? A. . . . Sacco.

"Q. What were you doing in West Bridgewater? A. I went to Bridgewater to see my good friend.

"Q. Who is your friend in Bridgewater? A. Poppy.

"*Q.* What is his first name? *A.* That is not his name. I don't know his name. They call him just 'Poppy,' what you call a nickname.

"*Q.* Where does he live in Bridgewater? *A.* I don't know.

"*Q.* How long have you known him? *A.* A long time. I worked with him in the cordage company in Plymouth.

"*Q.* How long did you work with him? *A.* About two years.

"*Q.* And you don't know his name? *A.* They call him 'Poppy.' He is a strong, big man; wears a blue shirt.

• • • • •

"*Q.* Who did you go to see in Boston? *A.* Nobody. I go to see my friend in South Stoughton.

"*Q.* Do you mean Sacco? *A.* Yes. He is going to Italy. I get a letter from him, and he asked me to come as he is going to Italy soon. I did go to his house I think Monday, I am not sure."

• • • • •

"*Q.* What time did you leave Stoughton to go and see 'Poppy?' *A.* Maybe half past three.

• • • • •

"*Q.* Do you know Mike Boda? *A.* No. [845]

• • • • •

"*Q.* You are sure you have seen no motorcycle in West Bridgewater tonight? . . . *A.* No, I have seen no motorcycle.

• • • • •

"*Q.* And you don't know Mike Boda?

• • • • •

"*A.* No." [846]

• • • • •

MR. KATZMANN. It is agreed, if your Honor please, that Chief Stewart, the same night at the Brockton police station, asked the following questions and received the following answers from the defendant Sacco. . . .

[*Mr. Katzmann reads as follows:*]

"My name is Stewart. I am a police officer. I am going to ask you some questions, which you are not obliged to answer, and if you do answer, what you say may be used against you in court.

"*Q.* What is your name? *A.* Nicola Sacco.

• • • • •

"*Q.* Do you know Bartolomeo Vanzetti? *A.* Yes. He is my friend.

• • • • •

"*Q.* What time did you leave your house? *A.* After supper.

"*Q.* What time was that? *A.* Maybe half past six.

"*Q.* What did you go to West Bridgewater for? *A.* My friend, Mr. Vanzetti, go to see his friend, and he asked me to come.

"*Q.* Who is his friend? *A.* I don't know. I never see him.

"*Q.* Did you see him tonight? *A.* No. We ride a long ways, and get off the car at Elm Square.

. . . . .

"*Q.* What did you then? *A.* We walked a long ways. We go to the square. My friend says we is too late, maybe his friend sleeping. So we walked back.

. . . . .

"*Q.* Who were the men on the motorcycle tonight in West Bridgewater? [847]

. . . . .

"*A.* I no see any motorcycle.

. . . . .

"*Q.* Do you know Mike Boda?

. . . . .

"*A.* No." [848]

————BEFORE resting its case, the prosecution returned to identification and devoted three days to testimony intended to show that the cap found in the street beside Berardelli's body was Sacco's, that the bullet that killed Berardelli came from Sacco's Colt .32, and that the pistol found in Vanzetti's hip pocket was Berardelli's.————

Q. [*By Mr. Williams*] Now, when you arrived at the scene, was there anything which you noticed on the street near the body of Berardelli? *A.* [*By Fred Loring, a shoe worker employed by Slater & Morrill.*] A cap.

Q. Where was the cap? *A.* It was about 18 inches from Berardelli's body, towards the street.

Q. Did you do anything in regard to that cap? *A.* Yes. I picked it up.

Q. What did you do with it. *A.* Carried it down to the shop . . . and gave it to Mr. Fraher.

. . . . .

[*Mr. Williams hands a bundle to the witness.*]

Q. Will you open that bundle, and see if you can tell the jury what it is? *A.* That is the cap.

. . . . .

Q. Can you tell whether it is in the same condition now as when you found it? *A.* Just the same. [798]

Cross-Examination

Q. [By *Mr. McAnarney*] You heard some remarks about somebody was shot? *A.* Yes, sir.

Q. Did you look out? *A.* I looked out of the window, and saw a crowd out there.

.   .   .   .   .

Q. How many were in that crowd? *A.* About 40.

Q. About 40. Moving around? *A.* Yes.

.   .   .   .   .

Q. Did you see anyone out there without their hats? *A.* I didn't see anyone out there without a hat on.

Q. Did you notice every man out there at that time had a hat on? *A.* No.

Q. You don't know whether they had hats on? *A.* No, I am not sure.

Q. Didn't notice whether they had hat, cap or were bareheaded? *A.* No.

Mr. McAnarney. That is all. [802]

.   .   .   .   .

Mr. George T. Kelley, Sworn

Q. [By *Mr. Williams*] Where do you live? *A.* Stoughton, Massachusetts.

Q. What is your business? *A.* Superintendent of a shoe factory.

Q. Known as what? *A.* 3-K Shoe Company.

Q. Do you know the defendant Nicola Sacco? *A.* Yes, sir. [851]

Q. How long have you known him? *A.* I have known him for ten or twelve years.

Q. Was he employed at the 3-K in Stoughton, in the early spring and summer of 1920? *A.* Yes, sir.

Q. Do you know for how long he had been employed by you there on April 15, 1920? How long prior to that time? *A.* I should say possibly six or eight months.

Q. In what capacity was he employed? *A.* When he first went to work for us he was employed as an edge trimmer . . . Then he has worked taking care of the boiler nights, part time, not staying all night, but part time. [852]

.   .   .   .   .

Q. What kind of head gear was Sacco accustomed to wear, if you know? A. There were times that he wore a cap. There was other times he wore a hat.

Q. What kind of a cap have you seen him wearing? A. I have seen him wear a dark cap . . . of a salt and pepper design.

Q. What have you seen in regard to this cap, if anything? A. Nothing more than coming in to work and hanging it up on a nail. [853]

Q. What can you tell us in regard to its condition? As to whether it was old or new clean or dirty? A. Why, I should say it was naturally dirty.

Q. I wish you would look at what has been introduced for identification as No. 11, [cap picked up by Loring, later designated Exhibit 29] and let me ask you, to the best of your recollection, knowledge and belief, if that cap is alike in appearance to the cap that you have described as being worn by Sacco? A. [*Witness examines cap.*] The only thing I could say about that cap, Mr. Williams, from hanging up on a nail in the distance, it was similar in color. As far as details are concerned, I could not say it was.

Q. You have been shown that cap before? A. Yes, sir. Of course, you realize that inside there [*indicating*] the earlappers, and so forth, I never had any way of examining that cap to see if the ear laps were in there. The only method I had of looking at the cap from observation was if it hung up on a nail somewhere, just passing by and knowing whether it was black, white or green.

. . . . .

Q. Do you know if anything had occurred to his cap by reason of being hung up on a nail? A. No, sir.

Q. Have you examined the lining of this cap? A. I did.

Q. What do you notice to be the condition of the lining? A. Torn. [854]

. . . . .

Mr. Williams. If your Honor please, I offer this cap in evidence. It has been marked for identification, and I now offer it as an exhibit.

Mr. Jeremiah McAnarney. I object.

The Court. I would like to ask the witness one question: whether, —I wish you would ask him, rather,—according to your best judgment, is it your opinion that the cap which Mr. Williams now holds in his hand is like the one that was worn by the defendant Sacco?

Mr. Moore. I object to that question, your Honor.

The Court. [*To Mr. Williams*] Did you put it? I would rather it come from Mr. Williams. Will you put that question?

Q. Mr. Kelley, according to your best judgment, is the cap I show you alike in appearance to the cap worn by Sacco? *A.* In color only.

THE COURT. That is not responsive to the question. I wish you would answer it, if you can.

THE WITNESS. I can't answer it when I don't know right down in my heart that that is the cap.

THE COURT. I don't want you to. I want you should answer according to what is in your heart.

THE WITNESS. General appearance, that is all I can say. I never saw that cap so close in my life as I do now.

THE COURT. In its general appearance, is it the same?

THE WITNESS. Yes, sir.

MR. MOORE. I object to that last question and answer.

THE COURT. You may put the question so it comes from counsel rather than from the Court.[3]

Q. In its general appearance, is it the same? *A.* Yes.

MR. WILLIAMS. I now offer the cap, if your Honor please.

THE COURT. Admitted.

MR. MOORE. Save an exception.

MR. JEREMIAH MCANARNEY. Save an exception.

[*The cap is admitted in evidence and marked "Exhibit 29."*]

MR. WILLIAMS. [*Passing Exhibit 29 to the jury.*] Notice the outside and inside. [857]

. . . . . .

————IN THE INTERESTS of continuity, the defense's handling of the issue of Sacco's cap is presented here. Actually, this testimony was given on the thirtieth day of the trial in the course of Sacco's examination by his lawyers, whereas the immediately preceding testimony on the cap was given on the seventeenth day of the trial.————

[*July 6, 1921*]

Q. [*By Mr. Moore*] By the way, Mr. Sacco, there has been introduced in evidence here a cap that is marked Exhibit 29. Is that your cap? *A.* [*Witness examines cap.*] I never wear black much. Always a gray cap; always wear gray cap. Always I like gray cap.

MR. MOORE. That is not an answer to my question. [1850]

MR. KATZMANN. I ask that answer be stricken out. The question is, is it your cap, not what color he wears.

---

[3] The judge's request was evidently directed to the stenographer, who failed to comply with it.

THE WITNESS. No, sir.

THE COURT. The other answer may be stricken out.

Q. Do you know anything about that cap? A. No, sir, never saw it.

Q. Did you ever have a cap of any color made in that form with the fur lining? A. Never in my life.

Q. See if this is your size. A. [Witness puts cap on head.] The way I look. Could not go in. My size is 7-⅛.

THE COURT. Put that on again, please.

[The witness places cap on head again.]

THE COURT. That is all. [1851]

.   .   .   .   .

Q. [By Mr. Katzmann] I show you a cap. Will you look it over, please, and tell me if you know whose cap that is? [This is Exhibit 43, Sacco's cap taken from his house by police.] [1927]

.   .   .   .   .

A. [By Sacco] It looks like my cap.

Q. Did you have such a cap as that in your house at the time of your arrest? A. Yes, sir, something like.

Q. You think it is.

.   .   .   .   .

Q. Isn't it your cap? A. I think it is my cap, yes.

Q. Well, wait a minute, please. Look at it carefully, will you? A. [Witness examines cap.] Yes.

Q. There isn't any question but what that is your hat, is there?

.   .   .   .   .

A. No, I think it is my cap.

.   .   .   .   .

Q. Will you try that cap on, please, and watch yourself when you put it on, just how you put it on? A. [Witness does so.]

Q. Will you turn around so the jury can see, all the way, please? A. [Witness does so.]

Q. The other side, this side. Is there anything you want to say? Did I catch you as wanting to say something? I thought perhaps you did. A. I don't know. That cap looks too dirty to me because I never wear dirty cap. I think I always have fifty cents to buy a cap, and I don't work with a cap on my head when I work. I always keep clean cap. Right when I go to the factory, take all my clothes off and put overalls and jump. It look to me pretty dirty and too dark. Mine I think was little more light, little more gray.

Q. Is that your hat?

.   .   .   .   .

Q. Is it your cap? I should not say "hat." Cap? *A.* I think it is. It looks like, but it is probably dirt,—probably dirty after.

. . . . .

Q. Will you try Exhibit 29 on, and use the same amount of force [1928] in putting it on that you used in putting that hat on? *A.* Yes [*doing so*]. Can't go in.

Q. Can't go in? *A.* No.

Q. Try and pull it down in back and see if it can't go in. *A.* Oh, but it is too tight.

————*THE BOSTON HERALD* of July 8 described the appearance of Exhibit 29 on Sacco as follows: "It stuck on the top of his head and he turned with a satisfied air to let the jury see."————

. . . . .

Q. I call your attention to Exhibit 43 to that in the lining. What is it? *A.* I never saw that before.

. . . . .

Q. Don't know what that is? *A.* It is a hole.

. . . . .

Q. Never saw that before. Was there any hole in your hat when you last saw it? *A.* Hole, no.

Q. Sure of that? *A.* Pretty sure.

Q. Where did you hang your hats up? If this is your hat, did you ever wear it to work? *A.* Yes.

Q. What do you hang it up on? *A.* On a wall . . . [on a nail.] [1929]

[*July 11, 1921*]

George T. Kelley, Recalled

Q. [*By Mr. Jeremiah McAnarney*] Mr. Kelley, I show you Exhibit 29 in the record and Exhibit 43, and ask you to examine both caps and see which appears more like the cap which you saw in your factory as being the one that Sacco used to wear. *A.* [*Witness examines cap, hanging one of the caps on a hook on the door and leaves the witness stand to look at it.*] [2003]

Mr. Jeremiah McAnarney. The witness indicates cap Exhibit 43. [2004]

. . . . .

Q. [*By Mr. Jeremiah McAnarney*] You say Exhibit 43 looks more like your husband's cap? *A.* [*By Mrs. Sacco*] Yes.

Q. Did your husband ever wear a cap like that "29," this cap? Did he ever have a cap like that? *A.* My husband never wore caps with anything around for his ears, never, because he never liked it and because, besides that, never, he never wore them because he don't look good in them, positively. [2065]

. . . . .

————VANZETTI'S gun had the same potential significance as the cap found at the scene of the crime. If it could be shown beyond reasonable doubt that Vanzetti had Berardelli's gun in his hip pocket when he was arrested, the prosecution's case against him would probably have been clinched even though no conclusive evidence was presented to prove Vanzetti was present at the shooting. To attempt to prove this crucial point to the jury, the prosecution called first on Berardelli's widow.————

Q. [*By Mr. Williams*] Do you know whether . . . [Berardelli carried a] gun while he was at work . . . ? *A.* Yes, sir.

Q. Could you describe his gun to the jury? *A.* I suppose I could if I would see it.

. . . . .

Q. I will show you that revolver [taken by police from Vanzetti at his arrest], which is Exhibit 27, and ask . . . have you ever seen a gun like that before? *A.* I think I did.

Q. And where have you seen a gun like that? *A.* If I seen just like it? [806]

Q. I say, where? I thought your answer was "like that." Now, I ask you where? *A.* I have seen one that my husband carried.

Q. At some time before the shooting, do you know whether or not your husband had done something with the gun which he carried? *A.* Why, yes, three weeks before he got shot, why, he brought it in the place to have it repaired.

. . . . .

Q. Was the name Iver Johnson Company? *A.* Yes, sir.

. . . . .

Q. Well, do you know what the matter with the gun was? *A.* It was a spring broke. [807]

. . . . .

Q. Now, at some time after that did he do anything about getting the gun back? *A.* No. He returned the check to Mr. Parmenter.

. . . . .

Cross-Examination

Q. [*By Mr. McAnarney*] You don't know whether he got that re-volver back, or not? *A.* No. He returned the ticket to Mr. Parmenter, and I don't know if Mr. Parmenter got it for him, but I know Mr. Parmenter let him take another one.

Q. And the one he let him take was a black handle one? *A.* Yes, sir.

Q. And it looked like the other one? *A.* Yes, sir.

Mr. McAnarney. That is all. [809]

. . . . .

————LINCOLN WADSWORTH, an Iver Johnson employee, testified that he had made a record of Berardelli's gun when it was brought in.

Q. [*By Mr. Williams*] . . . [W]ill you tell the jury the facts as to that revolver? *A.* .38 Harrison & Richardson revolver, property of Alex Berardelli, was brought in for repairs, and sent up to the shop on March 20, 1920. [814]

. . . . .

Q. Can you tell the jury whether or not the revolver which was brought in on that date is of the same type and calibre of revolver as the one I have now shown you [namely, Vanzetti's]?

Mr. McAnarney. To that I object.

Q. That simply calls for a Yes or No answer. Can you tell? *A.* Yes.

Q. You need not answer this until my friends have a chance to ob-ject. I am going to ask you whether or not that revolver is the same make and calibre of revolver as the one which was brought in?

. . . . .

The Court. I suppose you are going to show, are you not, later by evidence tending to prove that the revolver in front of the witness was the same revolver that Berardelli had at the time of the alleged shoot-ing?

Mr. Williams. I am, if your Honor please.

The Court. With that assurance, the witness may answer.

Mr. McAnarney. Save an exception.

Mr. Moore. Save an exception.

The Court. Certainly. And reserving a right, as in all other matters, to have the evidence stricken from the record if the connection is not made. [815] . . . . .

Q. Now will you tell us? *A.* It is the same calibre and make. [816]

————AFTER George Fitzmeyer, an Iver Johnson gunsmith, testified that he put a new hammer in Berardelli's revolver, Mr. Williams handed him Exhibit 27.————————————————————————

Q. Now will you tell us if, in your opinion, any repairs have been made to that revolver recently? *A.* Well, a new hammer, I should call it, a new hammer.

Q. And how can you tell a new hammer has been put in there? *A.* Well, the firing pin does not show of ever being struck. There isn't any burnt mark or powder mark or anything on it. [822]

————TO DETERMINE if Berardelli got his revolver back after it was repaired, the prosecution questioned James Jones, manager of the Iver Johnson shop. He testified that there was no record of Berardelli's having received it, but since the gun was no longer in the shop and since there was no record of its having been sold as a used gun, Jones inferred Berardelli had gotten it back. The defense summoned two firearms experts both of whom denied that Exhibit 27 had a new hammer. One of them, James E. Burns, for thirty years a ballistic engineer with U. S. Cartridge Co., demonstrated the age of the hammer to the jurymen, one by one.————————————————————

[June 28, 1921]

Mr. Burns. The double-acting sear [*indicating*] is the part that engages the hammer. The notch in the hammer raises the hammer and when it gets up to a certain distance it lets go and lets the hammer fall. When that sear comes back, just a slight spring tension on it, [it] has worn the face of the hammer so that it is highly polished, and that is a case-hardened hammer. It would take some use, some time to polish that.

.   .   .   .   .

The double-acting sear rubs the face of the hammer, see it? When the hammer goes down the double-acting sear rubs across the face of the hammer, see, and it has polished it, from there down . . . Now I will cock it. See that double-acting sear comes up. It is done so quick, rubbing across there, it has polished the face of that hammer. . . . See the wear on it? . . . Get the light shining on it just right. See the wear on it? . . . It is case-hardened, case-hardened. Is that all?

Mr. Jeremiah McAnarney. Mr. Katzmann, the hammer on the revolver the jury has just looked at is, is it not, the hammer that Mr. Fitzmeyer, whom you called last week, said was a new hammer?

Mr. Katzmann. It is.

Q. Is there any doubt in your mind, Mr. Burns, but that it is a used hammer? *A.* It is not any more than the rest of the gun. Doesn't show any more use than the rest of the gun.

Q. Is it anyway, is it a hammer that has been used? *A.* Yes, sir. [1418]

Q. And are you able to say the extent? . . . In other words, how old is that gun? *A.* Well, that gun is sixteen years old. [1419]

————PROBABLY no task of identification was more laborious, controversial, and crucial to the prosecution's case against Sacco than the task of linking bullet III and Sacco's Colt .32. Of the six bullets recovered from the bodies of Berardelli and Parmenter, five, according to the testimony of the prosecution's ballistics experts, could not possibly have been fired from either of the pistols found by police on the defendants. But the sixth bullet, they agreed, had been fired from a Colt .32. Moreover, the physician who performed the autopsy on Berardelli testified that it was the sixth bullet that had caused his death. To identify it, he scratched a "III" on its left base with a surgical needle. In its efforts to link bullet III and Sacco's gun, the prosecution called first on Capt. Wm. Proctor of the Massachusetts State Police, a ballistics expert who had testified in more than 100 capital cases.————

[June 21, 1921]

Q. *[By Mr. Williams]* How certain can you be then of your opinion that . . . [all the bullets but III were] fired from a Savage automatic .32? *A.* I can be as certain of that as I can of anything. [891]

.   .   .   .   .

Q. Have you any opinion as to whether bullet III was fired from the Colt automatic which is in evidence [Sacco's gun]? *A.* I have.

Q. And what is your opinion? *A.* My opinion is that it is consistent with being fired by that pistol. [896]

————THE PROSECUTION also summoned Capt. Charles Van Amburgh, an assistant in the ballistics department of the Remington Co., who was asked to compare bullet III with test bullets fired from Sacco's gun.————

Q. *[By Mr. Williams]* Now, Captain, . . . having in mind your examination of No. III, your examination of the six bullets fired by you and Captain Proctor at Lowell, have you formed an opinion as to whether or not the No. III bullet was fired from the Colt automatic gun [Sacco's] which you have in front of you?

. . . .

A. I am inclined to believe that it was fired, No. III bullet was fired, from this Colt automatic pistol. [920]

. . . .

Q. Now what is the basis of your opinion, Captain, or bases? *A.* My measurements of rifling marks on No. III bullet as compared with the width of the impressions which I have taken of No. III or of this particular barrel, together with the measurements of the width or dimension of rifling marks in bullets recovered from oiled sawdust in Lowell, inclines me to the belief.

Q. Now, what marks have you observed which occasioned you to have that belief? *A.* You mean, in addition to the dimensions of rifling marks?

Q. Yes. I mean, are there any peculiarities or irregularities of those bullets which you have observed which assist you to form an opinion? *A.* There are.

Q. And will you describe them to the jury? *A.* There are irregularities evidently caused by similar scoring or irregular marks in rifling which appear on all bullets which I have examined that I know have been fired from this one automatic pistol which is before me.

Q. Yes. And what about No. III? *A.* No. III bullets, [*sic*] I find on No. III bullets [*sic*] such evidence of scoring in the barrel. It takes on the bullets the form of a, well, a long streak bordering close on the narrow cut, the land cut, on the bullet.

Q. Is there anything in the barrel of that revolver which can be shown to the jury so they can see it which will help them to understand what you mean by irregularities caused by something in the pistol? *A.* I believe it can be shown to the jury.

Q. Well, will you show it, if you will, and I will manipulate any lighting apparatus which is necessary. You are at liberty to step down from the witness stand and do anything that is necessary.

[*The witness leaves the stand.*]

THE WITNESS. It is a difficult matter to point it out. I can indicate it.

MR. WILLIAMS. If you can tell them what you see in there, then, possibly, by looking themselves they will be able to see part at least of what you see.

THE WITNESS. Close to the land which is now on the bottom portion of the bore of the barrel, on the right side as you look in, you will see a rough track.

MR. WILLIAMS. Would a microscope assist?

THE WITNESS. It might.

MR. WILLIAMS. Mr. Katzmann suggests that the jury be allowed one by one to go to the window and look at the bullet.

THE COURT. I would suggest that the witness go to the window and see if it may be explained better at the window.

THE WITNESS. I believe the light is better.

MR. WILLIAMS. Don't you think that will help? [921]

THE WITNESS. Yes.

MR. WILLIAMS. You can hold it in proper position. The jury may step up one by one.

THE COURT. Explain to the jury what you have in mind, but explain it in such a way that all can hear.

MR. WILLIAMS. Did you hear, Captain, the Judge's suggestion?

[*The jurors go one by one to the window to examine the barrel as shown by the witness.*]

THE WITNESS. On the bottom portion of the barrel as you look into it, beside that land on the right side of it is a rough track, at the bottom of the barrel.

THE COURT. Would you like some fans, any of you? Oh, you have them, all right.

THE WITNESS. At the bottom of the barrel is a rough track.

THE COURT. Mr. Foreman, you might come right around and be ready, and then follow right around so you will be there.

THE WITNESS. On the bottom a rough track. At the bottom of the barrel is a rough track.

[*The witness returns to the witness stand.*] [922]

. . . . . .

Cross-Examination

Q. [*By Mr. McAnarney*] You have now been telling us about the pitting of the barrel of a pistol, haven't you? *A.* I have some knowledge——

. . . . . .

Q. And you have found a condition inside of the barrel of that automatic caused by allowing the gun to rust, haven't you? *A.* It could be caused.

. . . . . .

Q. You will say it was? *A.* That is generally what causes pitting in most cases, therefore, I am inclined to believe it was caused by rust.

Q. You believe and you are inclined to believe. [923]

. . . . . .

Q. You know it was, don't you, by your months of study, that [it] has been rusty? *A.* I believe it has been caused by rust.

Q. When you say "I believe," have you anything back of that that you don't quite feel sure of? *A.* Yes, I have a slight reservation.

. . . . . .

————TO COMBAT the prosecution's ballistics experts, the defense summoned James E. Burns, who has been mentioned above, and J. H. Fitzgerald, who was in charge of testing in the Colt factory at Hartford.————————————————————————————————————

Q. [*By Mr. Jeremiah McAnarney*] Well, having in mind the appearance of No. III on the photograph there, bullet No. III, and having in mind the grooves made on the [1413] bullets fired from the Colt automatic and designated as the Sacco gun, have you an opinion as to whether the so-called fatal bullet No. III was fired from the Sacco gun? *A.* [*By Mr. Burns.*] I have.

Q. Was it fired from the Sacco gun? *A.* Not in my opinion, no.

Q. [O]n what do you base that opinion? *A.* On the 11 bullets that I examined that were fired from the Sacco gun. [1414]

————FITZGERALD'S testimony was substantially the same as Burns'.

. . . . . .

Q. [*By Mr. Jeremiah McAnarney*] In substance, repeating my former question, are you able to form an opinion,—were you able to form an opinion as to whether bullet No. III was fired from Exhibit 28 [Sacco's gun]? *A.* [*By Mr. Fitzgerald*] I was.

Q. What is your opinion? *A.* My opinion is that No. III bullet was not fired from the pistol given me as Exhibit 28.

Q. Kindly now explain to the jury the reasons that you have for that opinion. *A.* The land marks on the No. III bullet do not correspond, in my best judgment, to bullets I have seen fired from this pistol. [1466]

. . . . . .

THE COURT. Then, having reached the hour of five . . . May I ask you, Mr. District Attorney, about when the prosecution will finish its evidence. . . ?

. . . . . .

MR. KATZMANN. . . . [W]e believe we have nothing further to offer. [937]

. . . . . .

[*June 22, 1921*]

. . . . .

THE COURT. Does that close——

MR. KATZMANN. The Commonwealth rests, if your Honor please.

. . . . . .

B. THE CASE FOR THE DEFENSE

————WHEN Mr. Katzmann closed the case for the Commonwealth, it marked the end of 940 pages of testimony directed against Sacco and Vanzetti. Now, after nineteen days, it was the turn of the McAnarney brothers and Messrs. Moore and Callahan to refute, weaken, or somehow deflect the charges made against the defendants. The efforts of the defense took up sixteen days in court and filled 1,133 pages of the *Transcript of the Record.*————

[*June 22, 1921*]

THE COURT. [*To the jury*] Mr. Foreman and gentlemen, it is my duty to make the same suggestions to you immediately preceding the opening by counsel for the defendants that I did preceding the opening by Mr. Williams, counsel for the Commonwealth. As I said to you then, and I repeat now, these are simply opening statements, sometimes called the opening arguments, but they are statements to give you an intelligent idea of the evidence that the defendants propose to introduce for your consideration, and that being true, you must bear in mind, as I said then, that statements by counsel in any opening should never be considered evidence. . . .

The Commonwealth has now rested. . . . You have not heard the testimony of the defendants and, therefore, you should still keep your minds open and in a state of absolute impartiality, with a view of deciding these cases after you have heard all the evidence, and after you have heard the arguments, and after you have heard the charge, and then you will return to your jury room and, as I said, I hope your minds then will be in as near a perfect state of impartiality as the general lot of humanity will permit, with a view of determining from all the evidence introduced on both sides as to what is the truth.

You may proceed with the opening, please.

MR. CALLAHAN. May it please the Court, Mr. Foreman and gentlemen: You have now heard the Commonwealth's direct case. That is to say, you have heard now substantially all the evidence which they base their proof of the allegations stated in the indictments upon which these men at bar are charged with.

. . . . .

I want you to pause for a moment and consider what is before you: The lives of two human beings. And when you deal with the evidence that has been offered here by the Commonwealth and when you deal with the [941] evidence that is to be offered here by the defendants and their witnesses, you are dealing with the lives and the existence of the two defendants.

You have had an experience to date, day after day, week after week, sitting here in the jury box listening to the various witnesses, their testimony, the various arguments between counsel and some with the Court, and you have heard the Court make various rulings as to the admissibility of certain evidence, and you have heard after those rulings were made by him, exceptions taken by the defendants' counsel, and you will hear, perhaps, in the introduction of the defendants' testimony those things happen, and I am going to . . . say to you that those exceptions are of no consequence to you.

The fact that exceptions were taken by defendants' counsel are as a matter of right, and they have a right to go to a higher court to ask for another adjudication.

. . . . .

We start at the opening of the defendants' case in the same legal predicament as when the Commonwealth opened their case, that is, the defendants now are innocent of this crime, and they remain so until you have determined the evidence and changed their legal category from that of innocence.

The presumption of law still is that they are innocent of the crimes stated in these indictments, and the burden of proof is still upon the Government, or Commonwealth, to prove to you all the allegations set out in the indictments beyond reasonable doubt.

As a matter of law, the defendants are not obliged to offer any testimony whatsoever, and the mere fact that they do offer themselves as witnesses or offer other witnesses to explain situations that developed in the Commonwealth's case, they do not sustain any burden. The Commonwealth still carries the burden that they must prove to you beyond a reasonable doubt the allegations set out in the indictments. But the defendants do intend to offer themselves as witnesses, and they do intend to call other witnesses who will explain certain situations that were brought out by the Commonwealth's witnesses.

The defense will be made up of practically two parts. We shall offer

witnesses that were at or near the scene of the shooting April 15 that
[942] will tell you what they saw and who they saw, and by that,
when I say "who they saw," I mean with reference to the defendants.
The defendants will explain to you in person what they were doing on
the day of April 15, . . . not only at the time when the crime was
committed—or crimes were committed—but also throughout the entire
day.

The defendant Vanzetti will offer himself as a witness and tell you
his experience from the time that he landed in this country, I think
New York, and his life experience of the years he remained in New
York City, working around restaurants, washing dishes and maintain-
ing himself as best he could, until some few years ago he made his
home in Plymouth, Plymouth County, down on the Cape, and for a
few years he worked there in a mill, doing unskilled labor.

After saving a few dollars he bought out a small fish business, a fish
business that consisted of a push cart only for several years, and sold
fish around the streets in Plymouth with his push cart. When the fish
business was not good, he did outside labor, worked for independent
contractors there, as an unskilled laborer, and that has been his life
since he has been in this country up to the date of May 5th, when he
was arrested.

Now, as to Sacco, Sacco will also tell you that some few years
ago, 1908, I think, he landed in Boston, went to live first in Milford,
Massachusetts, obtaining employment as a water boy with some contractor there who was doing paving work in the streets of Milford.

Later, he got promoted to the occupation of carrying paving stones,
and from there he worked during the summer and fall of his first year
in this country, and when winter came he went into one of the machine shops and did unskilled labor. He worked there for nearly a year
and then went to a school to learn edge-trimming, and I mean by
"school" he went to what was known then in Milford as the 3-K Shoe
Factory, which is now in Stoughton, and a Mr. Kelley—not the man
who testified here a few days ago, but I think his father—taught him
for a certain sum of money the trade of shoe trimming or edge-trimming.

And from there he went to Webster and worked in the shoe factory
there, in his trade of edge-trimming. Then he came back to Milford
again and worked in another factory, in his trade as edge-trimmer.
Then he came down locally here to Stoughton. I think he worked in
Rice & Hutchins in South Braintree for a short time as edge-trimmer.
Then he worked in Cambridge for a short time edge-trimming. Then

he worked in Somerville and then in Chelsea, until later he came to live in Stoughton and went to work again for the 3-K Shoe Factory and worked there for several years at his trade of edge-trimming, and worked there up to May 1st or 2nd of last year previous to his arrest.

He will tell you of his home conditions, of his mother passing away some time in the early part of March of last year, and the receipt of a letter from his father asking him to come home on account of his mother's [943] death and on account of the illness of his father, and after the receipt of that letter he went to his employer at the 3-K Shoe Factory in Stoughton, showed the letter, or at least talked about the letter, and told his employer that he had decided to go back home, and then asked that arrangements might be made that he could go to Boston some day the latter part of the week of which April 15 fits in.

And when Mr. Kelley took the stand I wish you to notice that he testified that Sacco had asked him, not only that week, but some week before, about getting away some day, but there wasn't any particular or definite day mentioned by Sacco, but some day during that week, on which he might go into Boston and make application and obtain his passport, and that he was told by his employer that after he had caught up his work he could so do, and he went and obtained the services of another man who he "broke in" as they say in a factory, taught or instructed or demonstrated the work; that a man and he worked together for several days until the work was caught up, which happened to be Wednesday, April 14; and that night he called the condition of his work to Mr. Kelley's attention, and Mr. Kelley said, "Very well, go tomorrow."

And he will tell you that he went in on the early train from Stoughton Centre, Massachusetts, to Boston. He will tell you about going to the office of the Italian Consul, having with him a picture, [of] himself and his wife and child, as a requirement for the application of a passport. And he will tell you his experience there in the office of the Italian Consul, in that the picture was not in the right form or the right size, and that he had to go out and obtain another one, and he went back again after he had left the employ of Mr. Kelley, namely, May 2nd, when the passport [was] issued, three days before his arrest.

We will offer you in corroboration of that fact a deposition that was taken in Italy from the man whom he saw in the Italian Consul's office on the date of April 15. We will show you that that man worked in the Consul's office up until some time in that fall of 1920, when, on account of his health, he went back to Italy, and in that deposition, which will be presented to you later, it will show of the visit of Sacco to his office and of the business transaction between him and Sacco, the time of day. Then we will show you by Sacco [how] his time [was] taken up in Stoughton on the 2nd, 3rd, 4th and 5th of May, up to the night of his arrest. In those two courses I have followed now, they will show what these men were doing the day of April 15. They will also explain to you the reason for them having guns, and ammunition, in their possession.

Now, going back to South Braintree for a moment, we will offer some 12 or 15 witnesses who were stationed or working at certain points, and they will tell you what they saw of the shooting, what they saw of the men that did the shooting, and what they saw of the automobile and what they saw of the men in the automobile. [944]

We will produce a witness [Burke] who was at or near the crossing directly opposite to the cobbling shop towards the railroad track . . . [and who] was within six or eight feet of the automobile when it came across the railroad crossing from the lower part of Pearl Street, a man who was in South Braintree there that day on business. He arrived at the South Braintree station some time in the neighborhood of 2:30, had some paraphernalia with him that he brought along in the train with him. He was on his way to give an exhibition in one of the schools there in glass-blowing. . . .

. . . . . .

He looked down Pearl Street and he saw the men in the street. He saw the shooting, and he started off to go down and he got nearly to the railroad tracks when the automobile came up, so he got a full-face view of the automobile, and he got a full-face view of three of the occupants in the automobile. . . . [945]

. . . . . .

Then we will offer you a witness [Liscomb] who worked . . . at the window directly above [the one from which Miss Splaine looked] . . . and apparently got the same view. . . .

. . . . . .

And I want to say to you in conclusion that when you are taking in this evidence that you will give the defendants and their witnesses the [946] same consideration, the same attention and the same patience that you have given the witnesses for the Commonwealth.

MR. JEREMIAH McANARNEY. Your Honor, in view of the statement of Mr. Callahan, and it is so substantially covering the whole affair, I do not think I will make any opening on behalf of the defendant Vanzetti: the two being interwoven together, it would be a good deal of repetition. Where our cases differ will be shown by the evidence.

THE COURT. We will proceed with the evidence, if you please, if counsel for the defendants are now ready. [947]

———OF THE many witnesses who testified for the defense that the bandits they had seen in So. Braintree were not Sacco and Vanzetti, only two are presented here: Burke and Liscomb. The testimony of these two shows clearly the problems the defense faced in its efforts to overcome the prosecution's identification testimony; it likewise shows the methods used by Mr. Katzmann to weaken the credibility of these witnesses. The first of these witnesses, Burke, the itinerant glassblower, testified that the bandit car approached him on Pearl St. shortly after the shooting.———————————————

Q. [By Mr. Callahan] Now, when you got to the point near the railroad crossing . . . will you tell me what you observed? A. [By Mr. Burke] As I said, I seen an automobile coming slowly up the incline toward the railroad track. Just at that time two men run in a diagonal direction and jumped on the running-board of that car and got into the back part of the car. The car proceeded then toward the railroad track. . . .

. . . . .

As the car approached the crossing, . . . one of the men who was in the back of the car started to climb over the back seat into the front seat with the driver. About that time a shot was fired from the car, what part I couldn't say, but there was a report from the car. This man climbed over into the front seat and sat himself in alongside of the driver.

Q. How near did the car get to you when this man had got seated in the front seat? A. Probably within ten feet, I should judge. Quite close. He lumbered over and got set, but at the time he was set, he was surely within ten feet of me.

Q. After he got seated . . . did you observe him doing anything? [972] A. After he got seated in the front seat, he faced toward me. There was a man running up the street behind the car hollering, "Stop them! Stop them!" And this man who was on the front seat, he leaned slightly forward, grabbed hold of the door, leaned forward and poked a gun, a revolver, at me, and snapped it, and said, "Get out of the way, you son of a b."

Q. Using the English language? A. Fully.

Q. Did you get a view of that man? A. Yes, sir.

Q. Will you describe that man to the jury. A. This man appeared to be a thick, short,—thick set, shortish looking man, the way he was crouched in the seat, with a very full face, a pronounced full face, flat, and a broad, heavy jowl. . . . [973]

. . . . .

Q. Did you observe anybody else in the car?

. . . . .

A. There was two men that I noticed in the car in the rear seat, but one in particular was sitting, leaning out over the back door of the car.

Q. On the side of the car nearer you? A. Yes.

Mr. Katzmann. Don't lead him. One moment, I object to that.

Q. On which side of the car? A. On the side towards me.

Q. Will you describe that man to the jury? A. The first I seen of him that I took particular notice was after this fellow started to climb over the back seat. I noticed this man that was—I am speaking of now —sitting there with his hand over the back door, with a revolver, waving it in this manner [indicating] toward the depot and in that general direction, swinging it like this [indicating]. As the car got——

Q. You mean, the South Braintree station? A. Yes, sir. As the car got up closer to me, first, and my mind was engrossed with the fellow that pulled the gun, he I paid more attention to, but the fellow in back seemed to be a dark man, with a short cropped moustache, very, —medium short, cropped. Also had a cap on. Dressed dark.

Q. Any further description of him? A. No, sir. [974]

. . . . .

Q. . . . . Now, having in mind the descriptions of the men that you have given to the jury, are you able to state whether any of those men are either of the two defendants in the dock?

Mr. Katzmann. One moment, I object.

The Court. I will hear you. It is leading, of course.

Mr. Katzmann. That is the objection. And also, that he is asked to give it from his description. Of course, that is for the jury to say. He gives it from what he saw. Besides, it is leading.

Mr. Callahan. I will withdraw the question. [976]

Q. Having in mind, Mr. Witness, what you saw of the men in the automobile that you now describe, are you able to say whether or not those men were either of the two defendants in the dock? A. I would say they were not.

. . . . .

Q. Did you later after that day learn of the arrest of the two defendants? A. Yes, sir.

. . . . . .

Q. Did you go to the Brockton police station? *A*. Yes sir. [977]

Q. Do you know what day it was with reference to the day of the arrest of the two defendants? *A*. It was within two or three days.

Q. And did you see the two defendants at the Brockton police station? *A*. I saw three men that were under arrest.

Q. Did you see these two men? *A*. Yes, sir. [978]

. . . .

Cross-Examination

Q. [*By Mr. Katzmann*] What moment on April 15th did you first learn somebody had been killed? . . . *A*. After the automobile had passed the point where I was.

Q. Yes. So up to that moment you had no knowledge of what had caused this excitement, had you? *A*. No, sir.

Q. And you were not particularly interested in the car or its occupants for that reason, were you? *A*. I was interested because,—yes, I was.

Q. You were not interested in the occupants of the car until somebody leaned out and pointed a revolver at you, were you? *A*. I was interested when I saw the men running and jumping aboard the car after the excitement down the line. [979]

Q. Did you know there had been shooting there? *A*. I heard shots fired.

. . . . .

Q. Did you know that the men who were running to the car were in any way connected with the shooting? *A*. I inferred, yes.

. . . . .

Q. You did not know anybody had been killed? *A*. No.

Q. You did not know these two men had shot at any human being, did you? *A*. No.

Q. You just knew you heard some shots. On which side of the car did those two men get in, the left or the right? *A*. On the south side.

Q. You mean—— *A*. On the north side of the car, that would be the left side.

Q. In which direction was the car traveling? *A*. Towards me.

Q. By point of the compass? *A*. Traveling west.

Q. They got in on the north side? *A*. On the north side. Yes.

. . . . .

Q. That is the same side as the tank is situated on? This side, the north side of Pearl Street, there is a tank? *A.* That is on the south side of Pearl Street, isn't it?

Q. Well, what do you say? *A.* I say it is on the south side.

Q. What does that [*indicating*] say? Don't you see that? Can't you see that? *A.* Yes.

Q. What does it say? *A.* "North."

Q. Yes. Then, what side of the street is it on? *A.* It is on the north.

Q. Then you needed to change your answer, didn't you, that they got in from the other side? *A.* Yes. [980]

. . . . .

Q. How long was it after you first heard the shooting that you saw these men in motion? *A.* Probably three quarters of a minute, I should say.

Q. What had happened in that forty-five seconds? *A.* I had walked down the street. [981]

. . . . .

Q. The direction you were walking in would bring you back of that wooden fence, wouldn't it, or high board fence by the tank? *A.* I couldn't say where I would have wound up if I kept on going, just where I would have landed, but I walked down about the point I showed you.

Q. Do you know there is a high board fence—— *A.* Yes.

Q. ——in front of the tank? *A.* Yes.

Q. If you were walking in that direction, it would bring you back of the fence, wouldn't it? *A.* I couldn't say anything about that.

Q. Are you telling this jury, sir, you could see from the point you have indicated near the word "dirt" in the extended north line of the Pearl Street sidewalk, you could see down to the point you previously indicated where you first saw those men? Are you telling that to this jury? *A.* Yes, sir, I am telling them, telling them as I saw the thing.

Q. Are you familiar with a Buick car? *A.* No, sir.

Q. Have you ever seen a Buick car? *A.* Yes, sir.

Q. How could you tell it was a Buick? *A.* Well, I saw one this morning. I rode over in it and noticed the name plate on it while I was waiting to take a ride over.

Q. Whose Buick was it you rode over in this morning? *A.* What say?

Q. Whose Buick was it you rode over in this morning? *A.* [*Witness hesitates.*] Lawyer Callahan's.

. . . . .

Q. Did you look at the name plate on Mr. Callahan's car this morning? *A.* I did, yes, sir.

Q. Was it a Hudson or a Buick? *A.* I believe it is a Hudson, now that you call my attention to it. It shows my lack of knowledge of cars. [982]

Q. You admit that, do you? And your eyesight was so good this morning that after looking at the name plate in front of the car, you called a Hudson car a Buick; is that correct? *A.* Yes.

Q. How close were you to the front part of Mr. Callahan's car this morning? *A.* I think I was resting my hand on the radiator when I was looking at it. He was filling the radiator.

Q. And you read the name Buick on a Hudson car, did you, as close as that? *A.* Well, I formed that impression. I thought it was——

Q. Your eyes are not very good, are they, Mr. Burke? *A.* Fairly good, sir.

Mr. Jeremiah McAnarney. Pardon me.

The Court. Is your eyesight good?

The Witness. Fairly good for a man of my years, yes.

Q. How old are you? *A.* Fifty-five.

Q. You squint a great deal, don't you? *A.* Always did.

Q. Yes. You couldn't see that plan without putting your glasses on, could you? *A.* I always when I am reading put my glasses on, or most always.

Q. What was the shape of the figure on the front of Mr. Callahan's car that you saw this morning? *A.* Now, that you——

Q. What was the shape of it? I haven't "now" anything about that. What was the shape of it? *A.* Triangular.

Q. That isn't a Buick, is it? *A.* I do not know the shape now of the Buick one. If I see a name plate I can tell what they are.

Q. You saw a name plate this morning? *A.* Yes.

Q. You could not tell what it was, could you? *A.* You mean to say I could not read?

Q. Well, you didn't, did you? *A.* What?

Q. You did not read it right, did you? *A.* I did, but I——

Q. You what? *A.* The impression wasn't enough on my memory to remember that.

Q. It impressed you enough to go around the radiator and look at it, didn't it? *A.* No, I didn't go for that purpose, sir. [983]

. . . . . .

Q. Where was the car when you first began to take any notice of the occupants? *A.* When it was coming across the crossing, when it got to the crossing.

. . . . .

Q. Which man did you notice first? *A.* The man that was climbing over. The man was driving the car, I seen the man driving the car.

Q. How long did you watch him? *A.* I didn't watch him any length of time at all.

Q. How long did you watch him? *A.* I couldn't say.

Q. Give us your best judgment. *A.* It was less than a minute.

Q. How much less than a minute? *A.* I don't know. I cannot be pinned down to things of that kind, because I don't know, Mr. Katzmann. I am going to try to do the best I can, but I want you to be as fair with me as I want to be with you. I am here to tell the story as I saw it.

Mr. Katzmann. I ask that be stricken from the record.

The Court. That may all be stricken out. [988]

————MRS. LISCOMB was called to the stand. She testified that during the holdup she looked out on Pearl Street from a third floor window in the middle of the Rice & Hutchins factory.————

Q. And when you looked out that window, what did you see? *A.* I saw two men lying on the ground, and one man, a short dark man, standing on the ground facing me, with his head up, holding a revolver in his hands.

Q. Did you get a clear view of his features and his face? *A.* Yes, sir, I would always remember his face.

. . . . .

Q. Now, did you see the automobile when it went away? *A.* No, sir. I imagine I was at the window about two seconds.

Q. Did he have a revolver, this man you saw? *A.* Yes, sir.

Q. And what did he do with it? *A.* He was holding it, pointing it toward the factory, toward the window which I was looking out of.

Q. What did you do then? *A.* I sort of fainted away.

Q. Were you later taken, either by the officers or by some one in the factory, to see some men? *A.* Yes, sir.

. . . . .

Q. How soon was that after the shooting? *A.* Well, I really do not know, but I think it was about four or five days after, this last time.

. . . . .

Q. When you went to the Brockton police station were you shown some men? *A.* Yes, sir.

Q. And you have looked at these men in the dock? *A.* I have.

Q. Are either of the men in the dock the man you saw pointing the revolver at your window? *A.* No, sir.

Q. Are you sure about that? *A.* I am positively sure.

Mr. Jeremiah McAnarney. That is all. [1191]

Re-Cross-Examination

[*June 25, 1921*]

.   .   .   .   .

Q. [*By Mr. Katzmann*] Mrs. Liscomb, do you remember what you said yesterday afternoon as to where the man was who had something in his hand, whether he was in front of you, to your right or to your left? . . . *A.* As I remember, I said yesterday afternoon he stood in front of me.

.   .   .   .   .

Q. . . . . Well, it is certain, is it not, Mrs. Liscomb, from your recollection that yesterday afternoon you put the man whom we called Berardelli, the guard, on the sidewalk to your left, didn't you? *A.* Yes, sir, I did.

Q. Ten or twelve feet to the left of the corner of the building? *A.* Yes, sir.

Q. Now, Mrs. Liscomb, did you not yesterday afternoon place the standing man, the man standing in the street, opposite that man? *A.* No, sir.

Q. You are certain of that? *A.* I am quite certain.

Q. Are you positive of it? *A.* No, I am not positive. [1206]

Q. So your recollection goes back to the description of a man's face on April 15, 1920, and you are positive about that, and you cannot tell this jury what you said yesterday afternoon between twenty minutes of five and five o'clock. Is that right? *A.* No, sir.

Q. What is wrong about it? *A.* I am telling you as near as I can.

.   .   .   .   .

————THE DEFENSE attorneys next turned to identification of the cap, guns, and bullets; however, in the interests of continuity, this testimony was presented immediately following the prosecution's handling of these matters. Then, on July 5, the twenty-ninth day of the trial, the first of the defendants took the witness stand.————

Mr. Jeremiah McAnarney. Will the defendant Vanzetti be brought forward?

Bartolomeo Vanzetti, Sworn

Mr. Jeremiah McAnarney. Now, before I ask you any question, I want to say this to you: if any time you do not understand the question, you please say so, because we are going to try and go along in English, and we would all like you to tell us when you do not understand the question or any word in the question, and if you make an answer and use the word and you think you have not used the right word, if you will tell us the Court will gladly let you explain it or make it right.

The Witness. Yes, sir. [1689]

. . . . .

Q. Now, what is your full name? *A.* Bartolomeo Vanzetti.

Q. And Mr. Vanzetti, where were you born? *A.* I born in Italy.

Q. What town and province? *A.* Town of Villeefalletto; province of Cuneo; region of Piedmont.

Q. How old are you? *A.* I am thirty-three years old.

Q. How long did you attend school, Mr. Vanzetti? *A.* I go to school from six years old to thirteen years old.

Q. . . . What did you go doing then? *A.* . . . I left my town and my family. I went to the city of Cuneo to learn pastry cooking and candy making.

————FOR THE next six years, according to his testimony, Vanzetti worked as a pastry and candy cook until his departure for the United States in 1908 at the age of twenty. For nearly two years he worked as a helper in the kitchens of a number of New York City restaurants. Out of work, he went to New England where he spent a year and a half working in quarries, brickyards, and on street construction. He laid railroad track near Springfield, carried stones for two years in the construction of the Worcester municipal water reservoir, and cut ice in Plymouth. In 1913 he settled in Plymouth.————

. . . . .

Q. What was your first employment after you got to Plymouth, Massachusetts? *A.* I worked for a year or a year and a half for Mr. Stone.

. . . . .

Q. What was his business? *A.* I do not know what it was, his business, because he is a rich people and he go there only in the summer. He got a big villa for his family.

. . . . .

Q. How long did you say you worked there? *A.* More than a year, about a year and a half, fourteen or fifteen or eighteen months.

. . . . .

THE COURT. Stone & Webster, was it? [1693]

Q. Was the name,—does Stone & Webster sound natural to you? *A.* No. There is only one family. We call him Mr. Stone and Mrs. Stone.

Q. You knew his first name? *A.* No, I don't know his first name.

. . . . .

Q. . . . After getting through working for Mr. Stone, where next were you employed? *A.* I was employed by the Cordage.

Q. The Cordage Company at Plymouth? *A.* Yes . . . I was there for more than a year, a year and a half, something like that.

Q. Where was your next employment, Mr. Vanzetti? *A.* Then I start to work outside, to make the water breaker up near the Pilgrim place in Plymouth. [1694]

. . . . .

————IN THE SPRING of 1920, Vanzetti said, he sold fish from a cart he pushed through the streets of Plymouth. By the middle of April the fish were hard to come by, so he started digging clams and selling them. He peddled fish for the last time, he said, on April 15, 1920.

Q. . . . On the 15th, where did you peddle? *A.* On the 15th, I have a few, not very many, fish in the morning of the 15th, and I peddled in Cherry Street, Standish Avenue and Cherry Court, down Suosso's Lane, around that place, around that centre. Castle Street is the last place I sell fish on the day of the 15th.

Q. Now, tell us anything else that you did on the day of the 15th. *A.* On the day of the 15th, when I was going by Suosso's Lane, from Suosso's Lane I reached Court Street and then I turned towards Plymouth, toward south, and I was intentioning to go in Castle Street. Almost on the corner of Castle Street I met this man [Rosen] that go around with cloths.

Q. Yes. *A.* And he asked me,—I can't say that.

Q. You met that man with the cloths? *A.* Yes.

Q. Did you do anything with him? *A.* Yes. He stopped me. He says something to me.

Q. Very good. You are not going to give the conversation. That is right. Now, you talked, I assume. He talked, too. Did you do anything? *A.* Yes, I buy a piece of cloth from him.

. . . . .

Q. . . . You talked about the cloth, didn't you?
THE COURT. In consequence of that, what did you do?
A. . . . I bring him to the Brini house. I knew that the Brini wife was in the house, and I know she worked in the woolen mill and she know the cloth. [1701]

. . . . .

Q. What did you pay for it? *A.* I should say something like twelve dollars, but I don't remember exactly. Not twelve dollars, not twelve dollars, but $12.75 or something like that. I give him fifty cents after to buy because he say he lost.
Q. What time in the day was that . . . ? *A.* Near one o'clock, about half past eleven, something like that, half past twelve, about one o'clock. [1702]

. . . . .

———AFTER selling his fish, Vanzetti testified, he went down to the shore to converse for an hour with a friend of his named Corl who was painting a boat. For the next week, he said, he looked for work. On April 22, he went to East Boston to meet with friends at the Italian Naturalization Club where it was decided that Vanzetti would be sent to New York City to learn as much as he could about the imprisonment of an Italian radical, Salsedo.———

Q. What did you go to New York for?
MR. KATZMANN. How is that competent, if your Honor please?
THE COURT. How is that involved in this matter at all, Mr. Mc-Anarney?
MR. JEREMIAH MCANARNEY. Well,———
THE COURT. I haven't heard any claim of the Commonwealth which has in any manner attacked his whereabouts on these dates, or on this date in particular.
MR. JEREMIAH MCANARNEY. Unless it is, then I won't press it.
Q. You are in New York. I assume you went there on some business. How long did you stay in New York? *A.* I stayed three days. [1710]

———UPON his return from New York, Vanzetti said that he visited Sacco in Stoughton.———

. . . . .

Q. Now, tell us how long you stayed there, meaning for this first question, did you stay there that afternoon, in the evening or not? *A.* Yes, I stayed there in the afternoon, in the evening, and I spent the night with him.

Q. Now, May 4th? *A.* In the Sacco house, too.

Q. Did Sacco go away to work on May 4th or was he around the house that day? *A.* No, he went to Boston on May 4th.

. . . . .

Q. When he came home from Boston did any one come with him, or did he come alone? *A.* He come with Orciana.

. . . . .

Q. Did you see a motorcycle there that evening? *A.* No.

Q. Do you know how he came there, how Sacco came there? *A.* Yes, because they speak of the motorcycle, and Orciana got some dress like a motorcycle.

. . . . .

Q. You mean clothes that they use when they ride? *A.* I mean clothes that the men who go on a motorcycle, something like that, use, yellow dress, yellow pants.

. . . . .

Q. All right. Was there anything said there? Did you have a conversation there with Orciana and with Sacco with reference to what Sacco was going to do and what you were going to do the next day, May 5th? You may answer that yes or no. *A.* Yes.

Q. And was there any time fixed that you were to see Sacco or Orciana? *A.* Yes.

Q. What time? *A.* On the afternoon of the other day, May 5th. [1713]

Q. May 5th, what did you do? . . . *A.* We stay until the evening, around the Sacco house, and then we go.

Q. What did you do during the day, if anything? *A.* We do many things. Split some wood, cut some wood, we go in the forest and cut some wood for the fire, and we speak about many things, and he was busy too, put some stuff in order.

. . . . .

Q. You know you can't tell us anything you said. You told us one thing you did. You split some wood. Did you see Mrs. Sacco doing anything? *A.* Oh, yes, Mrs. Sacco was preparing the stuff, clothes and everything like that for to be ready to go away.

. . . . .

Q. For what trip? *A.* To put in order to go to Italy.

Q. What did you see her doing? *A.* I saw her put the stuff in the trunk from the commode.

Q. Did anyone there give you anything? *A.* Yes, before we go away I take the three gun shells.

Q. Three gun shells? *A.* Yes.

Q. You call them. And how long are they? You make and show us on your pencil how long they are? *A.* Something like that [*indicating*].

· · · · ·

Mr. Jeremiah McAnarney. Two inches and a half. [1714]

· · · · ·

Q. How came she to give them to you? How came you to get them? *A.* Because I say, "I will bring to my friends in Plymouth." My friends, I know they go to hunt in the winter time.

· · · · ·

Q. What did you do with those shells? *A.* I put in my pocket. I want to give to him when I reach Plymouth.

Q. Now, speaking back a few months. When you were arrested, you had a revolver on you? *A.* Yes.

Q. Where did you carry that revolver? What part of your clothes did you carry it in? *A.* I carried on my back pocket, pants back pocket, but I don't remember if in right or left side.

Q. When, about when, did you get that revolver? *A.* It was two or three months.

· · · · ·

Q. Why did you get the revolver? *A.* I got the revolver because it was a very bad time, and I like to have a revolver for self-defense.

Q. How much money did you use to carry around with you? *A.* When I went to Boston for fish, I can carry eighty, one hundred dollars, one hundred and twenty dollars.

Q. What do you mean by "It was a bad time"? *A.* Bad time, I mean it was many crimes, many holdups, many robberies.

· · · · ·

Q. Do you remember what you paid for the revolver? *A.* I think $5.

Q. Now, I will bring you back to May 5th. On the afternoon of May 5th, what happened at Sacco's house? Perhaps it will be plainer to you; did any one come there? *A.* Yes.

Q. Who came? *A.* Orciana came there with Mike Boda.

Q. How did they come? *A.* I should say they came in a motorcycle.

Q. Well, you saw the motorcycle? *A.* Yes, after a little while, after they arrived.

Q. How long did they stay there? *A.* I should say two hours, an hour or a half, two hours. [1715]

Q. About what time did they leave the house? *A.* They leave the house, I do not know, because I leave the house before them.

Q. What time did you leave the house? *A.* About seven o'clock, something like that.

Q. Did you leave alone, or someone with you? *A.* With Sacco, me and Sacco leave the house.

Q. Where did you and Sacco go? *A.* We went to Bridgewater.

. . . . .

Q. You looked for a car to Bridgewater? *A.* We wait in the street, we wait a little while. . . . [T]here is a lunch room and we went there and we drink a cup of coffee in the lunch room, and I take a pencil and piece of paper and I started to write.

. . . . .

Q. And what did you write? *A.* I write public invitations for a meeting next Sunday. [1716]

. . . . .

Q. After you wrote that, what did you do with it? *A.* I read it to Nick.

Q. You read it to Nick? *A.* And it was found a little too long. . . . When we take a car to Bridgewater I condense that. I fixed him up to leave the same sense and with . . . less words.

. . . . .

Q. . . . What did you do with the one you wrote again? *A.* I give it to Nick, to Sacco.

———THE SHEET of paper with Vanzetti's notice written on it was found in Sacco's pocket by the police at the time of his arrest. The text of the notice, which was translated by the defense and read into the record near the end of the trial, is as follows: "Fellow Workers, you have fought all the wars. You have worked for all the capitalists. You have wandered over all the countries. Have you harvested the fruits of your labors, the price of your victories? Does the past comfort you? Does the present smile on you? Does the future promise you anything? Have you found a piece of land where you can live like a human being and die like a human being? On these questions, on this argument, and on this theme, the struggle for existence, Bartolomeo Vanzetti will speak. Hour——— Day——— Hall———

Admission free. Freedom of discussion to all. Take the ladies with you." [2120]———————————————————————

Q. What was he to do with it? A. He was to bring it to the printer in Brockton, or in Boston, for next Saturday, and to have it printed and give it to the population. [1717]

. . . .

Q. Was there any arrangement made about a hall? A. Yes, the hall, I know that the hall was already rented.

. . . .

Q. That would be May 9th. At what hour in the day were you to speak there? A. I do not remember what hour we fixed, because I do not write in that invitation, I do not write the hour nor the street nor the place. I left to him or to somebody else that fixed the place and everything, because I do not know that. [1718]

———————VANZETTI testified that he and Sacco were to meet Orciana and Boda near Elm Square where Boda expected to get his Overland from Johnson's garage. When they got off the streetcar, they walked toward a motorcycle headlight and found Orciana.————————

. . . .

Q. You stepped up . . . and you spoke to Orciana? A. Yes.

Q. Now, did you see any one at this house near which the motorcycle was standing? A. After a little while we seen a woman coming to the house.

Q. Where did she come from? A. She come toward Brockton.

Q. She come toward Brockton? Well,—— A. She come from toward Brockton.

. . . .

Q. Where did she go? A. She go in the house in front of the motorcycle.

. . . .

Q. Where the motorcycle was standing in front? A. Yes.

Q. Did you see a woman go out of that house before that? A. I did not see.

. . . .

Q. Now, when you came up to Orciana you had a talk with him? A. Yes.

Q. Boda was not in sight then? A. No, I don't see Boda at that time.

Q. All right. After you talked with Orciana beside the motorcycle, what did you and Sacco do? *A.* We stayed and entertained ourselves to talk with Orciana. [1720]

Q. Anything else? *A.* Yes, and after a little while Boda come on the street.

Q. Where did he come from? *A.* From the house.

Q. The house near the motorcycle? *A.* Yes.

Q. Did you hear any talk between Boda and anyone before he came out? *A.* No, I don't hear no talk.

Q. Did Boda have talk with you or with Orciana in your presence after he came out? *A.* Yes.

Q. What did Boda say?

. . . . .

A. He say that we cannot take the automobile because Mr. Johnson say that he cannot take it without having a new number.

Q. No number? *A.* New number—that Boda must have a new number for to take the automobile, something like that, simply in reference to the number.

Q. All right, then. What else did Boda say, if anything? *A.* Then he say, "Well, I and Orciana, we,—I and Orciana go with the machine and you take a car and you go home. We will look for a new number. When I am ready I will tell you and we will come here some other day. We will come to take the automobile."

Q. What were you going to get the automobile for? *A.* For to take out literature, books and newspapers, from the house and the homes.

Q. What house and homes did you want to take the books and literature from? *A.* From any house and from any house in five or six places, five or six towns. Three, five or six people have plenty of literature, and we want, we intend to take that out and put that in the proper place.

Q. What do you mean by a "proper place"? *A.* By a proper place I mean in a place not subject to policemen go in and call for, see the literature, see the papers, see the books, as in that time they went through in the house of many men who were active in the radical movement and [1721] socialist and labor movement, and go there and take letters and take books and take newspapers, and put men in jail and deported many.

Mr. Katzmann. I ask it be stricken out.

The Witness. I say that in that time——

Mr. Katzmann. Wait one moment.

THE WITNESS. And deported many, many, many have been misused in jail, and so on.

Q. Where were you going that night if you could have got the automobile? *A.* I intended to go to Plymouth and speak to some of my friends of Plymouth who is owner of the house.

Q. And do what? *A.* And if they are willing to receive such literature and newspapers in his house.

Q. Now, where were you going to take these papers and literature you were going to take from these houses? What were you going to do with them? Suppose you had got the automobile that night and you had gone down to Plymouth to these houses? What were you going to do with the papers you would pick up here? *A.* Before to pick the paper, I want to find the place and ask if my friend in Plymouth, if he was willing that we bring the paper in his house.

. . . . .

Q. Now, [was] this going around to get these papers . . . a result of what you learned when you went to New York? *A.* Yes. What we read in newspapers, too.

Q. Well, you did not get the automobile that night? *A.* No, we were arrested that night. [1722]

. . . . .

Q. . . . Did the officers have a talk with you when they arrested you on the electric car? *A.* The officer who arrested me on the electric car come in the front of the car and walked toward the back of the car, and when he come near the chair where we sit down, I and Sacco, he say, "Where do you come from?" And we answered, "We come from Bridgewater." Then he took out a revolver. He pointed to us a revolver at me, yes, sir, and say, "You don't move, you dirty thing."

. . . . .

Q. While you were in the electric car before the police automobile came up, did you try to get your hand in your clothes to take the revolver out? *A.* No.

Q. Did the police officer say to you, "Don't put your hand in there or I shoot"? Did that take place? *A.* No, absolutely.

. . . . .

Q. Now, you are brought to the police station in Brockton, finally? *A.* Yes. [1724]

. . . . .

Q. And you were then put in a cell. Did they talk with you and ask you some questions before you were put in a cell, or after, which?

A. After I was put in the cell.

. . . . .

Q. . . . [D]id they say what you were arrested for? *A.* They say, "Oh, you know, you know why." And when I try to sleep in the cell, there is no blanket, only the wood. Then we called for the blanket, because it was rather cool. They say, "Never mind, you catch warm by and by, and tomorrow morning we put you in a line in the hall between the chairs and we shoot you."

Mr. Katzmann. Shoot?

The Witness. Yes.

The Court. Get shot?

The Witness. Yes. And one policeman, he started in the same night to walk toward me, and he started to spit toward my face and walk toward my cell, and I was there, stood in back of the door; the door, as you know, the jail door is barred. Then he spit three or four times, and come all the time more near, and I stand more near the bars. I will see if that gentleman is so generous to spit in my face, but he spit. When he reach my face he spit. Then he go back and took a revolver from his pocket, put out the bullet of the revolver and show me the bullet and then put the revolver,—put the bullet in the revolver again and put the revolver like that [*indicating*] on the top of the gate and point the revolver toward my cell [1725] near where I stand. He maybe want to look if I go away, if I get scared and go away from the door. And I don't go away. I don't move. That is all, and he don't shoot, anyhow.

Q. When did they tell you, if they did, why you were arrested that night? *A.* Absolutely no, they don't tell me.

Q. Did they tell you the next day? *A.* Neither the next day.

Q. Just when,—did they any time while they had you in detention at the Brockton police station, tell you why you were arrested that night on the electric car? *A.* No.

. . . . .

Q. Now, in talking to Officer Spear and to any other official, District Attorney or others, did you at any time tell them what you have now told us, that you were going to get any of this literature, or anything of that sort? *A.* No, I don't tell them that thing.

Q. You withheld that from him. You never told that to them before? *A.* No.

Q. Why not? *A.* Because in that time there, there was the deportation and the reaction was more vivid than now and more mad than now.

Q. The action? *A.* The reaction. What you call "reaction." It mean the authority of this country and every country in the world was more against the socialist element in that time than before the war and after the war. There were exceptional times.

· · · · ·

Q. Now, going back, you said you had lived at Plymouth about all the time, or you made some qualifying remark. Did you at one time go away from Plymouth? *A.* Yes, sir. [1726]

Q. And when was that, please? *A.* I should say it was in the year 1917, before the registration, the years of registration.

· · · · ·

Q. How long were you gone? *A.* I should say a year or a year and a half after.

Q. Why did you go away? *A.* I go away for not to be a soldier.

· · · · ·

Q. Where did you go to? *A.* At first time I went to Mexico.

Q. How long did you remain in Mexico? *A.* Three or four months, four or five months.

Q. From there, where did you go? *A.* From there I come back in the United States.

Q. Where to? *A.* The first city I stopped was St. Louis, Missouri. . . . From St. Louis I went to Youngstown, Ohio. . . . From Youngstown I went to Farrell, Pennsylvania.

Q. And from there, where did you go? *A.* I come back to Plymouth . . . [in 1918]. [1727]

Q. Now, I was asking you, do you drive an automobile? *A.* No.

Q. Did you ever drive one? *A.* No, sir, I am not able. [1728]

· · · · ·

Q. Tell us all you recall that Stewart, the chief, asked of you? *A.* He asked me why we were in Bridgewater, how long I know Sacco, if I am a radical, if I am an anarchist or communist, and he asked me if believe in the government of the United States.

Q. Yes. *A.* If I believe in the violence, if I believe in the use of violence against the government of the United States. Some thing I think generally, I don't remember exactly what he asked me, but of that nature he asked me. He asked me about some such subject. [1732]

· · · · ·

Cross-Examination

Q. [*By Mr. Katzmann*] So you left Plymouth, Mr. Vanzetti, in May, 1917, to dodge the draft, did you? *A.* Yes, sir.

Q. And you stayed away, did you not, until the class in which men of your age came had all been drawn in the draft. Is that true? *A.* Not exactly.

Q. What part of it isn't true? *A.* It isn't true because men of my condition were never compelled to be a soldier.

Q. No men of your condition were compelled to be soldiers? *A.* Yes, sir.

Q. Were you physically unable to be a soldier? *A.* I don't speak of the physical condition. I speak of the civil condition.

Q. Were you physically sound? *A.* I hope so.

Q. Do you know? *A.* I ought to be.

Q. Did you believe you were? *A.* Yes, sir.

Q. Physically sound as you were, and after you had been in this country since 1908? *A.* Yes, sir.

Q. When this country was at war, you ran away so you would not have to fight as a soldier? *A.* Yes.

Q. Is that true? *A.* It is true.

Q. Did you ever work in Springfield, Massachusetts? *A.* Well, I have worked not really in the town of Springfield, Massachusetts, but in a shanty near Springfield.

Q. In a shanty near Springfield? *A.* Yes, in a shanty, you know, the little house where the Italian work and live like a beast, the Italian workingman in this country.

Q. Where the Italian man lives and works like a beast? *A.* Yes.

Q. That is, they locate near the place where you worked? *A.* Yes.

Q. The "beast" part of it locates it, does it? *A.* Yes.

Q. Did you think I asked you what kind of a building the Italian workingman lived in? *A.* I don't think, but I told that because——

Q. What did you put it in your answer for? *A.* To give the characteristic of the place, because I can't tell the place of the work, the place where this shanty here, I can't tell the name. It is somewhere near Springfield, Massachusetts, in a little shanty where the Italian live like a beast.

Q. And did you think if you put in your answer that it was a shanty where the Italian lived like a beast then I would know where that shanty was? Did you think that part of your answer would tell me? *A.* No, not exactly.

Q. What did you put it in for, then? *A.* I put it for to tell you if I refused to go to war, I don't refuse because I don't like this country or I don't like the people of this country. I will refuse even if I was in Italy and you tell me it is a long time I am in this country and I tell you that in [1737] this country as long time I am, that I found plenty good people and some bad people, but that I was always working hard as a man can work, and I have always lived very humble, and——

.   .   .   .   .

Q. What kind of work was it you did there? *A*. We make new railroad track. New track.

Q. Was an automobile truck used in that work? *A*. Automobile truck, no. We make——

.   .   .   .   .

Q. Are you certain that you did not drive that automobile truck? *A*. Oh, yes, I am certain of that.

Q. Sure of that? *A*. Nobody can prove I ever drove one automobile in my life.

Mr. Katzmann. I ask that be stricken out, if your Honor please.

The Court. It may be. Mr. Vanzetti, I would answer only the questions, and nothing else, please.

The Witness. Yes. [1738]

.   .   .   .   .

Q. Do you remember where you were at twelve o'clock and thirteen minutes to fifteen minutes after on April 15, 1920? *A*. I remember where I was.

Q. Yes. Where were you? *A*. I was in Plymouth.

Q. Whereabouts in Plymouth? *A*. In near or in the Brini house at that time.

Q. Were you in the Brini house at 12:13 on that day? *A*. I could not say exactly. I could not say exactly how many minutes after twelve o'clock.

Q. Thirteen minutes after twelve? *A*. But it was between twelve and one o'clock.

Q. Were you in the Brini house at 12:13 that day? *A*. I can't say surely.

Q. Did you not say in your direct examination that it was between twelve and one o'clock that you were at the Brini house? *A*. Yes, sir.

Q. And that it was nearer one o'clock than twelve? *A*. More probably, yes.

.   .   .   .   .

Q. Do you say, Mr. Vanzetti, that on the night of May 5, 1920, an officer came to the cell room in the Brockton police station, unloaded a revolver, showed you the bullets, reloaded them into the gun, and then [1739] rested his hand on the bar of another cell and pointed the revolver at you? Do you say that, sir? . . . *A*. Yes, sir.

. . . . .

Q. What is his name? *A.* I do not know the names,—I do not know
the name of one policeman of Brockton.

Q. Among the police officers who testified in the course of this trial,
did you see that man on the witness stand? *A.* No. [1740]

. . . . .

Q. Did I treat you with any discourtesy? *A.* Oh, you treat me as a
gentleman ought.

Q. You were willing, were you not, to answer such questions as I
asked you? *A.* I am not willing or unwilling. I was there like a piece
of paper in my hand, and the policemen take me out and down as they
[1742] liked. I do not know the rule of the jail. I do not know very
well the language. I speak a little better now after one year in jail than
then. I never was arrested before. I never,—I don't know anything
about trials, jails, but I know I read that time that some men were
called in jail. I know that, and I don't refuse when the police come to
take me and bring to you, to take me and bring to be photographed,
and to take me and bring me to be recognized by the people who come
there. I don't refuse that because I don't know that I have a right to
refuse. You tell me if I don't want to speak you don't compel me to
speak.

Q. Then when I talked with you, you knew you did not have to
talk, didn't you? *A.* Yes, I knew that. [1743]

. . . . .

Q. You were not frightened then, were you? *A.* I was not frightened that you punch me. I was disturbed. [1744]

. . . . .

Q. Do you remember my asking you:
   "*Q.* How long have you owned that revolver?"
And your answer:
   "*A.* A long time."
A. Yes, sir.
Q. Do you remember my asking you then:
   "*Q.* Where did you get it?"
And your reply:
   "*A.* In Boston."
A. Yes, sir.
Q. Was that answer that you had owned the revolver a long time
true? *A.* No, sir.
Q. Do you remember,—was the answer that you had gotten it in
Boston true? *A.* I have in East Boston. I told you in Hanover Street.

Q. Do you remember my then asking you?

"*Q.* Whereabouts in Boston?"

And you said:

"*A.* On the north side of Boston." [1749]

.   .   .   .   .

Q. Mr. Vanzetti, is there any reason connected with collecting literature that made you say on May 6th to me that the revolver cost you $19, when it cost you only five, as you now say? *A.* No, there is no reason. [1750]

.   .   .   .   .

Q. Then, Mr. Vanzetti, within three weeks of the time that I was talking to you, or less, you had slept twice in Boston, hadn't you? *A.* Yes.

Q. Did you tell me the truth about it? *A.* Now?

Q. Then? *A.* If I told you I only slept one time, I don't tell the truth.

Q. Was it because, as to that particular question, you did not want to tell the truth, or because you could not remember? *A.* It is the same thing for the books and for the revolver. I don't want to tell.

Q. The same thing as the books or the revolver? *A.* Yes.

Q. Do you remember my then asking you, Mr. Vanzetti:

"*Q.* How is it you can remember you were on the water last Saturday, referring to May 1, 1920, and can't remember where you slept last Sunday night? You can remember what happened the day before, but you can't tell us what happened the next night? How does that happen?"

Do you remember your reply to that?

"*A.* I am ashamed."

A. I am what?

Q. "I am ashamed." Do you remember that answer of yours? *A.* Oh, yes, yes.

Q. Yes? *A.* Yes.

Q. And do you remember then my asking you?

"*Q.* What are you ashamed of? You have not been telling us the truth?"

And your answer:

"*A.* Yes."

Do you remember that? *A.* Well, I remember something like that. [1753]

.   .   .   .   .

Q. Do you remember my . . . asking you:

"*Q.* Didn't you see a man sitting on a motorcycle when you walked by to get the car?"

"*A.* No."

Do you remember saying that? *A.* Yes, sir. I remember, I don't remember exactly, but most probably if you ask me two or three times I say two or three times "No," sure.

Q. Every time you said it it was untrue, wasn't it? *A.* Yes, even if you ask me one hundred times I answer one hundred times, "No," because I have some purpose.

Q. You intended to deceive myself and the officers who were present, did you not? *A.* I intend to not mention the name and the house of my friends.

Q. You intended to not mention names or addresses of your friends? *A.* Yes.

. . . . .

Q. Why, you told us where Pappi lived, didn't you? *A.* I tell I know the town.

. . . . .

Q. Did you think by not telling me the name of the street or the number of the house, we could not find Pappi? Did you think you were safely covering Pappi up from us? *A.* No, I don't think that. [1758]

. . . . .

Q. You knew we could find Pappi, if there was such a man, didn't you? *A.* Oh, yes.

Q. You told us Pappi's name then? *A.* Yes.

Q. You told us where he lived? *A.* Yes.

Q. And how we could get him? *A.* Yes. I told you the town. I can't tell you the number to the house.

Q. No, but you told us enough so we could locate him, didn't you? *A.* You can find him, yes.

Q. Yes. *A.* Yes, if you send some policeman there to find Pappi, sure.

Q. And he was one of the men, was he not, that you considered among your friends that was mixed up with this literature? *A.* Not at all. It is the only man among my friends who has no paper, no literature in [his] house. [1759]

. . . . .

[*July 6, 1921*]

Q. Did you have any talk with Sacco about hiding his books or papers before you left there May 5th? *A.* That we will take out from Sacco's house.

Q. Did you take them out? *A.* No, . . . [1766] we got no means to take out that much.

Q. "We had no means to take out?" Didn't you have your hands with you? *A.* Why, yes.

Q. Weren't the woods nearby Sacco's house? *A.* . . . Yes, there is woods near Sacco's house, but we do not want to spoil the books. . . . We want to keep the books.

Mr. Jeremiah McAnarney. Will you talk so Mr. Sacco can hear you?

The Witness. Yes.

Q. You have a good strong voice, haven't you, Mr. Vanzetti? *A.* Not very much now. It is more than one year I am in jail.

Q. Was your voice weak the day Michael J. Connolly was on the stand and you called him a liar when he said how you made a move to your hip pocket?

Mr. Jeremiah McAnarney. Wait a minute.

A. I don't speak very high when I called that man a liar.

Q. You did not speak very high?

Mr. Jeremiah McAnarney. I submit that is hardly,—I object to the question. His voice was whatever his voice was. My brother is putting this argumentative question to embarrass the witness, not to elicit any information.

The Court. I can't say it is for that purpose.

The Witness. I don't speak more high than I speak now when I call that man a liar.

Q. [*By Mr. Katzmann*] Is that your recollection of the tone of voice you used that day? *A.* Maybe the tone was different, because the sentiment was different.

Q. What day of the month was it that you called Michael J. Connolly a liar? *A.* I do not remember exactly what day it was.

Q. Was it less than twenty days ago? *A.* No; it was less than twenty days ago, yes.

Q. And you can't remember the day? *A.* No, I don't take a note.

· · · · · ·

Q. Did you take any note of where you were on April 15th? *A.* Mr. Katzmann,——

Q. Pardon me, sir. Answer that question. [1767]

· · · · · ·

A. No, I don't take any note. I make the best for recollection, for remember the day when I was arrested, and when I was charged with one thing and then Sacco was charged with another thing, then I make the best to recollect.

Q. And when did you first know that you were charged with the murder at Braintree? *A.* The people in jail of Plymouth tell to me, the personnel tell to me that more probably I will be charged with that thing.

. . . . . .

Q. Can't you remember the day when you first knew you were charged with this murder?

Mr. Jeremiah McAnarney. Wait. I object.

Q. Can you remember that date? *A.* No, I do not remember the day when I was charged with this murder. [1768]

. . . . . .

Q. Do you tell this jury that while you can't remember the day when you first knew that you were charged with this murder; yet you can remember where you were more than twenty days before that date? Do you say that to this jury? *A.* Yes, yes, yes, sure, and you can be sure that I can remember that I never kill a man on the 15th, because I never kill a man in my life.

Mr. Katzmann. I ask that be stricken from this record.

The Court. Mr. Vanzetti, you are again making a talk to the jury which isn't responsive. That may be stricken out.

The Witness. Please, I like to have explanation to explain.

The Court. Your counsel will look after that later. It is not now the time for explanation where you are under cross-examination, and I dislike to be obliged to order this evidence stricken from the record, but of course I must when asked by the District Attorney when those answers are not responsive. You must not lose sight of the fact that Mr. McAnarney, if he desires an explanation from you later, will call for whatever explanation he desires.

Q. Where were you, sir, at two o'clock on the afternoon of April 14, 1920? *A.* I should say near the shore.

Q. What were you doing? *A.* Two o'clock on the afternoon of the 14th?

Q. On the 14th. *A.* I was peddling fish surely on that time.

Q. Where were you at two o'clock peddling fish? *A.* I can't tell you that place.

Q. Where were you at ten o'clock on the morning of April 14, 1920? *A.* I can't tell you that place.

Q. Name a single individual to whom you sold fish, if you sold any fish, on the 14th of April, 1920. *A.* Well, I sold fish—I got the customers, many customers. Them I see every time that I peddled fish.

Q. Did you have any more customers on April 14, 1920, than you had on the next day? *A.* No, I did not say that. No, I don't say that. [1769]

. . . . .

Q. How long, Mr. Vanzetti, was Mrs. Simon Johnson in the Bart-lett house on the night of May 5, 1920? *A.* I don't know about that.

Q. How long were you outside after you came up to where the motorcycle was before you first saw her coming back to her own house? *A.* I don't saw. I saw a woman come back from toward Brockton and turn in the house that I learn after was the Johnson house.

Q. I am asking you now, how long it was after you came up to Orciana on the motorcycle before you first saw that lady? *A.* A few minutes.

Q. How many minutes? *A.* Well, I can't say. Four or five or six minutes, something like that, a few minutes.

. . . . .

Q. I am asking you for your impression. You told us before, haven't you, that you didn't have any watch on you that night? *A.* Even if I have a watch, I don't watch, no man was observe such a thing, see.

Q. Could you see, when that motorcycle light was facing toward Brockton, could you see the telephone wires running into that next house? *A.* I have no idea of the place. I don't know about that. I cross the bridge without perceiving the bridge. I have no idea at all of the place there. When I walked with the friend I have the habit to speak with him, not looking around.

Mr. Katzmann. I ask that be stricken from the record, if your Honor please.

The Court. It may be.

Q. Now, will you answer my question? *A.* Yes, sir.

Q. With your motorcycle light facing towards Brockton, could you see the telephone wires going into the next house, the Bartlett house? *A.* I never saw them. [1774]

. . . . .

Q. Were you in any hurry when you left there, Mr. Vanzetti? *A.* No, we weren't in a hurry. We were not in a hurry.

. . . . .

Q. Were you calm and collected? *A.* Yes. [1776]

.   .   .   .   .

Q. Did I ask you at Brockton anything about where you were at
the time of the registration under the selective service draft? *A.* No,
you don't ask me that.

.   .   .   .   .

Q. Did I ask you a single question about your evasion of the draft?
A. No. [1777]

.   .   .   .   .

Q. . . . [A]re you the man, Mr. Vanzetti, that on May 9th was
going to address a meeting down at Brockton to your fellow citizens,
saying: "You have fought in the wars, and you have worked for
capitalists, and tried their ways"? Are you the man, sir, that was going
to address the returned soldiers? *A.* Yes, sir.

Q. You were going to advise in a public meeting men who had
gone to war? Are you that man? *A.* Yes, sir, I am that man, not the
man you want me, but I am that man.

.   .   .   .   .

Q. Mr. Vanzetti, do you remember this question and this answer
at the Brockton police station that I made of you, and which you
gave in reply:

"Q. Well, do you remember the holiday we had in April, the
19th of April, they call it Patriots' Day, the middle of April? *A.*
Yes. I heard that before, but I did not remember that was in April."
Do you remember saying that to me at Brockton? *A.* What holiday?

Q. The 19th of April? *A.* What holiday it is?

Q. Patriots' Day. *A.* Patriot?

Q. Patriots' Day. *A.* Oh, patriotics day.

Q. Yes, do you remember my asking you that question and your
making that reply? *A.* No, I don't; I don't remember.

Q. Will you say you did not make that reply to that question? *A.*
No, I don't say that I didn't.

Q. Do you remember the next question:

"Q. This year it came on a Monday."
You remember the answer:

"*A.* I don't remember."
Did you make that reply? *A.* No. I don't remember.

Q. Will you say you did not make it? *A.* Well, maybe I did. I
might have, yes.

Q. Do you remember this question and this answer:

"Q. You don't know where you were the Thursday before that
Monday, do you? *A.* No."

Do you remember that answer to that question? *A.* Oh, yes, I answered some other thing no, that I don't remember in that time, but I remember it now, not only this.

Q. On May 6th, 1920? *A.* Yes.

Q. You did not remember where you were on the 15th of April, did you? *A.* More probable, yes.

Q. But after waiting months and months and months you then remembered, did you? *A.* Not months and months and months, but three or four weeks after I see that I have to be careful and to remember well if I want to save my life. [1802]

. . . . .

Re-Direct-Examination

Q. [*By Mr. Jeremiah McAnarney*] In answer to Mr. Katzmann there at one time you said you were afraid. What did you mean by that?

MR. KATZMANN. One moment, if your Honor please. That was mentioned two or three times.

Q. Any one time you mentioned that you were afraid, what did you mean by that? *A.* I mean that I was afraid, for I know that my friend there in New York have jumped down from the jail in the street and killed himself. The papers say that he jump down, but we don't know.

Q. You now allude to who? Who is that man? *A.* Salsedo.

Q. When did you learn of Salsedo's death? *A.* On the day, in the day, fourth of May.

Q. Fourth of May. Now, you were appointed, you say, by a committee, to go to New York? *A.* Yes, sir. [1808]

Q. I ask you whether or not that was in connection with this man Salsedo? *A.* Yes. I was sent to New York for the principal purpose to look for him.

MR. KATZMANN. One moment, if your Honor please.

THE COURT. Anything, as I said yesterday, that operated on his mind at this time is competent. That may be from conversation with others or it may be from different sources. The thing that he must be limited to is the effect that whatever he heard and from whatever source he may have obtained the information had upon his mind, and I will allow that.

. . . . .

Q. What effect did what you learned in New York, if any, have upon your actions? After you came from New York, how did what you learned operate on your mind, if it did? . . . *A.* It operated very bad, especially after my arrest and after I hear that he was——

THE COURT. I did not get that.

THE WITNESS. He was killed before my arrest and I hear that the day before my arrest. [1809]

. . . . . .

Q. What did you hear in New York? What did you learn? *A.* I learned that most probably for the May 1st there will be many arrest of radicals and I was set wise if I have literature and correspondence, something, papers in the home, to bring away, and to tell to my friends to clean [1810] them up the house, because the literature will not be found if the policemen go to the house.

Q. And was it in consequence of that that you were there that night, May 5th, to get this car? *A.* Yes, not only for that, not necessarily for that,—we want to go to Bridgewater to speak to Pappi for the conference, for the speech, too.

Q. Well, the two things? *A.* The principal purpose is to go to Plymouth, suggest a place where we can put the literature and then bring around the literature to that place.

. . . . . .

Q. How much literature,—what is your judgment, how much literature there was down in Plymouth, so far as you know? *A.* It would be five hundred pounds, sure,—four or five hundred pounds, sure. [1811]

Q. Did either Chief Stewart at the Brockton police station or Mr. Katzmann tell you that you were suspected of robberies and murder? *A.* No.

Q. Was there any question asked of you or any statement made to you to indicate to you that you were charged with that crime on April 15th? *A.* No.

Q. What did you understand, in view of the questions asked of you, what did you understand you were being detained for at the Brockton police station? *A.* I understand they arrested me for a political matter.

. . . . . .

Q. You mean by reason of the questions asked of you? *A.* Because I was asked if I am a socialist, if I am I.W.W., if I am a Communist, if I am a radical, if I am Blackhand.

MR. JEREMIAH MCANARNEY. All right. That is all. [1812]

——AMONG the witnesses called by the defense to buttress Vanzetti's alibi was Angel Guidobone, one of Vanzetti's customers in Plymouth, who testified that he purchased some fish from Vanzetti on April 15, 1920. He gave his testimony through an interpreter.————

Q. [By Mr. Callahan] Could you tell me the time of day you saw him there that you got the fish? A. I saw him on the 15th day of April, about thirteen minutes past twelve or quarter past twelve; well, I was going to my dinner.

. . . . .

Q. How do you fix the date as being April 15th that you saw him there? A. Well, I have a mark here [pointing to his right side]. I had appendicitis. I had an operation.

Q. When did you have the operation? A. I had it on the 19th day of April. [1587]

. . . . .

Cross-Examination

Q. [By Mr. Katzmann] I take it Mr. Guidobone, that the fact you were operated on on April 19th makes you remember you bought some fish on the 15th. Is that it? A. Yes.

Q. And that is the only thing that makes you remember it? A. Well, the operation and that, because I was very careful what I was eating.

Q. Do you think the codfish caused the appendicitis? A. No, no, no.

Q. What is the connection between the operation on the 19th and your buying codfish on the 15th? A. It had nothing to do with it with me.

Q. The codfish had? A. Because I remember. The fish has nothing to do with the operation.

Q. How long were you troubled with the pain that resulted in the operation? A. Oh, over a year before. I did not have the courage to do it.

Q. Then you had the pain for quite some time, didn't you? A. Yes. . . .

Q. Did you have a pain on the 15th? A. No, sir. I did not. On the 17th I did.

Q. Did you have any,—what was the last date before the 17th you had a pain? A. Well, there were other days, different days, that I had pains, but I do not remember now what days.

Q. But you remember codfish on the 15th day, is that right? A. Yes. [1588]

. . . . .

————SACCO took the stand on July 6. In most respects his testimony merely confirmed what Vanzetti had previously testified to: the meeting at the Italian Naturalization Club in Boston, the plan to use Boda's car to haul away radical literature, the episode at the Johnsons' the defendants' belief that they were arrested for radicalism. And like Vanzetti, Sacco testified that he had repeatedly lied to Chief Stewart and Katzmann immediately after his arrest. He admitted lying about not knowing Boda, about where he bought his cartridges and gun, and about other matters. But what strikingly distinguishes his testimony from Vanzetti's, is the lengths to which Katzmann led him to discuss his radical views.————

THE COURT. Let me suggest, Mr. Sacco, to you, the same as I did to Mr. Vanzetti, if you do not understand any questions put to you either by Mr. Moore or by,—either in direct examination or by Mr. Katzmann in cross-examination, it is your right to say so and have the questions put so that you may understand each one and all. You may proceed, Mr. Moore.

Q. [*By Moore*] Mr. Sacco, state your name in full please. *A.* Nicola Sacco.

Q. Where were you born? *A.* Toremaggione, Italy.

Q. What year were you born? *A.* 1891.

Q. Your father, what business was he in there? *A.* He is a business man of olive oil.

· · · · ·

Q. How long did you go to school? *A.* Seven to fourteen.

Q. And why did you leave school? *A.* Well, my father was need very bad on our property,—vineyards.

Q. Needed working on the vineyards? *A.* Yes.

Q. How many children were there in your family? *A.* Seventeen.

Q. And after you quit school at fourteen, what did you do then? *A.* I went to work in,—after fourteen I went to work with my father.

· · · · ·

Q. How long did you continue to work at the family place? *A.* I continued to work until fourteen to sixteen.

Q. Then what happened, Mr. Sacco? *A.* Well, I did not like very much agriculture.

· · · · ·

Q. No. *A.* No, so I went and learned mechanic.

Q. Where did you go to take up mechanical work? *A.* In the same town. [1817]

· · · · ·

Q. . . . What year did you leave Italy? *A.* 1908.

Q. And how did you happen to come here? What was the occasion for your coming here? Who did you come with? *A.* . . . [M]y brother when he came back from the army, he desired to come to this country, so I was crazy to come to this country because I was liked a free country, call a free country, I desire to come with him.

Q. So you two came together, did you? *A.* Yes.

Q. How old were you at that time? *A.* Seventeen years old.

.   .   .   .   .

Q. What kind of work did you take up? *A.* I loaf a couple of weeks. I had an idea to go in a shoe factory to learn a job, but that time in the shoe factory was very slack and I go to see if I could go get another job. . . .

Q. What kind of work did you take up first? *A.* Water boy.

Q. In what character of work was that, construction work, do you mean? *A.* Contractor work, sanitary for Milford. Who done the work, the contractor was the Draper Company. [1818]

Q. How long did you follow that line of work? *A.* About six months, six or seven months, anyway. I am not certain.

Q. Then what did you do? *A.* In the winter time, it was kind of cold, you know, so I decided to work in the factory. I decided to learn a job, a trade, so I did.

Q. Where did you learn edge trimming? *A.* Michael Kelley, 3-K. He used to run the little factory over there at that time. He used to do about eighty dozen a day.

.   .   .   .   .

Q. When did you start in there as an edge trimmer? *A.* 1910. [1819]

.   .   .   .   .

Q. What month, if you know, when you left the Milford Shoe Company? *A.* The last of March [in 1917], before the registration.

.   .   .   .   .

Q. What did you do in June of 1917? *A.* I left Milford.

.   .   .   .   .

Q. Were you outside of the state of Massachusetts during that period of time? *A.* Outside of this country, the United States.

Q. What month, if you know, did you come back? *A.* [August, 1917.]

.   .   .   .   .

Q. Why did you come back? *A.* Well, I could not stay no more. I leave my wife here and my boy. I could not stay no more far away from them.

Q. You were married when? *A.* 1912.

Q. You had a child at this time, did you, when you—— *A.* Yes, sir.

Q. How old was your boy at that time? *A.* When I left Milford?

Q. No. When you came back from outside of the States. How old is your boy now? *A.* He is going on nine years. He finished eight years the 10th of May, last May.

Q. When you returned here in the fall or summer of 1917, what did you do then? *A.* I went straight to see my wife in Cambridge.

Q. Did you go to work then? *A.* Yes, sir. After a few days.

Q. Where did you go to work? *A.* Cambridge, in a candy factory. . . .

Q. And what name had you been using during this interval?

. . . . .

A. . . . Nicola Mosmacotelli, my mother's second name.

Q. When did you take that name? *A.* When I left Milford. [1820]

Q. How did you get that name? *A.* Well, to not get in trouble by registration.

. . . . .

Q. What was the next place you worked after leaving the candy company at Cambridge? *A.* I used to buy the *Globe* every morning, so I find a job over in East Boston, the Victoria Shoe Company, so I left there for a week or two. Those women's shoe, I never trimmed on women's shoes before. It was very hard for me to trim them, the heel was too high, so I couldn't make no more than two dollars a day. I decided to leave the job and go pick and shovel be better, make more money if I couldn't find a job.

. . . . .

Q. What was the next piece of work you did? What company did you work for next? *A.* Rice & Hutchins' shoe factory.

. . . . .

Q. Were you doing edge trimming? *A.* No, sir.

. . . . .

Q. How long were you there? *A.* Seven or eight days, no more.

Q. Why did you leave? *A.* Because that was not my job. I was to get only $13 a week.

Q. Then where did you go? *A.* I go straight to Haverhill. [1821]

Q. Now, when did you go to work for Mr. Kelley at the 3-K shoe at Stoughton? *A.* It began in November of 1918.

. . . . .

Q. Now, Mr. Sacco, are your father and mother living? *A.* My father is living. My mother died.

Q. Had you any communications from your,—when did your mother die? *A.* 7th of March, 1920. [1822]

. . . . .

Q. Mr. Sacco, where were you on April 15th, Mr. Sacco? *A.* I was in Boston.

Q. What hour that day? Or, first, I will ask you what you went to Boston for? *A.* To get my passport.

. . . . .

Q. What time did you leave Stoughton that day? *A.* I leave Stoughton on the 8:56 train.

. . . . .

Q. And where did you go on arrival in Boston? *A.* I left the South Station. I went in the North End. I went buy a paper, *La Notizia.*

. . . . .

Q. What did you do then? *A.* Oh, I stayed over there about fifteen minutes, I guess. I read a little. So then I take a walk, and I went on Hanover Street. [1823]

. . . . .

Q. Where did you go? *A.* I started to walk, and I met a friend [Angelo Monello].

. . . . .

Q. Then where did you go? *A.* We walked until Washington Street, and I go back again, so I stopped in the stores and been looking at a straw hat, some suits,—a price, you know. Then I go back. I have my mind to go in the afternoon and get my passport. I say probably I go to get my dinner first, so I have a little time and I go there, so I went over to Boni's restaurant.

Q. And who did you see there? *A.* I met Mr.—Professor Guadenagi.

. . . . .

Q. Any one else? *A.* Mr. Bosco.

Q. Is there any one else? Well, how long were you in the restaurant? *A.* I should say about an hour and fifteen minutes,—fifteen or twenty minutes.

. . . . .

Q. Where did you go then? *A.* I went right straight to the consul's, —Italian consul.

Q. About what hour, if you know, Mr. Sacco, did you get to the Italian consul? *A.* It was about two o'clock. [1824]

Q. And what occurred on your going into the consulate? Who did you talk with there and what happened? *A.* . . . I went in and a man came around . . . I said, "I like to get my passport for my whole family." He asked me,—he said, "You bring the picture?" I said, "Yes," so I gave it to him, see, a big picture. He says, "Well, I am sorry. This picture is too big." "Well," I says, "can you cut, and make him small?" "No," he said, "the picture we cannot use, because it goes too big." I says, "No, no use, because got to make a photograph just for the purpose for the passport, small, very small."—so I did.

Q. Now, I call your attention to the photograph marked "B" attached to the depositions in this case.

. . . . .

Q. Then what did you do? A. I go back to buy my stuff, groceries, so before I got my groceries, I went to get coffee in a coffee store in the North End near the Boni restaurant. . . .

. . . . .

Q. . . . And did you see any one while you were there? A. Yes.

Q. Who? A. Professor Guadenagi.

Q. Any one else, if you know? A. Yes. Professor Dentamore.

Q. Then where did you go? A. I went to buy grocery. [1825]

. . . . .

Q. Do you know about what hour you left for Stoughton that night, that afternoon? A. I should say about twelve minutes past four.

Q. And you went immediately back to Stoughton and then to your home? A. Yes. [1826]

. . . . .

[*July 7, 1921*]

Q. Mr. Sacco, how did it happen that you were carrying on the evening of May 5th a revolver or a pistol? A. Well, to use like that. My wife used to clean the house, get ready, because we are to go Saturday to New York to get the steamboat, and she was getting ready, and so she cleaned the bureau . . . and she pulled out the bullets and the pistol, and then she ask me, she said, "What are you going to do, Nick, with this?"

MR. KATZMANN. One moment.

Q. Not what she said to you, but what you did. A. So I took that sometime in the afternoon, about half past three, I should say, about four o'clock, anyway. I said, "Well, I go to shoot in the woods, me and Vanzetti." So I did. I took it in my pocket. I put the revolver over here [*indicating*] and the bullets in my pocket, in my pocket back. Well, we started to talk in the afternoon, me and Vanzetti, and half past four Orciana and Boda came over to the house, so we started an argument and I forgot about to go in the woods shooting, so it was still left in my pocket. [1858]

. . . . .

Q. Now, when had you received word of your mother's death? A. I received a letter, the first letter from my father. It was sometime the last of March. My mother died on the 7th of March. The letter came about the 22d or 23d of March, I should say. I do not remember exactly the day, but I should say that time, about that time.

Q. Did you speak to Mr. Kelley about leaving his employ and going to Italy? A. Yes, sir.

Q. At the time, or about April 15th, what steps had you taken to secure some one to take your place, if any? A. I spoke with George Kelley. That is the son of Michael Kelley. He is running the factory there. He is the superintendent. So I say, "George, I desire to go to Italy."

. . . . .

Q. What steps were then taken to get some one to take your place? A. I told him about Monday before March, because I was ready to go before March. I told George to find a man as quickly as he can. I say, "I am not going to leave you."

. . . . .

Q. Do you know who came, or who was secured to take your place? A. Yes. He asked me if Henry Iacovelli could come with me. He was a witness here. [1859]

. . . . .

Q. . . . [W]hen you went to the 3-K, in addition to the regular work as a piece worker, did you do anything else? A. Yes.

Q. What? A. I used to light the steam heat in the shop in the winter time, the fireman, and assist watch the shop. [1860]

. . . . .

Q. Mr. Sacco, at the time that you were taken into the Brockton police station on May 6th or 7th, what did you do at the time that various people came into that room, into the jail, to look at you? A. I walked with a couple of police away up to the big room. . . .

. . . . .

Q. What did you do? A. So I went in. I stand up. Sometimes I turned around like that [indicating]. Sometimes faced like that [indicating] the first time. There was about six or seven people watching the way I was turning around. . . .

. . . . .

Q. What did you do when these various people were in the room? *A.* The first time I walked a couple of steps. Then I walked a couple of steps like that [*indicating*]. Then I walk a couple of steps like that [*indi-* [1861] *cating*] in this way. So the second time I cross like that [*indicating*]. They make me just to shoot, wait for somebody to hold up money, with a dirty cap on my head. The second time he put the hair like that [*indicating*] with the hands, and I turned around. On the second time make———

Q. How do you mean with your eyes, eyes looking up? *A.* Yes, still. The other time made me look on the right side with eyes raised, and four times this way [*indicating*] with the left side.

Q. Turned your eyes to the left? *A.* Yes. So when I stand again, they put a cap, the old cap on again. After that that was all.

Q. Did any of these people who were in the room at the time that you did these things, did any of these people do anything themselves? *A.* They watch pretty carefully, pretty close, and the most of the people I could see the head very sorry, shaken. [1862]

. . . . .

Q. How many times did Miss Splaine come and look at you? *A.* I should say three times.

. . . . .

Q. How many persons, all told, Mr. Sacco, looked at you during the time that you were in the jail there? *A.* I should say about one hundred.

Q. Mr. Sacco, at the time that you were arrested, did you have at that time all of the .32 calibre shells or any calibre shells of any kind or character that there was in your house? *A.* Yes, sir. [1863]

Cross-Examination

Q. [*By Mr. Katzmann*] Did you say yesterday you love a free country? *A.* Yes, sir.

Q. Did you love this country in the month of May, 1917? *A.* I did not say,—I don't want to say I did not love this country.

Q. Did you love this country in the month [*sic*] of 1917? *A.* If you can, Mr. Katzmann, if you give me that,—I could explain———

Q. Do you understand that question? *A.* Yes.

Q. Then will you please answer it? *A.* I can't answer in one word.

Q. You can't say whether you loved the United States of America one week before the day you enlisted [*sic*] for the first draft? *A.* I can't say in one word, Mr. Katzmann.

Q. You can't tell this jury whether you loved the country or not?

Mr. Moore. I object to that.

A. I could explain that, yes, if I loved——

Q. What? *A.* I could explain that, yes, if I loved, if you give me a chance.

Q. I ask you first to answer that question. Did you love this United States of America in May, 1917? *A.* I can't answer in one word.

Q. Don't you know whether you did or not?

Mr. Moore. I object, your Honor.

The Court. What say?

Mr. Moore. I object to the repetition of this question without giving the young man an opportunity to explain his attitude.

The Court. That is not the usual method that prevails. Where the question can be categorically answered by yes or no, it should be answered. The explanation comes later. Then you can make any inquiry to the effect of giving the witness an opportunity of making whatever explanation at that time he sees fit to make, but under cross-examination counsel is entitled to get an answer either yes or no, when the question can be so answered. You may proceed, please.

Q. Did you love this country in the last week of May, 1917? *A.* That is pretty hard for me to say in one word, Mr. Katzmann.

Q. There are two words you can use, Mr. Sacco, yes or no. Which one is it? *A.* Yes.

Q. And in order to show your love for this United States of America when she was about to call upon you to become a soldier you ran away to Mexico?

Mr. Jeremiah McAnarney. Wait.

The Court. Did you?

Q. Did you run away to Mexico?

The Court. He has not said he ran away to Mexico. Did you go?

Q. Did you go to Mexico to avoid being a soldier for this country that you loved? *A.* Yes.

Q. You went under an assumed name? *A.* No. [1867]

Q. Didn't you take the name of Mosmacotelli? *A.* Yes.

Q. That is not your name, is it? *A.* No.

Q. How long did you remain under the name of Mosmacotelli? *A.* Until I got a job over to Mr. Kelley's.

Q. When was that? *A.* The armistice.

Q. After the war was practically over? *A.* Yes, sir.

Q. Then, for the first time, after May, 1917, did you become known as Sacco again? *A.* Yes, sir.

Q. Was it for the reason that you desired to avoid service that when you came back in four months you went to Cambridge instead of to Milford? *A.* For the reason for not to get in the army.

Q. So as to avoid getting in the army. *A.* Another reason why, I did not want no chance to get arrested and one year in prison.

. . . . .

Q. Did you love your country when you came back from Mexico? *A.* I don't think I could change my opinion in three months.

Q. You still loved America, did you? *A.* I should say yes.

Q. And is that your idea of showing your love for this country? *A.* [*Witness hesitates.*]

Q. Is that your idea of showing your love for America? *A.* Yes.

Q. And would it be your idea of showing your love for your wife that when she needed you you ran away from her? *A.* I did not run away from her.

Mr. Moore. I object.

The Witness. I was going to come after if I need her.

The Court. He may answer. Simply on the question of credibility, that is all.

Q. Would it be your idea of love for your wife that you were to run away from her when she needed you?

Mr. Jeremiah McAnarney. Pardon me. I ask for an exception on that.

The Court. Excluded. One may not run away. He has not admitted he ran away.

Q. Then I will ask you, didn't you run away from Milford so as to avoid being a soldier for the United States? *A.* I did not run away.

Q. You mean you walked away? *A.* Yes.

Q. You don't understand me when I say "run away," do you? *A.* That is vulgar. [1868]

Q. That is vulgar? *A.* You can say a little intelligent, Mr. Katzmann.

Q. Don't you think going away from your country is a vulgar thing to do when she needs you? *A.* I don't believe in war.

Q. You don't believe in war? *A.* No, sir.

Q. Do you think it is a cowardly thing to do what you did? *A.* No, sir.

Q. Do you think it is a brave thing to do what you did? *A.* Yes, sir.

Q. Do you think it would be a brave thing to go away from your own wife? *A.* No.

Q. When she needed you? *A.* No.

Q. What wages did you first earn in this country? *A.* Wage?

Q. Wages, money, pay? *A.* I used to get before I leave?

Q. When you first came to this country? *A.* $1.15.

Q. Per day? *A.* Yes.

Q. What were you getting at the 3-K factory when you got through? *A.* Sometimes sixty, fifty, seventy, eighty, forty, thirty, twenty-five, thirty-five. Depends on how much work was.

Q. That was within eight years after you first came to this country, isn't it? *A.* After seven years,—no, after twelve years.

Q. 1908. I beg your pardon. That is my mistake, Mr. Sacco. I did not mean that. That is within thirteen years? *A.* Yes, sir.

Q. From the time you came to this country? *A.* Yes.

Q. From $1.15 a day to $5 a day or better? *A.* Yes.

Q. And your child was born in this country, wasn't it? *A.* Yes.

Q. And your marriage took place in this country? *A.* Yes.

Q. Is Italy a free country? Is it a republic? *A.* Republic, yes.

Q. You love free countries, don't you? *A.* I should say yes.

Q. Why didn't you stay down in Mexico? *A.* Well, first thing, I could not get my trade over there. I had to do any other job.

Q. Don't they work with a pick and shovel in Mexico? *A.* Yes.

Q. Haven't you worked with a pick and shovel in this country? *A.* I did.

Q. Why didn't you stay there, down there in that free country, and work with a pick and shovel? *A.* I don't think I did sacrifice to learn a job to go to pick and shovel in Mexico.

Q. Is it because,—is your love for the United States of America commensurate with the amount of money you can get in this country per week? *A.* Better conditions, yes.

Q. Better country to make money, isn't it? *A.* Yes.

Q. Mr. Sacco, that is the extent of your love for this country, isn't it, measured in dollars and cents?

Mr. JEREMIAH McANARNEY. If your Honor please, I object to this particular question. [1869]

THE COURT. You opened up this whole subject.

Mr. JEREMIAH McANARNEY. If your Honor please, I object to this question. That is my objection.

THE COURT. The form of it?

Mr. JEREMIAH McANARNEY. To the substance and form.

Mr. KATZMANN. I will change the form, if your Honor please.

THE COURT. Better change that.

Q. Is your love for this country measured by the amount of money you can earn here?

Mr. JEREMIAH McANARNEY. To that question I object.

THE COURT. Now, you may answer.

A. I never loved money.

MR. JEREMIAH MCANARNEY. Save my exception.

THE COURT. Certainly.

Q. What is the reason then?

THE COURT. I allow this on the ground that the defendants opened it up.

Q. What is the reason you came back?

MR. JEREMIAH MCANARNEY. My exception lies just the same?

THE COURT. Certainly.

MR. MOORE. Both defendants?

THE COURT. Certainly.

Q. What is the reason you came back from Mexico if you did not love money, then? *A.* The first reason is all against my nature, is all different food over there, different nature, anyway.

Q. That is the first reason. It is against your nature. The food isn't right. *A.* Food, and many other things.

Q. You stood it for four months, didn't you? *A.* Three months.

Q. Three months? *A.* Yes.

Q. You came back all right physically, didn't you? *A.* I should say yes.

Q. And you had Italian food there, didn't you? *A.* Yes, made by ourselves.

Q. You could have had it all the time if you sent for it, couldn't you? *A.* Not all the time. I don't know.

Q. Did you fail to have it at any time in the three months you were there? *A.* Yes, sir. Different.

Q. What is the difference about it? *A.* Oh, different food that we did not like.

Q. It was Italian food, wasn't it? A. No, sir.

Q. Didn't you say it was? *A.* Sometimes after.

Q. You could have had it all the time if you sent for it, couldn't you? *A.* Could have had beans sometimes and any other vegetable.

MR. KATZMANN. I ask that be stricken out and the witness required to answer the question. [1870]

Q. Could you have had it by sending for it? *A.* Could not get it all the time.

Q. Why couldn't you get it in Mexico the same as you get it here? *A.* I suppose Mexico is not very much industries as in this country.

Q. Couldn't you send to Boston to get Italian food sent to Monterey, Mexico? *A.* If I was a D. Rockefeller I will.

Q. Then, I take it, you came back to the United States first to get something to eat. Is that right? Something that you liked? *A.* No, not just for eat.

Q. Didn't you say that was the first reason? *A.* The first reason——

Q. Didn't you say that was the first reason? *A.* Yes.

Q. All right. That wasn't a reason of the heart, was it? *A.* The heart?

Q. Yes. *A.* No.

Q. That was a reason of the stomach, wasn't it? *A.* Not just for the stomach, but any other reason.

Q. I am talking first about the first reason. So, the first reason your love of America is founded upon is pleasing your stomach. Is that right? *A.* I will not say yes.

Q. Haven't you said so? *A.* Not for the stomach. I don't think it is a satisfaction just for the stomach.

Q. What is your second reason? *A.* The second reason is strange for me, the language.

Q. Strange language? *A.* Yes.

Q. Were you in an Italian colony there? *A.* If I got them? I can't get that, Mr. Katzmann.

Q. Pardon me. Were you in a group of Italians there? *A.* Yes.

Q. When you came to America in 1908, did you understand English? *A.* No.

Q. A strange language here, wasn't it? *A.* Yes.

Q. What is the third reason, if there is one? *A.* A third reason, I was far away from my wife and boy.

Q. Couldn't you have sent for your wife and your boy? *A.* I wouldn't send for my wife and boy over there, because it was the idea to come back here.

Q. I know that. You are back here. My question is, couldn't you have sent for Mrs. Sacco and your boy? *A.* Extreme condition, it would be bad. I could not go back in this United States, why I would get my wife and my boy.

Q. Your answer means, does it not, you could have had Mrs. Sacco and the boy come down there to live with you? *A.* Yes.

Q. You preferred to come back to this country? *A.* Yes.

Q. But you preferred to remain under the name of Mosmacotelli until the armistice was signed, didn't you? *A.* Yes. [1871]

Q. Now, is there any other besides those three reasons why you loved the United States of America? *A.* Well, I couldn't say. Over here there is more accommodation for the working class, I suppose, than any other people, a chance to be more industrious, and more industry. Can have a chance to get anything he wants.

Q. You mean to earn more money, don't you? A. No, no, money, never loved money.

Q. Never loved money? A. No, money never satisfaction to me.

Q. Money never a satisfaction to you? A. No.

Q. What was the industrial condition that pleased you so much here if it wasn't a chance to earn bigger money? A. A man, Mr. Katzmann, has no satisfaction all through the money, for the belly.

Q. For the what? A. For the stomach, I mean.

Q. We got away from the stomach. Now, I am talking about money. A. There is lots of things.

Q. Well, let us have them all. I want to know why you loved America so that after you got to the haven of Mexico when the United States was at war you came back here. A. Yes.

Q. I want all the reasons why you came back. A. I think I did tell you already.

Q. Are those all? A. Yes. Industry makes lots of things different.

Q. Then there is food, that is one? A. Yes.

Q. Foreign language is two? A. Yes.

Q. Your wife and child is three? A. Yes.

Q. And better industrial conditions? A. Yes.

Q. Is that all? A. That is all.

. . . . .

Q. Did you find love of country among those four reasons? A. Yes, sir.

Q. Which one is love of country? A. All together.

Q. All together? A. Yes, sir.

Q. Food, wife, language, industry? A. Yes.

Q. That is love of country, is it? A. Yes.

Q. Is standing by a country when she needs a soldier evidence of love of country?

MR. JEREMIAH McANARNEY. That I object to, if your Honor please. [1872] And I might state now I want my objection to go to this whole line of interrogation.

THE COURT. I think you opened it up.

MR. JEREMIAH McANARNEY. No, if your Honor please, I have not.

THE COURT. It seems to me you have. Are you going to claim much of all the collection of the literature and the books was really in the interest of the United States as well as these people and therefore it has opened up the credibility of the defendant when he claims that all that work was done really for the interest of the United States in getting this literature out of the way?

MR. JEREMIAH McANARNEY. That claim is not presented in anything tantamount to the language just used by the Court, and in view of the record as it stands at this time I object to this line of inquiry.

THE COURT. Is that not your claim, that the defendant, as a reason that he has given for going to the Johnson house, that they wanted the automobile to prevent people from being deported and to get this literature all out of the way? Does he not claim that that was done in the interest of the United States, to prevent violation of the law by the distribution of this literature? I understood that was the——

MR. JEREMIAH McANARNEY. Are you asking that as a question to me?

THE COURT. Yes.

MR. JEREMIAH McANARNEY. Absolutely we have taken no such position as that, and the evidence at this time does not warrant the assumption of that question.

THE COURT. Then you are not going to make that claim?

MR. JEREMIAH McANARNEY. I am going to make whatever claim is legitimate.

THE COURT. I want to know what that is. You are going to claim in argument——

MR. JEREMIAH McANARNEY. I am going to claim this man and Vanzetti were of that class called socialists. I am going to claim that riot was running a year ago last April, that men were being deported, that twelve to fifteen hundred were seized in Massachusetts.

THE COURT. Do you mean to say you are going to offer evidence on that?

MR. JEREMIAH McANARNEY. I am going to claim——

THE COURT. I am asking the claim. You must know when I ask the claim I mean a claim that is founded on fact, evidence introduced in the case, and not upon anything else.

MR. JEREMIAH McANARNEY. We have not concluded the evidence, if your Honor please.

THE COURT. Do you say you are going to introduce evidence to that effect?

MR. JEREMIAH McANARNEY. We have witnesses which we may introduce here. I do not know whether we will introduce them or not.

[1873]

THE COURT. When you address me, I wish you would direct yourself to either evidence introduced or evidence you propose to introduce.

MR. JEREMIAH McANARNEY. Your Honor now sees——

THE COURT. So I can pass judgment then upon that, and I cannot pass judgment as to the competency of something that may not be introduced and never come before me for consideration.

MR. JEREMIAH McANARNEY. Your Honor now sees the competency of my remarks, when I said to your Honor that I objected to the question in the present state of the evidence?

THE COURT. Are you going to claim that what the defendant did was in the interest of the United States?

MR. JEREMIAH McANARNEY. Your Honor please, I now object to your Honor's statement as prejudicial to the rights of the defendants and ask that this statement be withdrawn from the jury.

THE COURT. There is no prejudicial remark made that I know of, and none were intended. I simply asked you, sir, whether you propose to offer evidence as to what you said to me.

MR. JEREMIAH McANARNEY. If your Honor please, the remarks made with reference to the country and whether the acts that he was doing were for the benefit of the country. I can see no other inference to be drawn from those except prejudicial to the defendants.

THE COURT. Do you intend to make that claim?

MR. JEREMIAH McANARNEY. What claim, please?

THE COURT. The one that I am suggesting.

MR. JEREMIAH McANARNEY. When this evidence is closed, if your Honor please, I shall argue what is legitimate in the case.

THE COURT. All I ask is this one question, and it will simplify matters very much. Is it your claim that in the collection of the literature and the books and papers that that was done in the interest of the United States?

MR. JEREMIAH McANARNEY. No, I make no such broad claim as that.

THE COURT. Then I will hear you, Mr. Katzmann, on the competency of this testimony.

MR. KATZMANN. I am sorry I did not hear what Mr. McAnarney said.

THE COURT. Mr. McAnarney says it is not his claim, as I got it, he does not propose to make the claim that the collection and distribution of this literature was any matter to be done by either or both of the defendants in the interest of the United States.

MR. KATZMANN. Then, if your Honor please, I offer the line of cross-examination I have started upon as tending to attack the credibility of this man as a witness.

THE COURT. As to what part of his testimony? [1874]

MR. KATZMANN. As to any part of his testimony to affect his credibility as a witness *in toto*.

THE COURT. You can't attack a witness's credibility *in toto* excepting concerning some subject matter about which he has testified.

MR. KATZMANN. Well, he stated in his direct examination yesterday that he loved a free country, and I offer it to attack that statement made in his examination by his own counsel.

THE COURT. That is what I supposed, and that is what I supposed that remark meant when it was introduced in this cross-examination, but counsel now say they don't make that claim.

MR. KATZMANN. They say they don't make the claim that gathering up the literature on May 5th at West Bridgewater was for the purpose of helping the country, but that is a different matter, not related to May 5th.

.   .   .   .   .   .

THE COURT. [*To the jury*] Of course, gentlemen, you understand, and you should understand by this time, that the Court is simply to pass upon the competency of testimony that is offered. The Court has no opinion of any facts. You heard me say so. The Court has no opinion in reference to this matter. I made simply the inquiry with a view of ascertaining what the claim of counsel might be, what might be argued, and inasmuch as counsel said they made no such claim, then I have reserved the right to pass upon the competency after inquiry has been made with reference to said testimony of the witness. I think you should know, and I repeat it, anyhow, there is no disposition, nothing has been said to do the slightest thing in any manner whatsoever to prejudice the rights of either of these defendants, and anything that has been said you will not consider it if anybody can draw such an inference. You will give it not the slightest consideration in the world. It deserves none, and you will give it none. The only question I was passing upon was the competency of testimony and nothing else. Questions are not evidence. Statements of counsel are not evidence. Statements by the Court are not evidence. You will be governed by absolutely nothing but testimony that is admitted and heard by you from the witnesses upon the stand. You may proceed.

Q. What did you mean when you said yesterday you loved a free country? A. First thing I came in this country——

Q. No, pardon me. What did you mean when you said yesterday you loved a free country? *A.* Give me a chance to explain.

Q. I am asking you to explain now. *A.* When I was in Italy, a boy, [1875] I was a republican, so I always thinking republican has more chance to manage education, develop, to build some day his family, to raise the child and education, if you could. But that was my opinion; so when I came to this country I saw there was not what I was thinking before, but there was all the difference, because I been working in Italy not so hard as I been work in this country. I could live free there just as well. Work in the same condition, but not so hard, about seven or eight hours a day, better food. I mean genuine. Of course, over here is good food, because it is bigger country, to any those who got money to spend, not for the working and laboring class, and in Italy is more opportunity to laborer to eat vegetable, more fresh, and I came in this country. When I been started work here very hard and been work thirteen years, hard worker, I could not been afford much a family the way I did have the idea before. I could not put any money in the bank. I could no push my boy some to go to school and other things. I teach over here men who is with me. The free idea gives any man a chance to profess his own idea, not the supreme idea, not to give any person, not to be like Spain in position, yes, about twenty centuries ago, but to give a chance to print and education, literature, free speech, that I see it was all wrong. I could see the best men, intelligent, education, they been arrested and sent to prison and died in prison for years and years without getting them out, and Debs, one of the great men in his country, he is in prison, still away in prison, because he is a socialist. He wanted the laboring class to have better conditions and better living, more education, give a push his son if he could have a chance some day, but they put him in prison. Why? Because the capitalist class, they know, they are against that, because the capitalist class, they don't want our child to go to high school or to college or Harvard College. There would not be no chance, there would not be no,—they don't want the working class educationed; they want the working class to be a low all the times, be underfoot, and not to be up with the head. So, sometimes, you see, the Rockefellers, Morgans, they give fifty,—mean they give five hundred thousand dollars to Harvard College, they give a million dollars for another school. Everybody say, "Well, D. Rockefeller is a great man, the best in the country." I want to ask him who is going to Harvard College? What benefit the working class they will get by those million dollars they give by Rockefeller, D. Rockefellers. They

won't get, the poor class, they won't have no chance to go to Harvard
College because men who is getting $21 a week or $30 a week, I don't
care if he gets $80 a week, if he gets a family of five children he
can't live and send his child and go to Harvard College if he wants
to eat anything nature will give him. If he wants to eat like a cow,
and that is the best thing, but I want men to live like men. I like
men to get everything that nature will give best, because they belong,
—we are not the friend of any other place, but we are belong to
nations. So that is why my idea has been changed. So that is why I
love people who labor and work and see better conditions every day
de- [1877] velop, makes no more war. We no want fight by the gun,
and we don't want to destroy young men. The mother been suffering
for building the young man. Some day need a little more bread, so
when the time the mother get some bread or profit out of that boy,
the Rockefellers, Morgans, and some of the peoples, high class, they
send to war. Why? What is war? The war is not shoots like Abraham
Lincoln's and Abe Jefferson, to fight for the free country, for the
better education, to give chance to any other peoples, not the white
people but the black and the others, because they believe and know
they are mens like the rest, but they are war for the great millionaire.
No war for the civilization of men. They are war for business, million
dollars come on the side. What right we have to kill each other? I
been work for the Irish, I have been working with the German fellow,
with the French many other peoples. I love them people just as I
could love my wife, and my people for that did receive me. Why
should I go kill them men? What he done to me? He never done
anything, so I don't believe in no war. I want to destroy those guns.
All I can say, the Government put the literature, give us educations.
I remember in Italy, a long time ago, about sixty years ago, I should
say, yes, about sixty years ago, the Government they could not control very much these two,—devilment went on, and robbery, so one
of the government in the cabinet he says, "If you want to destroy
those devilments, if you want to take off all those criminals, you ought
to give a chance to socialist literature, education of people, emancipation. That is why I destroy governments, boys." That is why my idea
I love socialists. That is why I like people who want education and
living, building, who is good, just as much as they could. That is all.

Q. And that is why you love the United States of America? A. Yes.

Q. She is back more than twenty centuries like Spain, is she? A. At
the time of the war they do it.

Q. Are we in time of war now? A. No.

Q. Were we in time of war when you came back from Mexico?
A. Yes.

Q. What did you come back for, then? *A.* I told the reason why I came back.

Q. All right. You don't get a good education in this country? *A.* I don't see why they have a chance.

Q. Do you get a better chance for education in Italy, I take it, from what you said? *A.* I don't say Italy better education in this country.

Q. You said you could work less hours over in Italy? *A.* Yes.

Q. You could get fresher vegetables? *A.* Yes.

Q. Better food, and it was a republic? *A.* For the working class.

Q. Why didn't you go back there? *A.* Pretty hard for men to change when he establish in one place.

Q. Why, you were to go back, weren't you? *A.* Yes. [1877]

Q. Why didn't you intend to stay back there when you went back? *A.* Italy?

Q. Yes, your native country. *A.* I could not stay or not, because——

Q. Have you said whether you were going to stay or not? *A.* Yes, I was going to go.

Q. Were you coming back? *A.* I do not know, Mr. Katzmann.

Q. Did you tell me you were coming back? *A.* I couldn't say so.

Q. Can't you remember what you said to me over in the Brockton police station? *A.* I could not remember all the words, but I do remember some conversation between me and Mr. Kelley.

Q. Never mind Kelley. I am talking about myself now. Didn't you tell me that you were coming back to this country in two or three months? *A.* Well, if I did——

Q. Did you? *A.* I could not remember, Mr. Katzmann, if I did.

Q. Wasn't that your intention to come back? *A.* I couldn't say yes, because probably I could remain in Italy because my father is old. I could get his business over there.

Q. Were you going to have your father support you? *A.* What? Support me, my father?

Q. Yes. *A.* No.

Q. Were you going to take your wife and child over? *A.* Yes.

Q. You could not go back to Italy, you say, because it would be a hardship, but you could take your wife and child back for a vacation; is that right? *A.* No, not vacation.

Q. Wasn't it a vacation? *A.* No, sir.

Q. Were you going to work while you were over there? *A.* Certainly. I could not [live] without work. I love work.

. . . . .

Q. Do you love it as much as you love this country? *A.* Well, I think men is a great work,—greater profit for the country, too.

Q. Do you love work as much as you love the United States? *A.* The reaction of the United States I did not like.

Q. When you came over to this country, you had certain ideas, didn't you, of what was here? *A.* No.

Q. Didn't you say when you came over you were thinking about education, building for your family, and raising a family? *A.* Yes, but I was a republican in my country.

Q. Didn't you say that you had those ideas of this country when you came here? *A.* Yes.

Q. And didn't you say when you came you saw a difference? *A.* Yes.

Q. And the things were better in Italy than they were here? *A.* No, not that.

Q. In substance, haven't you said that in this long answer you gave? [1878] *A.* No. Buy fruit more fresh for the working class, but no education and other things. It is just the same.

Q. Didn't you say you did not have to work so hard in Italy? *A.* Yes.

Q. That you could live just as well in Italy? *A.* Yes.

Q. And that there was better food? *A.* Yes.

Q. And fresher vegetables in Italy? *A.* Yes.

Q. Why didn't you go back? *A.* Well, I say already——

Q. Say it again. Why didn't you go back when you were disappointed in those things? *A.* I say men established in this country, it is pretty hard to go back, change mind to go back.

Q. Pretty hard to change your mind? *A.* Yes.

Q. You say on April 15, 1920, you were in Boston getting a passport to go back with your wife and children? *A.* Yes. That is not the reason I go back to the old country, for the fruit, but to see my father. For twelve years I never saw him, my brother, my sister, or my folks.

Q. It is just as easy, isn't it, to go back to see your father as to go back for fruit. You go back in either case? *A.* I do the greatest sacrifice in the life to go there.

Q. To go back to a country where you get those things and could not get them here,—is that a sacrifice? *A.* No. The great sacrifice is to see my folks.

Q. The great sacrifice. All right. Do you believe in obedience to constituted governmental authority?

MR. JEREMIAH McANARNEY. I object, if your Honor please.

. . . . .

Q. . . . Did you say in substance you could not send your boy to Harvard? *A.* Yes.

Q. Unless you had money. Did you say that? *A.* Of course.

Q. Do you think that is true? *A.* I think it is.

Q. Don't you know Harvard University educates more boys of poor people free than any other university in the United States of America?

MR. JEREMIAH McANARNEY. I object.

THE COURT. You may answer.

. . . . .

Q. Do you know that to be the fact? *A.* How many there are?

Q. What? *A.* How many?

Q. How many? Don't you know that each year there are scores of them that Harvard educates free?

MR. JEREMIAH McANARNEY. I object.

THE COURT. Wait until he finishes the question.

MR. JEREMIAH McANARNEY. I thought he had.

MR. KATZMANN. That was the end of it.

THE COURT. He may answer yes or no, whether he knows or not.

MR. JEREMIAH McANARNEY. Save an exception.

Q. The question is, do you know? *A.* I can't answer that question, no.

Q. So without the light of knowledge on that subject, you are condemning even Harvard University, are you, as being a place for rich men?

. . . . .

Q. Did you intend to condemn Harvard College?

. . . . .

A. No, sir.

Q. Were you ready to say none but the rich could go there without knowing about offering scholarships?

. . . . .

A. Yes.

Q. Does your boy go to the public schools? *A.* Yes.

Q. Are there any schools in the town you came from in Italy that compare with the school your boy goes to?

MR. JEREMIAH MCANARNEY. I object.

THE COURT. Isn't this quite a good way now from that? Of course, I see, or think I see, what you have in mind eventually, but it seems to me the boy going to school is quite a considerable distance.

Q. Does your boy go to the public school? *A.* Yes.

Q. Without payment of money? *A.* Yes.

Q. Have you free nursing where you come from in Stoughton? *A.* What do you mean?

Q. A district nurse? *A.* For the boys? [1880]

Q. For anybody in your family who is ill? *A.* I could not say. Yes, I never have them in my house.

Q. Do you know how many children the city of Boston is educating in the public schools?——

MR. JEREMIAH MCANARNEY. I object.

Q. [*Continued*] ——free?

MR. JEREMIAH MCANARNEY. I object.

THE COURT. Ask him if he knows.

MR. KATZMANN. I did.

THE COURT. Answer yes or no.

Q. Do you know? *A.* I can't answer yes or no.

Q. Do you know it is close to one hundred thousand children?

MR. JEREMIAH MCANARNEY. I object.

A. I know millions of people don't go there.

MR. JEREMIAH MCANARNEY. Wait. When there is objection, don't answer. I object to that question.

THE COURT. He says he doesn't know.

MR. JEREMIAH MCANARNEY. I object to that answer. I object to the question and the answer.

THE COURT. The question may stand, and the answer also. [1881]

———FOLLOWING his examination of Sacco's radicalism, Katzmann sought to weaken Sacco's credibility by questioning him about falsehoods he had told his employer and the district attorney.———

Q. Didn't [you] say anything to . . . [your employer, George Kelley] about trying to get back [from Boston, April 15] on the noon train? *A.* Oh, yes, I did tell him to go back if I could. [1940]

Q. Why didn't you go up to the consul's office in the morning and take the noon train out? *A.* Well, I think to pass all day when I been in Boston. I think better stay here. I have been working all the time. I will stay, take all day if I have a chance to stay it, because I got a pass to take all day off because they have enough work, the fellows after me working all day long, and if I was out just the same.

Q. Whatever the reason was that you did not get your passport in the morning, did you tell George Kelley the next morning that there was such a crowd in there you could not get your passport and the place closed and you missed the noon train for that reason? Did you tell that to George Kelley? *A.* Yes, I did.

Q. That was another falsehood, wasn't it? *A.* That was an excuse.

Q. It was a falsehood, wasn't it? *A.* Yes.

Q. It was a falsehood to the man that had trusted you, or his father trusted you, with watching his building. That is right, isn't it? *A.* Yes, . . .

Q. The man who lived there next door to you. That is right, isn't it? *A.* Yes.

Q. George Kelley is a personal friend of yours, isn't he? *A.* A friend of mine, yes, sir. [1942]

Q. He has been in your house times without number, hasn't he? *A.* Yes.

Q. And you have been in his house times without number? *A.* Yes.

Q. And you told him a falsehood the next morning, didn't you? *A.* Yes.

Q. There wasn't any reason, was there, why you should not have gone in the morning and kept your word with George? *A.* I don't know no reason.

Q. Is it true that there was a big crowd at the consul's office the day you were in? *A.* No, sir.

Q. There was a very small crowd, wasn't there? *A.* Yes. [1943]

. . . . .

Q. Do you remember my [then] asking you this question:
"Q. Did you ever hear about anything happening in Braintree in the last month?"
And your answer:
"A. Yes."
A. I don't know if I did say that.

Q. Well, it was true, wasn't it, that on May 6th you had heard of what happened in Braintree in the preceding month of April? That was true, wasn't it? *A.* I could not remember. . . .

Q. It was true you heard it about the time, wasn't it? You did hear of it the next day or day after, didn't you? *A.* Yes.

Q. Do you remember after I said:

"*Q.* Did you hear anything about what happened in Braintree?"
I then said, "What?" And you said:

"I read there was bandits robbing money."
Do you remember that answer? *A.* Yes, I do.

Q. Do you remember my asking then:

"*Q.* Where?"
And you said:

"*A.* In *The Boston Post.*"

. . . . .

Q. Do you remember my then asking you:

"*Q.* Where did they rob the money?"
And your answer:

"*A.* Over near Rice & Hutchins. I don't read English very good, but there was bandits in Braintree, and I think it was at Rice & Hutchins."
Did you say that? *A.* I think I did.

Q. We were not talking about any crime when you and I talked together? Do you still say that? *A.* I remember you asked me if I did work in April 15th. [1946]

Q. Wait. We will get to that in a minute. But do you still say that you and I did not talk about this very crime in South Braintree when you talked to me on May 6th? *A.* Well, I don't think you mean say with me the crime about——

Q. What did you think the thirty people or so were looking at you for? *A.* I was thinking they were looking for some crime, now, anyway.

Q. Some crime? *A.* Sure.

Q. And wasn't this the only crime I talked with you about, what had happened at Rice & Hutchins the month before? *A.* No. You asked me if I was working in,—you asked me some other questions. I don't remember now. I don't remember.

Q. All right. But you do remember I talked about this one, don't you? *A.* Yes.

Q. And that you made that reply that it happened over near Rice & Hutchins, bandits robbing money? *A.* That is what the paper says.

Q. Yes. Do you remember my then asking:

"*Q.* Did you read it next day in the paper?"
And you said:

"*A.* Yes, with some of the friends in the shop."
Did you say that? *A.* Yes, we have an argument on it.

Q. And do you remember the next question:

"*Q.* Were you working the day before you read it in the papers?"
And you said, and your answer:

"*A.* I think I did."
Did you say that? *A.* Yes, sir.

Q. And do you remember the next question:

"*Q.* Well, do you know?"
And your answer:

"*A.* Sure." [1947]

.   .   .   .   .

Q. And why did you tell me that falsehood, Mr. Sacco? *A.* Well, of course, I never remember.

Q. Why didn't you say you did not remember? *A.* Well, probably I could not figure it out that time.

Q. You could not figure it that time? *A.* No.

Q. You figured you read it in *The Boston Post* the day after it happened, didn't you? *A.* Yes.

Q. That is true, you read it the next day? *A.* Yes.

Q. And you read it with friends in the shop? *A.* Yes.

Q. Well, that was the 16th of April, wasn't it? *A.* Yes.

Q. And then I asked you if you worked all day long the day before and you said, "Yes," didn't you? *A.* If I said it, it was true.

Q. Was it true you worked all day long April 15th? *A.* April 14th.

Q. April 15th, the day before the 16th, I ask? *A.* If I say I worked, I was lie.

Q. Why did you tell me that lie? *A.* Because I was not sure.

Q. Why didn't you say you weren't sure? *A.* I could not remember exactly.

Q. If you were in Boston on the 15th day of April, getting your passports, why didn't you tell me that the night I talked with you at Brockton? *A.* If I could remember I would tell you it right off. [1948]

———FOLLOWING Katzmann's cross-examination of Sacco, the defense neither vigorously denied Sacco's radicalism nor firmly seized on it as an explanation of his alleged consciousness of guilt; instead of adopting either of these two strategies, the defense tentatively explored both of them.———

Re-Direct-Examination

Q. [*By Mr. Moore*] Mr. Sacco, at the time that you went to Mexico in 1917, in what condition financially did you leave your wife?

Mr. Katzmann. One moment, if your Honor please. I object to the question. I have not raised any issue that he left them destitute.

Mr. Moore. That was certainly the impression I got.

Mr. Katzmann. Not by intent, and I will disclaim it. I will withdraw what I said if it will help. I asked him if he thought it would be a proper course.

The Court. I remember the question.

Mr. Katzmann. I did not mean to have that inference drawn, and I make no claim he left his wife in destitute circumstances.

The Court. You do not care about the question, then, do you?

Mr. Moore. Of course, frankly, I got an entirely different impression.

Mr. Katzmann. Then I will withdraw the——

Mr. Moore. You disclaim it now?

Mr. Katzmann. I absolutely disclaim it. I did not want the jury to have any such thing in mind.

Q. Well, Mr. Sacco, at the time you went away did you leave funds, ample funds for your wife? A. I remember that I leave to her either $350, something like $350 or $360.

Q. Mr. Sacco, do you believe in the use of force or violence in connection with any of your social opinions? A. You mean to destroy property or individuals?

Q. Yes. A. No, sir.

Q. You do not? A. Absolutely not.

Q. Mr. Sacco, at the time that you talked, or, rather, that Mr. Katzmann talked to you, did you know anything at all about the South Braintree murder, the tragedy at South Braintree, other than what you had read in the newspapers and the discussion that had taken place in the factory? A. No, sir. [1962]

————THE DEFENSE called Walter Nelles, a New York lawyer who had been consulted in behalf of Salsedo, the Italian radical whose mysterious incarceration in a New York office building was the subject of Vanzetti's trip to New York. The use of Nelles was, of course, an acknowledgment by the defense of the radicalism of their clients.——

Q. [By Mr. Jeremiah McAnarney] When were you consulted with reference to Salsedo? A. [By Mr. Nelles] About a week before his death. In the latter part of April, 1920.

Q. On what day did his death occur? A. The 3d of May.

Q. . . . And in what way were you consulted and by whom, I mean? *A.* Luigi Quintilino.

. . . .

Q. Who was Luigi Quintilino? *A.* He came to me on behalf of the Italian Workers' Defense Committee.

. . . .

Q. Now, I will ask you if, during those consultations, you advised him about disposing of literature, socialistic or radicalist literature? *A.* Yes.

Q. When was that? *A.* In the week preceding the 3d of May. [1982]

―――――SACCO'S alibi that he had been in Boston on April 15 during the time of the holdup depended on three sources of testimony for its support: (1) an official in the Italian consul's office in Boston; (2) two Italian journalists; (3) a passenger on a Boston to Stoughton train that arrived in Stoughton on the afternoon of the crime.―――――

Deposition of Giuseppe Andrower

The deposition of Giuseppe Adrower [*sic*] taken before James M. Bowcock, Vice Consul of the United States of America and Commissioner at the City of Rome, Kingdom of Italy, on the eleventh day of May, 1921. . . . [2266a]

. . . .

Early in April Mr. Sacco came to the Royal Italian Consulate for information how to get a passport for Italy. I gave him the information and told him that he should bring two photographs, one to be attached to the passport and the other for the records of the office. He then left and on April 15th, 1920 . . . he returned with a photograph. . . . I told him that this photograph was too large for use on a *foglio di via* or an Italian passport. He left saying that he would return with smaller photographs but I never saw him again.

. . . .

April 15th, 1920, was a very quiet day in the Royal Italian Consulate and since such a large photograph had never been before presented for use on a passport I took it in and showed it to the Secretary of the Consulate. We laughed and talked over the incident. I remember observing the date in the office of the Secretary on a large pad calendar while we were discussing the photograph. The hour was around two or a quarter after two as I remember about a half hour later I locked the door of the office for the day. [2266c]

. . . . .

Felice Guadenagi, Sworn

Q. [By Mr. Jeremiah McAnarney] What is your business? A. My business?

Q. Yes. A. Journalist and literature.

Q. How long have you lived in Boston? A. In Boston, seven years. Nine years in America.

Q. When did you first meet Nicola Sacco? A. I met Nicola Sacco in some hall where I was speaking, in Boston.

Q. Could you tell us about when? A. When? Two years ago.

Q. How often had you seen him, say, up to 1920? A. In 1920?

Q. How often had you seen him before 1920? A. I can't say, but ten or twelve times.

Q. In April, 1920, did you see Nicola Sacco? A. Yes, sir.

Q. On what day did you see him? A. April 15th.

. . . . .

Q. Where at? What hour did you see him? A. I seen him in the step door of Boni's restaurant in North Square at half past eleven.

Q. Did you and he do anything there? A. Oh, we ate together in Boni's restaurant. [1991]

. . . . .

Q. Now, how is it, Mr. Guadenagi, that you say that you saw him on the 15th day of April; how do you know that? A. I first recollect that it was the 15th, because in that day I had some discussion about a banquet which was given to Mr. Williams, the editor of *The Boston Transcript*, and I had some discussion about that banquet with . . . Professor Dentamore afterwards in the coffee house. I was invited to that banquet.

Q. When was the banquet to be? A. The night of the 15th.

Q. This man you say is the editor of the *Transcript*? A. Yes, and I was speaking about that banquet. [1993]

. . . . .

Cross-Examination

Q. [By Mr. Katzmann] Are you called "Professor Guadenagi"? A. Yes.

Q. Are you a member of the [Sacco-Vanzetti] Defense Committee? A. Yes, sir. [1995]

. . . . .

Q. Had the day you had last seen him [Sacco] before his arrest become of any importance until he was arrested? . . . *A*. [*Through the interpreter*.] Yes, it interested me because that day I was invited to a banquet.

Q. What had that to do with Sacco? *A*. Because at the time that Sacco came in I was talking about this banquet in the restaurant, in the coffee house.

Q. Is that the only banquet you have ever been invited to? *A*. [*Without interpreter*.] Yes, sir.

Q. The only one? *A*. Yes.

Q. To Mr. Williams? *A*. Yes.

Q. And to anybody else? *A*. No.

Q. Never was invited to an Italian banquet? *A*. No.

Q. When were you invited to go to that banquet, when did you receive your invitation? *A*. One week before.

Q. What day? *A*. I don't remember. I can take the invitation and see what date.

Q. I am asking you, to test your memory, what day did you receive the invitation? *A*. About a week ago.

Q. No, not "about." What day? *A*. What day?

Q. Yes. *A*. I don't think it is necessary to fix the day when I received——

Q. I did not ask you whether you thought it was necessary. I asked you what day it was. *A*. I can't fix the date.

Q. Can't fix that date.

Mr. Katzmann. That is all. [1998]

. . . . .

Antonio Dentamore, Sworn

Q. [*By Mr. Jeremiah McAnarney*] What is your name? *A*. Antonio Dentamore.

. . . . .

Q. What is your work? *A*. I am foreign exchange man in the Haymarket National Bank.

Q. Now, sometime in April did you meet Nicola Sacco? *A*. Yes, sir.

Q. When and where? *A*. April 15th, about quarter of three, in the coffee house, Giordani.

Q. When you met him was he alone or some one with him? *A*. Well, Mr. Guadenagi introduced him to me. [2024]

. . . . .

Q. In what way are you enabled to tell this jury and Court that you met Sacco on the 15th day of April? How do you know that?

A. I know because that day I went to the banquet in honor of Editor Williams of *The Boston Transcript.*

. . . . .

Q. What hour in the day was the banquet held? *A.* April 15th [at noon].

. . . . .

Q. So that you had been to the banquet when you met Sacco? *A.* Yes, sir.

Q. Who up to the time of this introduction was a stranger to you? *A.* Yes.

. . . . .

Mr. Jeremiah McAnarney. That is all.

Cross-Examination

Q. [*By Mr. Katzmann*] Have you given all the reasons, Mr. Dentamore, why you recall the date April 15th? *A.* Well, not all. There is another reason.

Q. What is the other reason? *A.* Well, about an argument I had with Mr. Guadenagi about that banquet.

Q. Yes, you had an argument. That is the way that places it?

. . . . .

Q. What time did you have the argument with Guadenagi? *A.* In Giordani's coffee house.

Q. At what hour? *A.* What hour? It was about quarter of three, ten minutes of three.

Q. Are you sure of the time, that it was quarter to ten minutes of three? *A.* Yes. [2025]

. . . . .

Q. When did you receive,—did you have an invitation to that banquet? *A.* Yes.

Q. When did you receive it? *A.* About a week before.

Q. Well, exactly on what day? *A.* Well, I can't remember.

Q. What did you do the next day after you received the banquet invitation? *A.* The next day. At that time I was the editor of the Italian newspaper [*La Notizia*].

. . . . .

Q. What did you do on the next day after you received the invitation? *A.* Just my routine work.

Q. Who did you speak to on that day? *A.* Not a particular man.

Q. You mean by that you did not speak to anybody? *A.* I spoke to many.

Q. To whom did you speak? *A.* I could not recall now.

Q. Was there anybody with you at ten minutes of three on the day after you received the invitation to the banquet? *A.* I was in the office.

Q. Was there anybody with you at ten minutes of three the day after you received the invitation to the banquet? *A.* I can't say that offhand. [2026]

Q. Where were you,—with whom were you talking, if anybody, at ten minutes to three twenty-two days ago from to-day? *A.* I can't say that.

Q. Twenty-one days ago? *A.* I can't say that.

Q. Twenty days ago? *A.* I am not a fortune teller.

Q. Twenty days ago, sir? *A.* With some client in my bank.

Q. Who was it? *A.* I don't remember now.

Q. What day of the week was twenty days ago? *A.* I don't remember.

Q. What day of the week was twenty-one days ago? *A.* I can't tell now.

Q. Were you at the bank twenty-one days ago to-day? *A.* I think so.

Q. Were you at the bank twenty-two days ago to-day? *A.* I think so.

Q. That would be Sunday, wouldn't it? *A.* Well, twenty, I don't mean Sunday.

Q. I asked if you were at the bank twenty days ago. You said you thought so. That would be on a Sunday, wouldn't it? *A.* I don't know.

Q. And you are the foreign exchange man in a bank? *A.* Yes.

Q. And you can't subtract twenty days from a Monday and make it Sunday? *A.* Just not now. You are asking me,—if you give me time to recollect. [2027]

───────ONE DAY as Sacco sat in the cage he looked out among the spectators in the courtroom and observed a man whom he later testified looked familiar to him. He called his lawyer, Jeremiah McAnarney, and reportedly said to him that the spectator in the courtroom had come on the train from Boston with him on the afternoon of April 15. This man, James Hayes, appeared as a defense witness.───

James Matthews Hayes, Sworn

Q. [*By Mr. Jeremiah McAnarney*] Were you and your wife seated in the court room here one day in the early part of last week? *A.* Yes, sir.

Q. Did I ask you to step out in the anteroom, that I would like to talk with you? *A.* Yes, sir.

·   ·   ·   ·   ·

Q. As the result of that conversation did you go back home and make an investigation with reference to trying to find out if you could place yourself on the 15th of April, 1920? *A.* Yes, sir. [2014]

·   ·   ·   ·   ·

Q. What investigation did you make? *A.* I found that on the 15th of April I had gone to Boston.

Q. Tell us now how you remember that you went to Boston on the 15th of April? *A.* I remembered that by a perusal of my time books and by other incidents that happened previous to that. [2015]

·   ·   ·   ·   ·

Q. Did you know Sacco? *A.* No, I never knew Sacco. Never met him.

Q. And until I spoke to you and asked you to try and place yourself on April 15th, had you ever given it a thought as to where you were? *A.* No, sir, I never had any occasion to.

Q. Whether Sacco was on that train or not you don't know? *A.* I don't know.

Q. But you came out on that train? *A.* Yes, sir.

Mr. Jeremiah McAnarney. That is all. [2016]

Cross-Examination

Q. [*By Mr. Katzmann*] What did you do on the 26th day of March? *A.* I couldn't tell you.

Q. What did you do on the 27th day of March? *A.* I couldn't tell you.

Q. The 28th? *A.* I couldn't tell you.

Q. The 29th? *A.* I couldn't tell you.

Q. The 30th? *A.* I couldn't tell you.

Q. The 31st? *A.* I couldn't tell you.

Q. Well, Mr. Hayes—— *A.* Yes, I can tell you the 31st, from the 29th on, I can tell you what I done. I worked over to Mead's factory. We started that job the 29th of March.

Q. That you looked up in your book? *A.* That I looked up in my book, yes.

Q. You did not remember that,—you remembered it from looking on your time book? *A.* Did not remember anything until I commenced to look up in my book.

Q. There isn't anything in your book, is there, about going to

Boston, on the 15th day of April? *A.* No, but there is things that would call my attention to going.

Q. When next did you go to Boston after the 15th day of April, 1920? *A.* I have not had occasion to look it up.

Q. Can't you remember? *A.* No, sir. [2018]

. . . . .

Re-Direct-Examination

Q. [*By Mr. Jeremiah McAnarney*] You were asked the question if there was anything in your book that showed you what you were doing April 15th and you answered there was something there that helped you or something. *A.* Yes, sir.

Q. What is there?

Mr. KATZMANN. One minute. That isn't the question I asked him.

Mr. JEREMIAH McANARNEY. Perhaps I have misquoted.

THE COURT. He also answered "No."

Mr. JEREMIAH McANARNEY. Said a little bit more than that.

Mr. KATZMANN. I could tell you what the question was.

Q. What is there that calls your attention to going— *A.* I received $50 from my brother the 15th at noontime, the 15th of April. I used that, part of that $50, in Boston. That is the thing that called my attention to going.

Nicola Sacco, Recalled
[*The testimony is given through the interpreter.*]

Q. [*By Mr. Jeremiah McAnarney*] Mr. Sacco, where did you see this man [Mr. Hayes]? *A.* I remember that I might have seen him in the—— [*The witness talks to the interpreter, Joseph Ross.*] I remember that I might have seen him the 15th day of April in Boston.

Q. Well, where did you see him? *A.* I saw him on the train coming home to my house.

Mr. JEREMIAH McANARNEY. Now, Mr. Ross, that there be no mistake, he did not say, "I might have seen him." You used the word "might." The witness did not use that.

. . . . .

Q. And from that time that you saw him on the train, when did you next see this man? *A.* I saw him in court last week.

Q. And what did you do when you saw this man in court? *A.* I looked at him for several times, for quite some time, to make sure. Then I called you. . . . [2021]

Re-Cross-Examination

Q. [*By Mr. Katzmann*] What car did you ride out in? A. [*By Mr. Sacco*] I don't remember.

Q. At what stations did that train stop? A. I don't remember about which stations that train did stop, but I remember that that train stopped at Canton Junction and several other stops after that.

.   .   .   .   .

Q. Is there any train that runs from Boston to Stoughton by the way of the Providence Division that stops at Stoughton that does not stop at Canton Junction? A. I don't know.

Q. Did you ever ride out on the Providence Division from Boston to Stoughton on a train that did not stop at Canton Junction? A. My best recollection, I remember that when I went from Boston to Stoughton I always stopped at Canton Junction.

Q. "I always stopped"—— A. The train.

Q. I understood. The train stopped. Were you in the first car back of the engine? A. I cannot say.

Q. How many cars were there on the train? A. I don't know.

Q. On what side of the coach did you sit? A. I remember that I sat on my right, as you go to Stoughton.

Q. In what part of the coach? A. What do you mean, what part?

Q. I mean, how far from the front or how far from the rear. Locate the seat. A. About the centre.

Q. Where did this man sit you are now speaking of? A. On the left, right aside of me.

Q. On the aisle side of the seat? That is, next to the aisle? A. Near the aisle, on the side.

Q. And where were you sitting? Next to the aisle or next to the window in your seat? A. I was sitting near the aisle. [2022]

.   .   .   .   .

Q. Was there any particular occasion for you to look at the man who was seated at your left on this particular trip? A. Nothing, no occasion, well—— . . . but he got off at the same place where I did, and I noticed his face and I remember faces.

Q. Was there anybody else who got off at the Stoughton depot besides yourself? A. Yes, sir, there were others.

Q. How many? A. I don't remember.

Q. Describe what any other person looked like who got off at the Stoughton station that day. A. I cannot do it, because I don't remember.

Mr. Katzmann. That is all.

Mr. Jeremiah McAnarney. That is all. Tell the officer to bring Mr. Hayes back for one question. [*Hayes was outside the courtroom while Sacco testified.*]

James Matthew Hayes,
Cross-Examination, Resumed

Q. [*By Mr. Katzmann*] . . . Do you remember, Mr. Hayes, in what coach you came out? *A.* It seems to me I came out along in the middle of the train.

Q. How many coaches were there on the train? *A.* I should say six or seven.

Q. Well, in coming out from Boston to Stoughton, on which side of the coach were you seated, left or right? *A.* I was seated on the left.

Q. And whereabouts in the car? *A.* About midway in the car.

Q. And on which side of the seat? *A.* On the inside of the seat.

Q. That is, next to the window or next to the aisle? *A.* Next to the aisle.

Q. Have you talked this over with Mr. Sacco before he took the stand? *A.* No, sir.

Q. Or his counsel? *A.* No, sir.

Q. Has anybody asked you before I asked you in which part of the coach you were seated? *A.* No.

Q. Or which part of the seat? *A.* No, sir.

. . . . . .

The Court. Well, gentlemen, the book of fate in these cases has been closed. You will undoubtedly get these cases for final determination Thursday forenoon, or Thursday morning. During your absence quite a number of things have been settled between counsel, one of which is that arguments will be made to-morrow, beginning at nine o'clock. It has been agreed that four hours shall be given to each side,— that is, four hours for the defendants and four hours for the Commonwealth.

. . . . . .

I must again suggest to you to still keep your minds open. The evidence has simply closed now. You have not heard the arguments of counsel and . . . you have not heard the Charge of the Court. You must hear what the law is of the Commonwealth in order that you may apply the law to established facts found by you to be true . . . With these few words the Court will now adjourn. . . .

C. THE SUMMATION FOR THE DEFENSE
THIRTY-SIXTH DAY

Dedham, Mass., July 13, 1921.

THE COURT. You may poll the jury, please, Mr. Clerk.
[*The jury are polled and both defendants answer "present."*]
THE COURT. Are you ready to proceed, Mr. Moore?
MR. MOORE. Yes.
THE COURT. You may, please.

Argument of Mr. Moore to the jury

If the Court please, Mr. Foreman and gentlemen of the jury, I know of no time when a lawyer quite as keenly feels his responsibility as he does at the conclusion of a capital case. . . . But if that sense of responsibility can be added to at all, it is . . . when the responsibility for a human life, the responsibility of whether a woman shall be a widow and children fatherless is dependent upon their efforts. [2122]

.   .   .   .   .

What is the issue in this case? The primary issue and the only issue here is the issue of identification. The one issue is: Has the Commonwealth proved beyond reasonable doubt that the defendant Sacco fired the fatal shot that caused the death of one or the other of these men? Or did the defendant Sacco aid or abet or contribute in any wise to that crime?

Gentlemen, I think I am correct when I say that some 70 odd witnesses have testified for the Commonwealth. When you analyze their testimony, however, it reduces itself to a comparatively small nucleus of solid matter. [2125]

.   .   .   .   .

. . . Now, in determining human testimony and the value of it, you are entitled to consider what various men say, having various opportunities of observation.

Now, you remember Bostock, a plain, level-headed substantial sort of fellow, called by the Commonwealth. . . . He walked right by here in front of Rice & Hutchins and on up here where he met the two deceased. He says he saw two men standing in front of Rice & Hutchins, two men standing there. He saw them. Ah, gentlemen, is it significant at all in this case that Mr. Bostock, a plain, solid, substantial type of American citizenship, that Bostock refused to make an identification? [2128]

.   .   .   .   .

Gentlemen, that brings me to another question that I have not referred to. There is a vast difference between the identification of a man that you know, a man that you have seen before, a man that you have talked with. There may be some peculiar quality about the way I walk, the way I carry my head, the way my shoulders set, some peculiar quality of personality that would enable you, Mr. Foreman, to identify me instanter six months or a year or five months hence if you saw me going down the street, the back of me. There is no question about that.

But those are things that do not enter into this case, because remember, that, gentlemen, there isn't a single witness produced by the Common- [2130] wealth, not one, who ever saw either of these men before and who claims to make an identification projected upon this acquaintance or previous knowledge of that man. Not one.

.   .   .   .   .

Now, gentlemen, we have a lady, Miss Mary Splaine. Miss Splaine is in this factory building of the Hampton House, second floor. Miss Splaine did not know Sacco, never had seen him before. Never saw him later until three weeks had elapsed. Only saw him at best for a matter of seconds, [2131] possibly minutes, because, remember that she says the car was running at a minimum speed of 18 miles an hour, 18 miles an hour.

.   .   .   .   .

Now, just listen to the rather infinite detail of this description secured of a man in a moving car on a floor below at a minimum distance of 80 feet away in a space the hypotenuse of a triangle of not to exceed 70 feet, if it was that. Listen.

"Q. Can you describe him to these gentlemen? A. Oh, yes. Yes, sir. He was a man of, I should say, was slightly taller than I am. He weighed possibly from 140 to 145 pounds. He was muscular. He was an active looking man. I noticed particularly the left hand was a good sized hand, a hand that denoted strength or a shoulder that——

"Q. Was that the hand you said you saw where? A. The left hand that was placed on the back of the front seat, on the back of the front seat. He had a gray, what I thought was a shirt. Had a grayish, like a Navy color, and the face was what we would call clear cut, clean-cut face; through here [indicating] was a little narrow, just a little narrow. The forehead was high. The hair was brushed back and it was between, I should say, 2 inches and 2½ inches in length, and had dark eye brows, but the complexion was a white, peculiar white, that looked greenish."

Now, gentlemen, that is rather infinite detail for 80 feet away of a car running at 18 miles an hour at least 12 to 14 feet below. . . .

And in this connection and in determining the credibility of that testimony, remember that the young woman says, and Mr. Sacco corroborates her, that she went down to Brockton once, yes, twice, yes, three times, yes. Why? Was it in order to get the infinite detail of this description, sir, or not? I do not know. But if she got all of these details—as she never got them—if she got them at all to be testified to in this case . . . she had to get them in that matter of seconds from the window there.

Then why did she go down three times to make an identification? Then why did she ask the boy, Mr. Sacco, why did she ask him to get down, to contort himself in response to various demands made, lean forward, lean [2132] backward, cast his eyes up, cast his eyes down, to go through all these actions?

.   .   .   .   .

Gentlemen, that description is built bone and sinew, from top to bottom, not from what she saw from the window but from what she saw in the Brockton police station. You know it. I know it. Gentlemen, are you going to use that kind of testimony to take a human life? [2133]

.   .   .   .   .

Now, gentlemen, something is wrong. I do not know what. I do know that testimony of that character is not the kind of testimony that warrants taking a human life. I might go on through reading you this record referring to point after point and place after place where the lady's testimony is subject to the same character of examination. . . . The same is true of all of the witnesses who definitely and with any degree of finality make an identification.

There is one witness [to] . . . whom considerable attention was given. I am referring to Mrs. Lola Andrews. . . .

Gentlemen, I say to you that even though we had not offered a single witness against Lola Andrews, she killed herself on the witness stand by her own personality, but Campbell, Fay, [and others] finished her up.

.   .   .   .   .

I pass on to Louis Pelser, the man up in the Rice & Hutchins factory who looked out through the crack in the window and saw Berardelli falling, and with the divided attention upon the one side he fastened his eyes down here on Sacco and fixed him in his mind forever as the guilty murderer. Over here with his other eye he fixed it on the number of the car, and that number of the car remained forever fixed in his mind, bullets flying in all directions. [2137]

. . . This fellow admits that the statements that we read to him as being given to Mr. Reid were made by him. He does not deny it. He admits it. . . .

. . . He told Mr. Reid that he did not see the shooting, that he did not see anybody shooting, that he jumped to the window and slammed it down immediately, that he did not see any particular act at all. Now, that is his statement to Mr. Reid, that he could not identify anybody, that he could not say it was anybody because he did not see enough to be able to say that it was not Sacco or that it was not Vanzetti. In other words, we would not have called him on the statement that he gave to us.

Ah, remember, consider this: He says he did not want to be called as a witness and that was the reason he gave this statement to Mr. Reid. Yet what had he done at that very time? He had given the automobile number, he says, to the Government, and he was the only witness that had it, and he knew it and he knew that the Commonwealth was bound to call him. He had nothing to gain by telling us this story, unless he was filled with malice and prejudice and ill will. [2138]

Gentlemen, there isn't a single witness called by the government who had an unqualified opportunity of observation who gives an identification. Not one. Bostock had the opportunity and wouldn't. . . . So on down the line. But it is the Lola Andrews . . . the Pelsers that made the identification. Miss Splaine . . . I reject, because [her] testimony is utterly unreasonable. . . . You know it and I know it.

Now, gentlemen, what is the government's case? If you consider this case from the standpoint of the testimony with reference to what took place at South Braintree, there is absolutely nothing to it. But as in every case, the Court will instruct you in due course of time that circumstantial evidence is a proper matter for a jury to consider. Circumstances may point to "guilty" many times even stronger than the human eye itself as a matter of direct testimony. [2140]

The Court, I take it, in its instructions will tell you that in determining the faith and credit and weight that you are to give to circumstantial evidence, you are always to give that interpretation to the facts which is reasonable, and if there are two interpretations, equally reasonable and consistent, one pointing to innocence and the other pointing to guilt, that then it is your duty to accept that interpretation which points to innocence. . . .

Now, what do we have here, from April 15th on to May the 5th? There are no untoward facts involved. Suddenly on the night of May 5th the defendants are arrested and taken into custody on a Brockton street car. The thing is that what the defendants then said to the arresting officers, to Mr. Stewart and subsequently to Mr. Katzmann is admitted for your consideration, not because it proves that the defendants committed the crime in question, but because what they said was contrary to the facts and that that false statement is to be interpreted as indicative of consciousness of guilt. [2141]

In other words, if you charge Mr. Jones with having stolen your car, and Jones on a collateral matter of where he got it, this car, makes a statement that you know is false, you very naturally and logically begin to think that Jones probably did steal your car. Perfectly proper that you should, until Jones may explain why he made the false statement of fact.

Now, that is your issue here and that only. It is admitted, uncontradicted by the defendants and by all parties concerned here, that the defendant Sacco when taken into custody did say that he did intend to go with his friend Vanzetti to see Vanzetti's friend Pappi that night. Now, those are the facts. It is admitted that that is a false statement of fact. I should say it is only partly true. They did intend to see Pappi, but they did also intend to do something else, namely, to get the Overland car.

Now, let us divorce our minds from one or two things. First, there is no evidence in this record anywhere, . . . in any form, connecting Boda with the commission of this crime. Nowhere does Boda come into connection with the murders at South Braintree on April 15th. That is clear. Again, there isn't a scintilla of evidence in this record anywhere, . . . connecting Boda with the ownership or possession of a Buick car. . . . Now, those two matters are clarified.

Now, what is the issue? Boda did have an Overland car. He did own that car. Johnson did go get that car from the place where Boda did live. Those are admitted facts, undisputed. Boda did live with a man by the name of Coacci. It is admitted that Coacci was deported. It is admitted that Coacci was deported for some reason in connection with his ideas or opinions. That is admitted. The only thing in the world that stands here contested is that the defendants made a false statement of fact when they said to Mr. Stewart that they did not go to the Johnson house to get the Overland car.

Now, they did not give a true statement of facts. That is true. Or, rather, they did not make a complete statement of the facts. Now, why? That is the issue. Why? Are you to say that because they did not, they committed the murders at South Braintree? The only way that the false statement given to Johnson or given to Stewart with reference to what they were doing that night becomes of any probative value to you, gentlemen, is that if you believe that it points to their guilt of this particular crime, namely, the crime of murder at South Braintree on April 15th. It might point to a thousand other things, but unless you believe it proves to your mind that they committed that murder it has no force nor effect and should have none to you.

Now, how do they explain it? In the first place, in April, in May or June, 1917 these young men went to Mexico. They violated the Selective Service Act. You and I and this Court are not concerned with the causes that provoked that attitude. Personally I may launch upon it the most bitter philippics, the most bitter attack, but that is beside the issue. They [2142] went. They violated the Selective Service Act. Sacco says he was gone three months. The defendant Vanzetti says he was gone a year.

They came back. Sacco comes back, and you heard his record of jumping from point to point from August or September of 1917 until the day after the Armistice was signed in 1918. A half dozen jobs in a half dozen different places in this district, all under an assumed name, his taking his mother's maiden name. All during that time he knew that he had violated the Selective Service Act and was subject to punishment therefor.

On April 25th he went to a meeting in East Boston, in which the question of aiding and assisting one Salsedo in New York was discussed. It was determined to send the co-defendant Vanzetti to New York. Vanzetti went to New York. In New York he saw Mr. Quintilino and asked about the Salsedo matter. Mr. Quintilino made arrangements with Mr. Nelles for his employment on that case. Mr. Nelles says that in his discussion with Mr. Quintilino he advised that books, papers, literature and pamphlets in connection with the radical movement generally should be carefully taken care of and gotten rid of in anticipation of possible trouble in and around about May 1st.

Now, gentlemen, anybody who 10 years ago would have said that a member of the American bar in 1920 would deem it proper or appropriate to advise any group of people . . . in America to take care of any books or papers or pamphlets of whatever character they might have, . . . would have been laughed out of court, but that is not the situation in 1920.

What we are concerned [with] is whether or not these defendants believed on the night of May the 5th that they were in fear of deportation, whether or not on the night May 5th they believed that their lives or their liberties were in danger. . . . "I advised Sacco back in January or February of 1920 that I have been told that he was being investigated." Investigated for what? I do not know. We are not allowed to develop what for. But investigated for something. Now, we do know this: It could not have [2143] been for the crime at Braintree on April 15th, because April 15th had not as yet come around. Therefore, it must have been for other matters.

Sacco had these things in his mind on May 5th. The advice from Mr. Kelley, the knowledge that he had in his house books, papers, pamphlets and literature, the knowledge of the death of Salsedo the day before in front of the Park Row building, the knowledge that Coacci and Fruzetti or some other name and a number of others had been deported in this community, the knowledge of all the things that you and I have common knowledge of as having taken place in the last couple of years, further added to and abetted by the knowledge that from June 5th of 1917 he had been a violator of the Selective Service Act, [and] punishable therefor. . . .

Now, let us take one issue. The propriety of questioning Sacco with reference to his opinions and ideas by Stewart I am not here to question. That is beside the issue. The point is that Stewart's action, when Mr. Stewart asked Mr. Sacco, "Are you an anarchist? Are you a member of any club or organization or association? Do you believe in the American government?" when he asked those questions did he add fuel and flame to the already existing suspicions in the mind of Sacco which accounts for the false statements that he made?

My friend Mr. Katzmann on behalf of the Commonwealth will urge that it did not. He will say, "Why did Sacco deny that he worked for Rice & Hutchins?" Very good reason, gentlemen. As plain as your nose on your face. Remember Sacco's testimony. "I worked for Rice & Hutchins under the name of Nick Mosmacotelli." I believe that is it. If Mr. Sacco said to Mr. Katzmann, "I worked for Rice & Hutchins," and Mr. Katzmann went to Rice & Hutchins and found that he did not work there, then Mr. Sacco had done one of two things. He had either branded himself as a liar to Mr. Katzmann—in which event suspicion was only added and his danger and his seriousness of his position only intensified—or he would then when Mr. Katzmann came back and said, "The records do not show, Sacco, that you worked for Rice & Hutchins," then he would have had to have said in order to clear the deck, "Why, I had worked there under the name of Nick Mosmacotelli," and when Mr. Katzmann found that out . . . [Sacco] would then be putting himself in line for a criminal prosecution in the Federal courts for liability under the Selective Service Act. Simple.

But Mr. Katzmann will then tell you some other things that Sacco did not remember or could not tell. Now, I am not going to pretend to you gentlemen that all that Sacco said to Mr. Katzmann was predicated upon the fear that he was going to get in trouble over Selective Service or over his war attitude or anything of that kind. That is not my position. I am explaining solely and exclusively the Johnson episode on that issue. Inso- [2144] far as Sacco's statements, to wit, the most flagrant example, "Did you work on April 15th?" there is a pure matter of recollection. It is manifest from the record that Sacco did his best to tell Mr. Katzmann all the truth as he was best able to recollect it. And I say to you, gentlemen, if there is any one of you that has ever been mixed up in the preparation of either a civil or a criminal case, any of you, I do not believe there is a man in this box but what if he came to any one of us of counsel in connection with a small sized petty civil matter and we began to check you back on your dates that you would have an awful lot of trouble to tell where you were 30 days, 60 days or 90 days back. It is a hard job, gentlemen, and remember that that boy was under arrest at that time. Is it any wonder that he was uncertain? Is it any wonder that upon questions of exact dates he wavered?

But that is not the issue. Insofar as the question of his working on April 15th is concerned there ought not to be any question. Why, gentlemen, what have you got to do in this case in order to return a verdict? You have got to say that the whole Kelley family lied. You have got to say that some 20 odd witnesses called in connection with various phases of the movement of the defendant are all liars, unequivocal, unmitigated, unfaltering liars, and on top of that you have got to say that we of counsel had aided, abetted, advised, encouraged this perjury.

.   .   .   .   .

. . . I imagine that he [Katzmann] is going to say something about the kind of a man, the kind of a heart, the kind of a soul of a man, the kind of the character of a man who deserts the colors and goes into a foreign land during a time of stress and strain inside of our own states. I do not know just how he is going to phrase it. I do not know. I wish I did, but he is going to in substance and in effect, I believe, say that a man who is so foreign to the sense of American patriotism as to do that sort of a thing is a man whose credibility you can't believe, whose integrity upon the witness stand is subject to question, whose evidence you are bound to discredit.

Gentlemen, I want to say this: Personally I believe that is a tragedy, a serious tragedy in our national life that men of this stamp are created. I do not like it. I know you do not like it. None of us like it. But they exist. They represent a peculiar type of zealot ever willing to suffer any sort of liability to carry their ideas into effect.

It is rather interesting to note that when Mr. Stewart questioned Sacco about his ideas Sacco said, "I am a little bit different. I am not quite satisfied. I do not quite like things as they are."

Now, Mr. Katzmann may advert to the character of the books that are in question here as to whether or not they constitute the substance that would go to create human fear in a human mind. I do not know, gentlemen. Let me see those books, please. These books are in a foreign language. Some of them have been translated into the English language. They represent social and economic thought,—they represent a brand of thought I take it, judging solely from their titles, that is foreign to your experience and to mine. But Mrs. Sacco said something under her own examination that adds strength and force and vigor to the statement of Sacco, namely, that she burned a lot more books, that this did not represent all the books. The titles of some, however, may be significant. I am not attempting to give the Spanish titles. One is *The Grand Revolution*, by Kropotkin. Another is *Social Control*, by Merlino. Another is a book by Zola. Another is *Religion and Science*, by Vella and another book by Kropotkin. . . . *The Ideal of the Workers*, a pamphlet. *Concerning Law and Authority*. *Letters on Socialism. The Social Transformation*, and so on.

What is in those books I do not know. I can't read it, but I do know that Mrs. Sacco immediately following the arrest of her husband, in the exercise of what she considered her best judgment, in view of the decision reached on April 25th and May 2nd, May 3rd, May 4th, that Mrs. Sacco burned up some more. Why, I do not know. [It is a] . . . tragedy of American life that anybody should be in fear of a book, but she was right or wrong, and Nick told the story that he told because he was in fear of Salsedo's death, his friends deported, and so on.

Now, gentlemen, that is the Government's case in its broad, general [2146] terms. The time limitations fix me. I cannot go any further. Just one word. Dentamore, [Guadenagi], Kelley, Mr. Hayes all have told you the movements of Sacco on April 15th. You have got to say that they have all committed perjury. You have got to say that these men who know Sacco, that these men who have talked with Sacco, that these men, some Americans and some Italians, that they have all stooped to the commission of perjury, to the dragging of justice in the mire in order to save this man, and you have got to say that Mary Splaine, Lola Andrews, and Neal and all of these people who never saw the defendant before—and when they did see him, saw him for a matter of seconds—that they are right and that the defendant, Dentamore and others are wrong.

There are some other questions, many, that I would like to discuss. The issue of the government, you have heard the testimony of the experts pro and con, back and forth. Gentlemen, if the time has come when a micoscope must be used to determine whether a human life is going to continue to function or not and when the users of the microscope themselves can't agree, when experts called by the Commonwealth and experts called by the defense are sharply defined in their disagreements, then I take it that ordinary men such as you and I should well hesitate to take a human life.

．　　　．　　　．　　　．

Now, one more thing, gentlemen. You are duty bound to give, each and all of you, your individual judgment to this case. You are duty bound when you go into the jury room to debate one with the other, to answer legitimate and proper argument one to the other, to discuss in a spirit of fairness and justice the issues in this case, but if after all discussion is had, if after all legitimate and proper arguments have been considered, if after full and mutual consultation, one with the other, there is one or more of you who have an opinion at variance with the others, then under your oaths as jurors you are duty bound to return a verdict in accordance with your conception of the law and of the facts of this case as you view them and as proven from the witness stand. [2147]

In other words, let no consideration of public policy, let no consideration of compromise, let no consideration of anything other than the proven evidence on the witness stand direct and command your minds. Gentlemen, please, I beg of you, and I speak on behalf of the defendant Sacco and I feel I may say on behalf of the defendant Vanzetti, I beg of you, gentlemen, one and all, please, no compromise verdicts in this case. There can be but one verdict here, either murder in the first degree with the death penalty or not guilty, one or the other.

The man that committed that crime must go to the chair. I beg of you in the jury room no argument addressed to second degree murder or anything else less than first degree. If that boy committed this crime, there is no penalty too severe to visit upon him. But when you are rendering your verdict, remember that you are duty bound to return a verdict based solely upon the law, solely upon the facts.

And, gentlemen, the Court will conclude this case with his instructions. We of counsel and the Court cannot divide or assume your responsibilities. You are the responsible men. You are the judges of the facts. The Court gives you the law, but you and you only can pronounce the verdict upon facts, and when you pronounce the verdict, gentlemen, remember that you are duty bound to give it in accordance with the facts as you believe them to have been found on the witness stand.

I thank you.

THE COURT. Take a recess, gentlemen, of five minutes. You ran over your time 20 minutes, Mr. Moore.

Argument of Jeremiah J. McAnarney, Esq.

Mr. Foreman and Gentlemen of the Jury, I hope you feel as relieved as I do that we have arrived at this point in the case where evidence is all through, where we are doing our best to assist you to arrive at a verdict in this case, and I say this at the start, gentlemen, before I get into the evidence. I think every word in argument to any jury should be, and every question asked in any trial of any cause, should be to assist the jury to find out what is the truth, rather than to confuse a witness or confuse the issue by questions on the stand to a witness. [2148]

. . . . . .

And so, gentlemen, I have just seen by my associate's experience that 2 hours is a mighty short time to cover a case that has gone 5 or 6 weeks, so I have got to sail right into the middle of this wonderful, extraordinary case, and at the start we may say, "For goodness sake, what case is this?"

There was a shooting over in Braintree on the 15th day of April; one Berardelli and one Parmenter were shot. We have drifted miles away from that case, miles away. We had almost forgotten that those men had been shot, . . . but we have drifted . . . just exactly where this case belongs. We have drifted right to the issue, we have drifted to the reason that these men were arrested. We have drifted to the fact that these men are radicals and that they were apprehended because they were radicals, as every bit of this evidence when it is weighed absolutely proves.

You cannot kick a ball around 5 or 6 weeks but what it will get its level. You cannot play with this case as a case of a murder at Braintree for 5 or 6 weeks and conceal the true issue in this case. This case cannot be won on the facts of that shooting or that identification at Braintree. You would not kill a dog on that identification at Braintree.

The men—just take the description—a tall, a light, a dark, a small, a square, heavy chest, a light chest, a mustache, no mustache. You have every conceivable kind of a man on that job at Braintree. . . . So you find they are light and they are dark and they are dark and they are light, and, gentlemen, when you apply the rule of law which is that on the essential features of this case, as in any other, that the burden is on the government, for goodness sake, where do you land on such identification as that? [2149]

.   .   .   .   .

Take Miss Splaine. If ever a man teased a woman, coaxed her to tell that which she had first said, I did. She comes on here, and I am sorry that she said what she did. If she came on here or if that woman had taken this stand on behalf of one of these defendants and had so completely changed her evidence as she did, this building, the roof, the walls would not stand the vibration of my friend's voice when he would say to her, "Madam, are you changing your testimony, committing falsehood to deceive these jurors?"

And when after my examination of that woman, asking her if she did not say these things in the lower court, almost begging her to admit that that is what she did say, she denied it and told me that was wrong; what a miserable crawl that poor girl had to perform the next morning when under the kindly questions of Mr. Williams she admitted that she did say the things which I asked her the day before if she did not say. [2150]

.   .   .   .   .

. . . Some of you men have had experience, some of you have had experience in police matters. Do you say, gentlemen, that it is a fair test, what transpired in Brockton there?

Supposing you were in charge of Brockton. Supposing you had in your custody a man who was accused of murder and you knew there were people coming to identify that man. Wouldn't you in that sense of duty you owed to every man and to your oath of office, wouldn't you have stood that man up with a half dozen or two or three other men and asked the identifying witness to come in and look them over and pick out the man?

That did not take place at Brockton when those 25 or 30, according to Miss Splaine, were looking that man over. And, gentlemen, what is the sense of such identification? They are brought up, they are hurdled up, they are packed up there, to do what? To pick out a man. What man? This man, the man they got down in the room. . . . It may be their conception of a fair way to identify a man.

Does it strike you as being a fair way? . . . You would say, "Why didn't you have half a dozen other men there and let these people pick out the man who they saw?"

Is there anything in those Italians they should not have been granted that right which you know in your heart every man should have been granted and is granted where they attempt a proper identification? [2151]

.   .   .   .   .

Bostock says—and what do you say of Bostock? Was there anything weak-looking about that man? He was right there, he saw them. He was within 50 or 60 feet of them when it began and started towards them. They turned and shot at him. He goes around the corner of the fence. He describes how the curtains were. Here is the fence [*indicating*]. He goes behind it. As it comes up he describes how those curtains were. "If I put my hand out I could have touched the automobile." Not a person leaning from one window to another trying to get a fleeting glance. No, with his eyes all the time. He could have touched the automobile if he wanted to. [2152]

.   .   .   .   .

And, gentlemen, it may be significant. What is the significance of not calling Miss—Mrs. Liscomb? . . . Mrs. Liscomb was right there on the second floor, basement or no basement. She says she went to the window. She saw the man pointing the gun up, and then she fainted.

I say to you as a matter of common knowledge to yourself, it isn't any different whether you see a person a half hour or whether you see them 10 seconds, if into the retina of your eye was photographed through that eye to your brain a face, it doesn't require an hour, it doesn't require 10 minutes. You will retain it if your observation was sufficient. That woman looked down into that man's face. She told you on the stand she never could forget that face, that that face wasn't the face of Sacco.

. . . . .

The fine tooth comb has worked in this case, gentlemen, and not one bit of evidence was brought forward to controvert what that woman said. . . . [2153]

. . . . .

I don't want you to feel for one minute this case is going any other than this way, and I am going to say something mighty plain, and I am going to say it because it is so, and it isn't one reflection on this district attorney, who, outside of the fact that he wants to win this case—and I want to win it also—is as good a friend as I have got, and he or Mr. Williams or any other man there, I have got to go before those men, I have got to contest them, with them other cases and before this court—one of the most learned judges we have, whose brains and whose ability is acknowledged by the bar, by the judges of the supreme and superior court and every court in this land.

It comes to my mind now I had a little controversy with him, where I said I thought he was prejudicing the defense by a question he asked. We have had a talk about that, and he did not have my conception of my evidence and I did not have what he was trying to do to me. It might well [2154] have been he was helping me, but I was standing up on my feet and I did not think it was there and I said—and I took an exception to his prejudicing my case by his remarks, but, gentlemen, don't you mind that.

This court would not have any respect for me if I did not fill my clothes when I am trying for a defendant whose life is at issue. I can't think of the district attorney or the court or anybody else but to protect everything which in my mind is the right of that man. So, then, don't think it is any reflection when I say—but to get to what I mean, it is this. The district attorney is trying the evidence as it comes to him from his sources of information, but he can well turn to me and say, "Mr. McAnarney, you don't expect I would put on evidence that would prove your men innocent, do you?" He can well say that. That is our lookout, and we have got to produce the evidence that will show these men are innocent. The government is producing evidence that will show them guilty. [2155]

. . . . .

. . . All right, so far as this case is concerned. Do you think for one minute—there is an axiom of logic that some propositions are so self-evident a statement of them proves it. Here you have it gentlemen. That Sacco, known as he was—on their own evidence—who is within 15 feet of the windows of the Rice & Hutchins factory, right there for hours, standing up in front of the drug store on the corner, the best place he could expose himself, . . . where every one saw him, knowing that he was known, knowing that he had worked there, getting the money and getting away? No. And he is back to work in the factory the next morning.

If this man pulled that job at night, if he was masked, if he was concealed in some way, he might take the chance of staying around, but here, in broad daylight, absolutely in the presence of every man that he could show himself to, no disguise at all, getting away with the money in Braintree and he is back in the factory the next morning where he can be picked up when they get ready to take him. The same with Vanzetti.

Now, gentlemen, isn't there enough right there to satisfy you that that isn't the way the ordinary mind acts? . . .

. . . . . .

These men are brighter than that. They don't understand our language very well, but when you strip those men from their broken English you have got more than the ordinary type of fellow.

The poise of Vanzetti as he spoke on that stand, courteously and gently to the district attorney, and after he was stripped of everything that a man holds dear, to wit, his honor, his poise was simply wonderful. [2157]

. . . . . .

. . . Up to this situation here they were as ordinary fellows. Now, Sacco has met with the situation, sickness at home. . . . His mother had died, and he has told you he had some letters. He showed to Kelley the letter that came to him . . . Kelley says so. . . . He had been, he said, the last week [2158] in March into the consul to get general information that he would have to have a photograph. Then he had hurried up and went in on the 15th.

Now, gentlemen, he was acting in a natural way. What kind of family did he come out of? What was there in the situation there at home other than kindly affection and a wish for that fellow to come home. He had been saving his money in the bank. He had his wife and child. Was he the type of man who would be out doing a hold-up job, he with his father ill, with his mother dead, and the people at home advising him to come home to his father?

He wished to see him before he died, no doubt, and he, wanting to go home, was he in the mental frame to go out and do a job of murder right there on the street? . . .

. . . . .

Now, the case has drifted on, and we are going to get into some law. That is always difficult. There is going to be into this case the question of conscious guilt. That is, the old identification is pretty near knocked out [2159] of this case. I say it advisedly that that evidence warrants you in discarding anything about that, holding these men on identification.

. . . . .

There have been men here, there are men here today, who know that that meeting on the 25th of April was held. Those men know that at that meeting the situation in New York was discussed. Those men know that Vanzetti was appointed a committee to go over there in regard to this Salsedo who met his death on the 4th, 3rd or 4th of May. They know he went over to confer. This attorney for Salsedo was brought here by our process to this stand and he tells you Quintilino conferred with him [2160] and he advised Quintilino in view of the situation, the action of the authorities toward this literature, the best thing to do was to get rid of it. Vanzetti came back and on that next Sunday he reported at that meeting.

There are many human beings in this state, they have been in this court room, who know that is the truth, who know that Vanzetti went out to do that which he says he went to do, know that they arranged to get this car, know that just what he was doing was what you would expect him to do, to slip around and get hold of that literature and put it out of the way.

Hasn't that been shown without any doubt? Wasn't it what they were arrested for? If the only thing was the fact these men had shot a man in Braintree, why these questions, "Are you a socialist, are you an anarchist, are you this and are you that?" How would that prove the revolver or anything else?

. . . . .

These men—no more popular thing was given to a district attorney to play a note up to a jury on than this case. No district attorney ever argued such a beautiful case.

He can stand up to this rail and say to you gentlemen "What have we been here for six weeks for, for two slackers, for two men who did not think enough of their country but what they would go to Mexico,—murderers, slackers, anarchists," ring the changes, gentlemen, and you can play any tune you want to on that. And you have got to be very careful that you don't vibrate in unison with those words. They are fearful, they are potent, they are laden to the limit. [2161]

. . . . .

Yes, we have got Officer Connolly here. On the words, the wonderful words of that man Connolly we are going to have the question of conscious guilt worked out. Officer Connolly takes this stand here. Officer Connolly says that—I will call your attention just to his exact words. He says that he got on the car. There was a telephone [call] and he got aboard that car.

And I was astonished when I saw Connolly. On the witness stand there he was going along mildly, had a quiet tone of voice, and when he got to the question what he did, Connolly began to smile. He began to inhale the air and began to smile. I could not get what was coming, when he squared off and said, "I said to him,"—well, gentlemen, bear with Connolly, let him enjoy that smile. Connolly was there then listening to the sweetest music of his young life, the sound of Connolly's voice when he was telling you what he did, and let us see what was the occasion of his doing that. Here we are, page 685 of the record here.

"Q. All right. A. I told them when we started off the first false move I would put a bullet in them."

Well, Connolly got going by that time, didn't he? He was going to put a bullet in them the first false move they made.

"On the way up to the station, Sacco reached his hands to put under his overcoat."

Reached his hands to put under his overcoat. He had an overcoat on, and he reached his hand to put under his overcoat. Marvelous. "And I told him to keep his hands on his lap." He sees poor Sacco there and he [2162] reaches to put his hand under his overcoat, and that smile came on again.

"A. And I told him to keep his hands outside of his clothes and on his lap.

"Q. Will you illustrate to the jury how he placed his hand? A. He was sitting down with his hands that way, and he moved his hand up to put it in under his overcoat."

. . . . .

Q. At what point? A. Just about the stomach there."

And Connolly smiles again. He asked him if he has a gun. "I ain't got no gun," he says. Connolly says he reaches over and puts his hand under his coat but he didn't feel any gun.

Well, gentlemen, there you are on Connolly in regard to Sacco.

Now, I will come to what he said in regard to Vanzetti in just a minute. It isn't as strong as that.

Now, gentlemen, I want to come down to the evidence in regard to the Johnsons. . . . She testified they . . . followed her. . . . and these men [acted] suspiciously. Where she got that inspiration, I don't know. [2163]

.   .   .   .   .

Johnson saw his wife come from the Bartletts. Johnson saw his wife walk down that 30 feet from her place where she came out to the motorcycle. Johnson has already testified and the record shows the men were up near the motorcycle, three men. . . .

Gentlemen, doesn't that fairly and squarely dispose of the matter and place it just where these two unfortunate fellows say it ought to have been, just exactly as they say that when they got up there to the bridge they saw the light over there and they went over to it and then the talk took place? Is there anything other than what Johnson says, . . . when he said he did talk with him and that he did not have the number plate? Is there anything other than what Vanzetti says, that they were coming again when he would arrange to get the automobile?

These men lied. They lied and lied when they were arrested. Please, why? What for? My brother says to Sacco, "When you were arrested, it had all happened. Nothing else counted when arrested." Yes, there could be more. A man is arrested, but that is different from being convicted. He said, "They had Orciana. You knew that. Why did you lie that you did not know Orciana?"

They were informed with knowledge of what had transpired in New York. They knew their position exactly without any question. They knew they were amenable to something. The answer to the whole situation is this. Not one man on that panel believes that Mrs. Sacco was cognizant of any murders or crimes like that. Why did she lie? Was that because she was conscious of any guilt of the shooting at Braintree? She did just [2164] what her husband did. She . . . did the same as Vanzetti did. She concealed from those officials the truth. . . . She burned the papers . . . [2165]

.   .   .   .   .

I could not help feel that when that man Levangie took that stand and looked me boldly in the eye and denied he had seen me two weeks before: What is there in this case, . . . in the conviction of those two poor, unfortunate men—what can there be that your fellow man will repudiate you? Gentlemen, justice doesn't go on those lines.

. . . . .

Now, gentlemen, there were experts on revolvers here. You heard them testify. . . . We had Van Amburgh. . . . He was put on here by the government. He testified, . . . that that No. III shell, the fatal bullet that killed Berardelli, came from the .32 Colt. Now, mark that, gentlemen.

And he says that the bullet III, the one the doctors say killed Berardelli came from the Colt revolver that was found on Sacco. That is a fearful statement to make. Now, I challenge the record and I will quote the record to you almost word for word. You know there must be some peculiar outstanding identifying thing about that revolver which would warrant any [2166] man in taking that fearful responsibility . . .

. . . . .

. . . [H]e said there is a marking on the side of the groove caused by a fouling of the barrel. I asked him where he finds the fouling, and he says it is right at the shoulder where the groove and the lands meet. I asked him if that is not where he usually gets fouling in a used revolver. "Yes." I asked him if there is any condition in [2167] that revolver that is not usually to be found in a used revolver, and he says "No." For goodness sake, where do we get when men have that elasticity of conscience [to] jump that fairly large gap and say this is the revolver that fired that fatal shell?

We have got something more than that. We have got here—here is Vanzetti, gentlemen. I am carrying you along because it is a frightful thing to cover this thing and cover it right. Take the revolver, the H. & R. revolver. . . .

. . . . .

————MR. McANARNEY told the jury about the defense efforts to trace the ownership of Vanzetti's gun. He told how the defense had brought two men from Maine to the Dedham courtroom to testify that they had owned the gun, sold it to a friend of Vanzetti's, who had sold it to Vanzetti. The serial number of the gun was not given in the testimony of any of these witnesses, however.————

Gentlemen, give us credit for something. There was numbers on the bottom of that revolver. If falsehood was going to help us win this case and if we were going to stoop to falsehood, gentlemen, we would have done it a thousand times. What would we have had to have done? There is your number right there on the bottom, G-82, 581. All you would have to do was take that revolver out and ask every one of your witnesses. It is a little old. "Take it home. This is the number on it. When you get on the witness stand don't make any mistake. That is the revolver you had, keep the number in your mind."

If we wanted to deceive, if we wanted to tell an untruth to escape death, we could do it, gentlemen, but that table has not stooped to that and never will while I am conducting a case. There is a proof of our honesty. If we, as the questions to him implied, were trying to deceive, we could have just taken that number and remembered. . . .

.   .   .   .   .

What of this revolver? . . . What is the meaning of this Iver-Johnson matter? What does it mean? Their last man says that that revolver had a broken spring. Here is the joke. Why ask a man up there about a hammer? The revolver, Mrs. Berardelli said, had a broken spring.

Gentlemen, why is this legerdemain and sleight of hand performance in a murder case? A spring—she says that the revolver, the spring of the revolver was broken. They put on the Iver-Johnson man to testify this was a new hammer. . . .

.   .   .   .   .

The Iver-Johnson man said that revolver had never been fired. Burns showed you. He said the hammer was as old as the rest of the gun, and Fitzgerald said the same, the man who has charge of this work for the Colt people.

What is the meaning of bringing this, call it what you want? I don't want to dignify it. Vanzetti discarding a powerful Savage revolver with which they say he was shooting, going in and getting and carrying around this branded gun in his pocket to help identify him? An old, obsolete revolver 16 or 18 years old, and giving away a good one that was a gun. Gentlemen, it is easy or hard, just as you want to take it. . . . [2169]

Well, we are passing along. Sacco and Vanzetti had some guns on them. Conscious guilt again—Connolly. Is it what transpired? Did it happen? Were they getting ready—were they going away? Is that true or is it not true?

How about Hayes? . . .

.   .   .   .   .

. . . When that man says he went to Boston and came out about that time, and when that man doesn't have to go beyond the truth and doesn't say, "I saw Sacco." No, no, he didn't see Sacco, but Sacco picked him out and said he saw him. Give Hayes credit for telling the truth, because were he disposed to help us, all he had to do was say, "Yes, I saw Sacco on that train." Please let the truth come in, even though it comes through our side of the case, and we gave you the truth there. It isn't of great consequence, but it only shows Sacco was on that train, if that be the truth, and Mr. Hayes has shown it fairly that it was, and I give him credit for that.

There is one thing you want to bear in mind. Please don't construe the ordinary man by an Italian. If you go out and flock a dozen Italians together, the chances are you will get a gun or two, anyway. You could handle one hundred—fifty other men and you won't find a revolver.

Were they cleaning house? Had the opportunity presented they were going to go. The passports were got. Sacco says he went the last week in March to get information in regard to a passport. He learned some things. He took the big photograph in on the 15th. Those show one thing or the other, they are telling the truth or not. Take it as you will. If all the men have lied about the 15th, it may be so. Believe it if you will. [2170]

.   .   .   .   .   .

. . . They had those guns. Then did that prove they were guilty of the Braintree murder? I say of Connolly—take him out of this case, no other man on that car saw anything like Connolly saw. No other man heard the ring—the welkin ring with that wonderful voice when he made those fearful remarks to these poor men because they couldn't move their hand toward their stomach outside of their coats. Out of this case goes that, and if out of this case goes that, all question of conscious guilt shown you on that Braintree matter is out of this case. They have got to get conscious guilt in there some way. They have got to get conscious guilt into this case because that identification will not stand the test. It will not stand the acid test of truth. Vanzetti can only say to you he did not have Alvin Fuller, he did not have Louis Frothingham down there on this case to come in and testify to you. He has only got the poor people he traveled with and who know him. . . .

.   .   .   .   .   .

Vanzetti, 11 years down there in Plymouth. You saw the mentality of that man. Is he intelligent? Would he be bobbing up and down at every station to see where East Braintree was? . . . [2171]

.   .   .   .   .   .

You have all gone in a hotel with your friends. You have ordered your dinner from the waiter and the waiter was slow in getting

around and you turned around and said, "Which one is our waiter?"
. . . Hasn't that happened to all of you? Identifications! Great Scott!
We all know. , . . . [2172]

* * * * *

But going back to my client, Vanzetti; all there is against Vanzetti
is what? That he happened to be alive at this time, that is about all.
We . . . have got Levangie, and take Levangie, and if you ever meet
him tell him what you think of him. He says that Vanzetti was driving
the car. And what else have you got now but the fellows up to
Bridgewater? That is all there is against this man Vanzetti, except that
he, unmarried, patriotic in his way, was, after having been to New
York, . . . going to go through and help his fellow men out. [2174]

* * * * *

I am reminded, gentlemen, of one thing. Once I was trying with a
man who . . . asked me to take the cross-examination. The witness
testified to a pretty important thing. I said to him, "What will I ask
him?" He says, "Take him over the hurdles." I says, "What do you
mean?" He says, "Take him over the hurdles. Ask him about every
other day but the day." He said, "He won't remember a blame one
of them." That is what we call "taking them over the hurdles."

You testify to something that happened, something that occurred.
You meet with an accident on the 4th of July and there is two or
three cars in collision and it happened you get the whole situation.
You go into court, you want to prove your damages. A year after or
six months after the attorney for the defendant says, "You say you
saw A. B. there. He had on a light suit of clothing." "Who did you
see two days before that day who had on a light suit of clothing?"
You don't know. "Who did you see 5 days before?"

* * * * *

I will take all the blame—I will take all the lies that they say we
lied about, we have lied all through every time they asked us where
we were or our whereabouts, we lied just as well as that little wife
did, and for that very reason. I am not asking sympathy for her in
any way, remarkable little woman that she is. If her husband is a
murderer, that is unfortunate for her, but that cannot stop justice
being done, but if this case were what they say it was, if this case
stood on its feet there would be no need to try to put Vanzetti in
possession of Berardelli's gun, that never on the records was taken
out of Iver-Johnson's. If this case had strength enough to stand on
its own feet, it never would have been propped up by fiction. . . .

. . . [Y]ou know all this camouflage about the Berardelli gun is
simply to put that gun into the possession of Vanzetti, and if that is

Berardelli's gun, of course he is guilty, unless he got it through some circle, but you would say he was guilty and I would say he was guilty, and when I can say to you—and oh, I hate to repeat it, but it must [w]ring your minds and hearts for that woman to say that the spring of that revolver was what was broken and they put a man on to tell you there is a new hammer in there; what can such work mean, not when two men have taken $125, but when the taking of all that is sacred in this world, when the [2178] preserving of the prerogatives of the Almighty are involved, and such fabrication as that is here, what can we think?

This case has no parallel in the history of Massachusetts criminal jurisdiction. I ask your consideration if at times we have taken time. . . . I thank every man of you from the bottom of my heart for the consideration you have given this case, and I want every man, too, of this panel to treat these two defendants as if they were your own individual brother. Take that as the test, not the other that we feel and what this evidence would make them out; treat them as though— as your brother. He came to this world by the same power that created you, and may he go from this world by the same power that takes you. I thank you, gentlemen.

D. THE SUMMATION FOR THE COMMONWEALTH

Argument of the District Attorney, Frederick G. Katzmann, Esq.

AFTERNOON SESSION

THE COURT. Poll the Jury, please.
[*The Jury are polled and both defendants answer "present."*]
MR. KATZMANN. I should like, if your Honor please, to conclude my argument this afternoon.
THE COURT. All right. You may have until 6:20, if you need it.
MR. KATZMANN. That is one-half hour less than the defendants had. They had between them four hours and a half.
THE COURT. All right then. You may have until seven, then, the same length of time.
MR. KATZMANN. I shall not use it unless absolutely necessary.

ARGUMENT

May it please your Honor, Mr. Foreman and gentlemen of this jury, I congratulate you sincerely that the hour of your several deliverances is about at hand. . . .

. . . . .

. . . [B]efore opening either upon the law or the facts in my argument, I want to congratulate both of these defendants upon the quality
of the defense that they have had through the medium of two trained,
skillful, and experienced attorneys. They could not be more ably
defended. Neither could they be defended with greater devotion to
duty than have the gentlemen who have been representing them
exercised and performed. But above that and above the fact that there
are 12 good men from Norfolk County who are not going to be
swayed either by prejudice or by fear, nor, worse than anything else,
by emotion, that would make them fail in their duty, you 12 men, this
trial has been presided over by a Justice of eminent person[al] at-
tainment.

It is to be assumed, gentlemen of the jury, that a lawyer, a member
of the bar, who is called to the high office of Justice of the Superior
Court, will have, as a matter of course, learning commensurate with
that office, and that is pre-eminently true in the case of the learned
justice who here presides. But there are some qualities, gentlemen, that
even a Justice of the Superior Court cannot acquire, he cannot gain
by experience, and those qualities must be born in him, and I refer
above all to the quality of real human nature; a kindly heart and an
inherent sense of justice that cannot be swerved from an impartial
performance of duty to both parties to a case. And in that fact, perhaps more than any one fact, more than the presence of you men,
more than the presence of able counsel, are the defendants to be con-
gratulated that they have such Justice presiding over their destinies
in a matter that has involved, as has been said over and over again,
their very existence.

May I say a word to you, gentlemen, about your duties, to correct
an unconsciously erroneous statement of the law given by my brother
Moore? [2180] . . . As he said, and well said, if there should come
a division of opinion among you, our Supreme Court has laid down
the law that while a juryman should never, never yield where he has a
reasonable doubt conscientiously, that is not the whole rule of conduct
that the Supreme Court has laid down for his guidance. It is further
than that, and the Supreme Court has asked those who may find themselves in a well defined minority to give heed to the opinions of their
fellows and to consider if they, the minority, possess such learning,
such experience and such mental attainments that they must be right
and the others wrong and to hearken to the voice and to the argument
of the others . . .

. . . . .

I have listened to the arguments of learned counsel through a long morning, and I have wondered why it was that the tremendous force of personality and argument exhibited by both counsel has been directed almost entirely, gentlemen of the jury, to the defense of the defendant Sacco and almost not an appreciable portion of either argument devoted to the defense of the defendant Vanzetti.

Is it, gentlemen of the jury, that neither counsel who have argued to you have confidence in the alibi of the defendant Vanzetti, and that it is hopeless in their opinion, and that all their tremendous effort and intelligence must be directed to pulling out a verdict in favor of the defendant Sacco if they can, and that the alibi of the defendant Vanzetti does not satisfy these two gentlemen themselves? It may well be, gentlemen, but whatever the opinion of counsel, myself or the defendants' counsel, that is of no consequence to you. . . .

It is akin, gentlemen of the jury, to the opening made by other learned, skillful and experienced counsel. He never whispered a word to you, gentlemen, when he opened this case, as to where Vanzetti was on April 15th. And more than that, gentlemen, he never even suggested on the day that he opened this case for the defense, that they were prepared [2181] to admit that the defendants, Sacco and Vanzetti, were down in West Bridgewater at Simon Johnson's house on the night of May 5th, and if I forget everything else in my argument in what I conceive to be the orderly presentation of it, I hope I won't overlook that, gentlemen, because it is of tremendous probative force. The acts of counsel, gentlemen, bind the defendants themselves.

Before I pass the facts, may I trespass but a short length upon what is peculiarly the domain of the Court himself, an exposition of such law as may seem to be important to you in the determination of fact. . . . It has been said by my brother . . . this is first degree murder and that there should be no compromise. Gentlemen of the jury, when Mr. Williams opened this case, he said the same thing, and in closing this case I say, in behalf of the Commonwealth of Massachusetts, to these two men: it is first degree murder or it is nothing. The Commonwealth seeks no compromise. The Commonwealth demands that you make no compromise.

. . . . .

One other thing, and one other thing only I conceive to be necessary [2182] to call to your attention in the law. My brother McAnarney said in his argument this morning, that the defendant Vanzetti would be foolish to take up a .38 calibre Harrington & Richardson revolver in place of a Savage automatic. Now, if my learned friend and brother can see that the Commonwealth has contended or ever will contend to the end of this case that the defendant Vanzetti fired any Savage automatic at either of the two decedents, he mis-states the evidence and our purpose.

We say in plain English that on the evidence we have proven to you beyond any reasonable doubt that the defendant Sacco fired a bullet from a Colt automatic that killed Alessandro Berardelli; that some other person whose name we do not know and who is not under arrest, . . . killed the man Frederick A. Parmenter with a Savage automatic, and that that was not the defendant Vanzetti.

. . . . .

. . . [W]hat we do say to you is that we expect you [to] find upon all the evidence that the .38 Harrington & Richardson revolver that was found upon the defendant Vanzetti was the .38 Harrington & Richardson revolver that poor Berardelli tried to draw from his pocket to defend himself . . . before he sunk to his knees with the blood coming out of his mouth dying on that sidewalk that afternoon. [2183]

. . . . .

What is the defense in these cases? It is three-handed, gentlemen. It started out on the day of the opening by the express words of my brother Callahan, as being a two-part defense. It has become a three-part defense, gentlemen, because of the exigencies that have arisen in the trial. . . . The ones to which he referred were: first, the evidence of witnesses that neither of these men were the men whom those witnesses saw in the escaping automobile. And the second part of the defense . . . was that these two defendants were respectively some place other than in South Braintree at 3 o'clock that afternoon.

There is a third defense, gentlemen, that . . . is an explanation or attempted explanation . . . of what otherwise is the most damning evidence from consciousness of guilt, and I refer to what transpired, first, at the Johnson house; secondly, when Officer Connolly went in to arrest these defendants in the car; and thirdly, to the series of unmitigated falsehoods that the defendants severally told the officers of the law, including myself . . . [T]he unmentioned defense when this case was opened is the one to which now for days they have been devoting their utmost effort to satisfy you that it was from consciousness of guilt of a trivial offense and not consciousness of guilt of the commission of this tremendous and atrocious crime of taking the lives of two innocent men with whom they had no quarrel, against whom they could properly have no basis for enmity, and in cold blood to take, steal, and rob money belonging to somebody else. A common motive, gentlemen, among murderers, to rob and to steal and if need be—and even if not need be—to take the lives of human beings, to steal $15,000 worth of money belonging to a capitalist, the Slater & Morrill Company.

Who have been the witnesses; whom have they produced to show that neither of these defendants was in that bandit car either before, during, or after the commission of these heinous crimes? [2185]

. . . [T]hey produced one Frank Burke from Brockton, one of their early witnesses, . . . and he tripped himself up and contradicted himself so many times in the course of his testimony that it seems to me it is idle for me to go over it step by step. I can recall off hand several things from memory. . . . This man who was so sure it was not a Buick car because he was familiar with Buick cars, who told he had ridden over the very day he was testifying in a Buick car; . . . he finally had to take that back [and to admit] that he came over in Mr. Callahan's Hudson. [2190]

. . . . .

The next portion of the defense is that of alibi; as to the defendant Vanzetti first and as to the defendant Sacco. I am going to do more than Vanzetti's own counsel, because I am going to discuss it, and I submit to you respectfully, they almost entirely neglected to discuss it. Maybe I may exercise poor judgment if that is the way they feel about it, but this is murder, gentlemen. This is a serious matter and I am seeking to have you, on your consciences, bring in a verdict of guilty, but I want it not upon snap judgment, nor upon snap argument. I want it upon careful consideration.

But before I discuss the specific testimony relating to alibi, I want to discuss the manner in which an alibi may be put together, and by that I mean no opprobrious term.

. . . . .

Guidobone is typical of the . . . manner of fixing the date . . . of every other witness for the defense in this case. Guidobone says [2192] to you under his oath, to you 12 men of common sense and intelligence, "I remember I had a cod fish put in my hand at 12:10 o'clock on April 15 because on the 19th day of April I was operated on for appendicitis." That is the testimony of Guidobone, gentlemen, and I am not seeking to be humorous, either.

The witness Corl says, . . . during the whole of the week that ended April 17, Saturday, Corl was painting a boat, and because on the 17th it was his wife's birthday and that he put the boat into the water and towed a boat from South Duxbury over to Plymouth, he remembers what he was doing on the 15th.

Why, gentlemen, the 15th was Thursday. He was painting that boat, Monday, Tuesday, Wednesday, Thursday and Friday, and what he said happened could have happened as well on the 14th or the 13th or the 12th as on the 15th. . . .

And those men from Boston who remembered that they saw Sacco at the Boni restaurant on the 15th day of April, except for Mr. Williams they all remembered it because as every one of them said he did not go to the banquet. Bosco and Guadenagi and another whose name escapes me. Dentamore, the one who testified within a day or two, was the only one who went to the banquet. They remembered it because down there that noontime they were discussing the question of the banquet that was to be given that night in honor of Mr. Williams of *The Transcript*, and at the very moment they were discussing it the banquet was going on and was nearly over. That is the accuracy of recollection of those alibi witnesses.

Why, gentlemen, I once knew of a preposterous story that was told by a man,—not a story, a statement of being caught out in a fog when he was leading his cow out from pasture not 500 feet distant from his barn. He said the fog set in so suddenly and terrifically and remained so long it was a week before he could find the barn. He became lost. And his listener refused to accept that story and doubted its veracity, and the teller of it indignantly replied, "If you don't believe me, you walk over there and I will show you the barn."

Gentlemen, if you do not believe that I had a cod fish placed in my hands at 12:13 on the fifteenth because of this appendicitis operation on the 19th, would it have added any verity to the story, any convincing quality that would have warranted merit, if Guidobone had bared his side and shown you the scar? "Gentlemen, if you do not believe I had the cod fish on the 15th at 12:13 and was operated on on the 19th, look at the scar, that proves it." [2193]

. . . . .

If there was any actual connection between the indisputable events upon which they predicate their recollection! Do you suppose that there wasn't a banquet to Mr. Williams of *The Transcript* on the 15th? You know better. You know there was such a banquet. Do you suppose Guidobone did not go to the hospital and was operated on for appendicitis? It would be idle, the Commonwealth has never taken a move to dispute it. Of course it is true. That is fixed. They start with something fixed. Do you suppose for a single moment Corl did not paint his boat that week? Of course he painted his boat that week. It is a probable fact, undisputable. He starts with that. [2194]

. . . . .

The third defense, gentlemen, from which I can't seem to get away in my own mind, is the one that was born after the opening of this case for the defense. Gentlemen, I say that to you advisedly. I am fully aware of the importance of the words I am using, and I ask you to follow me while I give you the reasons why I said that this explanation of the consciousness of guilt shown by the actions of these defendants at Simon Johnson's house, in the street railway car to the officers, and the police station is something the defendants themselves had never entrusted even to their own lawyers until the exigency of the case demanded it.

Why do I say that, gentlemen? Will you ever forget the cross examination of Ruth Johnson who was the first of the two Johnsons to take the stand, the little lady who lived near the bridge on West Main Street in West Bridgewater? Or will you forget the cross-examination that was made of her husband, Simon Johnson? It included many things, gentlemen.

. . . . .

Do you believe that two learned gentlemen of the experience of my brothers McAnarney and Moore would have taken the time or have made the physical and mental effort to break down the identifications had they been entrusted with their own clients' story that they were going to go on the stand and admit they were down there that night? An utter waste of time of which these two gentlemen would not be guilty; and when the learned Mr. Callahan opened his case he gave you no inkling after both the Johnsons had testified that the defense proposed to admit that Sacco and Vanzetti were down at the Johnson house the night of May 5th.

Well, why, gentlemen, is all this great disturbance about their presence down there, twenty days after the murder was committed? Manifestly, the murders at South Braintree had long since been committed and were over with. What is the connection and what is the importance of the [2197] West Bridgewater trip? It has a bearing and has been admitted affirmatively by the Court against the objection of the defendants solely, for it affords to you convincing evidence, not convincing evidence but evidence for whatever weight you may give it, that the actions of those two defendants that night showed consciousness of the guilt of the commission of those two murders. I want to read to you what I have culled from a learned decision, not in this state and not literally, not word for word, but as I have adapted it to this case, on the question of the telling of the truth and the failure to tell it as evidence of consciousness of guilt, and it was said that,

"There is no reason, if they are innocent, for withholding a single truth. There is every reason for uttering the truth if innocent. If they are guilty and if they have not confessed, the result in all cases either must be evasion, falsehood, or silence. Each falsehood uttered by way of exculpation becomes an article of evidence of greater or less incriminating value."

And it is for you to say what importance you will attach to those circumstances. [2198]

. . . . .

Can you tell me why four men, gentlemen, going in two different separate directions, should go down to West Bridgewater to get that ancient automobile? Was it necessary for the four of them to push it out? What were four men going after one poor old automobile for that was on its last legs and had to be brought over here on a truck? Four men going down to get an automobile, going down to see Pappi "if we had time."

Well, if that is all they were going to do, gentlemen, and if this mortal dread that made them utter falsehood after falsehood and deny up hill and down hill that they were there, was founded on apprehension of arrest on slackerdom, will you tell me why it was, gentlemen, that the four of them went down there and the defendant Sacco from whose house they went, who had this literature that on his wife's own story was of such character it was burned the day, the morning after his arrest and left these things—if she had to burn the rest of them you can imagine the difference in character between those they dared produce in Court and those she burned—will you tell me why, under every instinct of self-preservation, Sacco and Vanzetti, who then had a week's notice, and the 1st of May had gone by when these raids were to be made—I am talking now about the 5th of May—Sacco and Vanzetti walked out of Sacco's house and left scores of books of such a nature that his wife burned them the next morning, and he says it was because he was afraid of the possession of that literature that he falsified?

Gentlemen, can you reconcile that with truth? Can you possibly conceive of any human being so gone to humanitarian values that, fright- [2199] ened out of his life when he was arrested that he was to be charged with having some radical literature in his possession, he walked off and left his wife and baby with a load of books there that were of such a nature she destroyed them after his arrest, and never moved one of them.

Vanzetti, loafing around there from Monday afternoon to Wednesday night, the man who came back from New York with the terrible report, frightened to death, wanted to go notify people in Bridgewater, Brockton, Everett and Salem to be sure to get this stuff out of their house and Vanzetti was going to provide a hiding place, as he said, with some house owner down in Plymouth. Vanzetti goes over to New York for that information. He was so frightened, gentlemen, when he was down in Plymouth on the 29th and 1st, 29th and 30th of April and 1st of May, he never made a move to ask an individual to hide it.

. . . . .

Well, gentlemen, maybe you see the logic of that. That is their explanation! That is the whole of their explanation. They ask you to swallow that. Well, gentlemen, what was it that could happen? They say "deportation." Well, this, gentlemen, is an absurd defense. Mrs. Sacco took the stand yesterday or the day before yesterday, rather, and said "Why we were going to Italy on May 7th." He was so afraid of deportation, he says; he was going Saturday the 11th—he was so afraid of deportation back to his own country, Italy, a trip that would cost him money for himself, his wife, and child that he was going to pay money for—the country that he loved because it had fresh vegetables, the country that he loved because he could work easier and earn just as much pay, the country that harbored the rest of his family—and when he had been wanting to go for months, he falsified to the authorities because he would be taken back there free of charge. That is their defense, the essence of it.

And the defendant Vanzetti was afraid, mortally afraid, so mortally afraid of deportation to his own home, the place from which he had emigrated seven or eight years before, that he, too, falsified. Sacco was afraid to go back! Why, he was boasting that he was going back, and that is his defense; and in the next breath he tells, "I falsified because I was conscious of my guilt of having this literature and I did not want to be deported." [2200]

. . . . .

Is there any reason or any logic in that defense?
Let us pass on, gentlemen. [2201]

. . . . .

. . . [T]hese men who had not gotten the automobile, who had not taken it out of the garage and who did not have a single scrap of

socialistic, anarchistic or whatever type of literature they were afraid
of, or any books of the sort in their physical possession, who were
simply men who were on foot out there that night and had not ac-
complished their primary design of obtaining that automobile: What
was there for them to be afraid of?

To use the vernacular, "Nobody had the goods on them then."
There was no literature in any automobile in which they were seated.
There was no literature in their pockets. They were in the same
condition, as far as the literature was concerned, as they are now.
Whatever might have been in their minds could not be discerned by
the authorities nor apprehended. They had no literature.

But they had arsenals upon them. Vanzetti had a loaded .38 calibre
revolver, this man who ran to Mexico because he did not want to
shoot a fellow human being in warfare, a loaded .38 calibre revolver,
any one of the cartridges instantly death dealing. This tender-hearted
man who loved this country and who went down to Mexico because
he did not believe in shooting a fellow human being, going down to
get a decrepit old automobile, had a .38 calibre loaded gun on him.

And his friend and associate, Nicola Sacco, another lover of peace,
another lover of his adopted country who abhorred bloodshed and
abhorred it so that he went down to Mexico under the name of
Mosmacotelli to avoid bearing arms . . . for his adopted country,
. . . had with him, this lover of peace, 32 death dealing automatic
cartridges, 9 of them in the gun ready for action and 22 more of them
in his pocket,—carried where the ordinary citizen carries it there?
No, gentlemen, carried where [2203] those who have occasion to use
it quickly and want to slip it out and use it quickly would be prone to
carry it, that death-dealing instrument.

But more than that, gentlemen, and ammunition enough to kill
37 men if each shot took effect, they had or Vanzetti had four shells
—no weapon in which to fire them at the moment that we found, but
you will remember, gentlemen, that sticking out the back of the
bandit's car on April 15th was either a rifle or a shot-gun, and in
Vanzetti's pocket were four 12-gauge shells loaded with buck shot
that they were going out to shoot little birds with, with some friend
that had visited them at some time before.

Maybe, gentlemen, you think that is the way men would be armed
who were going on an innocent trip, innocent so far as death-dealing
matters are concerned at night time after closing hours of the garage
and when the man who ran it was in bed, going to make a social trip

down to see Pappi, the friend of Vanzetti, and he did not know where
he lived, save that it was in East Bridgewater, gentlemen.

. . . . .

But, gentlemen, that is not the whole story on consciousness of guilt,
not by a great deal. You will remember that Officer Connolly,—who
has been described humorously, described as a man with a smile, and
that [2204] is the first time that I have ever heard counsel find fault
with the police officer for wearing a smile when he is testifying. It
is usually they find fault with him because he is vindictive and fails to
wear anything but a scowl.

But Connolly's testimony is not to be forgotten. . . . [I]f what
Michael Connolly says is true, it was not fear of deportation, it was
not fear of imprisonment because of being slackers that they tried to
pull death-dealing instruments on an officer of the law, their natural
enemy.

. . . . .

. . . [T]hink of it, gentlemen, going out in the woods to fire off the
32 cartridges to get rid of them because they were going next day, and
tucked it in the waist band of his trousers and sat down to his supper
and never knew it was in there and did not know there was 22 cartridges in his pocket, wholly unconscious of that, woke up [to] the
fact and twice, I submit, twice, in the ride to Brockton police station,
tried to draw that death-dealing weapon.

What was Vanzetti going to do with the gun if he had drawn it?
What was the defendant Sacco going to do with the automatic if he
had drawn it? Can you conceive of but one purpose, gentlemen? They
were going to draw their respective weapons to kill those police officers and make their escape. Consciousness of guilt! If you accept my
explanation, to commit murder on police officers to escape being deported to their native country.

Gentlemen, where is your common sense? No wonder the attack
was made upon Officer Connolly in an effort to break his testimony,
his testi- [2205] mony that is confirmed almost one hundred per cent
by the admission of the defendant Vanzetti himself. He says that Connolly said to him, "Don't move, you dirty thing." And Connolly said,
"I said to him, if you move you will be sorry for it." What move
would he try to make save a move that would result in the death of
the officer if successful and his escape from the hands of the law?

Consciousness of guilt, gentlemen. Well, if you were arrested for
expectorating on the sidewalk in violation of some city ordinance and

when arrested you had a gun in your pocket, would you say if you made an effort to draw that gun upon the officer that you [were] consciously guilty of the minor offence of violating a health ordinance by spitting upon the sidewalk, or would you say, if you were going to go that far, if you were willing to go that far, if like Sacco you tried to pull that gun twice upon Spear or Connolly or upon whomever it was sought to make away with him, that you were conscious of guilt of a crime commensurate with the kind of action that you were about to take? Can you draw any logical conclusion save that?

Well, the argument may be carried forward still more. They got to the station. They were visited by police officers, and the next day as part of my duty I asked them if they were willing to talk with me. They both expressed willingness to talk with me and did talk. . . .

But they talked, as they said, for an hour or so apiece, and in every instance we bore down upon matters wholly outside of or extraneous to literature. Sacco says I never asked a question about his beliefs, but it is but fair to him to say that Chief Stewart had asked him the night before, and had asked Vanzetti.

Falsehood upon falsehood, as fast as they could be uttered, in response to questions, given by me, and the answer now is, "We were afraid you would find out we were slackers." I am not a federal official, and I have nothing to do with deportation. That is a federal function, violation of the laws of the United States, and that is not within my province.

Again you may say, "Perhaps they did not know it." True. But when I asked them questions, gentlemen, about where they purchased their revolvers and when I got the defendant Sacco and asked him if he knew who Berardelli was and he said "No, who is this Berardelli?", and you will remember that he had said in direct examination that I never asked him about any particular crime in the interview I had with him! [2206]

. . . . .

. . . Perhaps you believe that this man who brings volume after volume in, Nicola Sacco, to show his learning and his desire to improve himself mentally, perhaps you believe that he is such a dullard that when the question is put to him after step by step, if he knew about this——

"Q. Did you read it the next morning after it happened in the papers? A. Yes.

Q. Where were you the day before you read it in the papers?

A. I was working all days."

That he did not know it.

Will you tell me, in the name of reason, gentlemen of this jury, what consciousness of guilt of having possession of socialistic literature up in his little house in Stoughton had to do with that falsehood? Or was he denying where he was the day before he read it in the paper because he was conscious of his guilt from participation in that crime itself? Can there be any other conclusion that 13 [*sic*] men of common sense can draw?

And you remember a similar question of the defendant Vanzetti, . . . if he knew where he was on the Thursday before the holiday that fell on the 19th of April, first calling his attention to when that holiday fell, the fact that it fell on Monday of a week, and he said, "No, he did not know."

There is no suggestion from either of these defendants that the examination was conducted unfairly or that it was conducted hurriedly or that, as far as I was concerned, that there was any attempt to confuse or to frighten or to press down upon them. Even Sacco does not make that allegation as to the officers.

But it fell to the man Vanzetti, the man who showed the gruff voice because he could not control himself because again he was facing his natural enemy, a police officer, Connolly, when he was on the stand, and he showed that same quality of gruff voice that he shows under emotion and excitement that Austin Reed told you about, the crossing tender at Mat- [2207] field, when he wanted to know why in "H" they were holding him up, when Connolly got to that part of his testimony when he said, "When I came in the car, Vanzetti made a move to his pocket."

Will you ever forget the uncontrollable outburst of the defendant Vanzetti . . . that condemned any consciousness of guilt theory of a minor offense, of which the authorities had no proof whatever? "You are a liar" burst from his lips when Connolly told about that move.

. . . . .

That is not all, gentlemen, upon consciousness of guilt. There is something more telling than that, gentlemen, more convincing than anything I have yet said to you. You have seen enough of George Kelley, you have seen enough of George Kelley to feel, I should judge, that you know him.

. . . . .

. . . [T]hey were in intimate terms of friendship, and this man

George Kelley was the one who had arranged for Sacco to go to Boston some time after the defendant Sacco showed him a letter. . . . [2208]

.   .   .   .   .

And when he came back he told him that the consulate was so crowded that he had to stay there or that he could not get his passport—the inference being that he stayed there from the time he went in until too late to get the noon train and that is why he did not come back to work—and George Kelley uttered a significant remark in his original examination, either in direct or cross, "I accepted that as being the excuse."

If you find, gentlemen, as I suggest common sense and logic must force you to find, that this is a suspicious alibi that Sacco has built up around himself about being into Boni's restaurant and meeting people, talking with them, who do not remember the date and truly because of the time of the banquet, or remembering it logically who are friends and associates of his, some of them associated with his very defense here now, and Williams associated in a business way with those friends, if you do not believe that, gentlemen of the jury, don't you see that when he falsified again—and he admits that he lied to his friend George Kelley—that he was falsifying again from consciousness of guilt of the crime that had happened but the day before? It must have been something substantial, it strikes me, that would make him falsify to the man who had been as good to him as George Kelley had.

But that is not all, gentlemen. He has falsified to you before your very faces. When Exhibit 43, his own cap that Lieut. Guerin says he got out of his own house, was produced and shown to him, before Lieut. Guerin testified, he would not admit, gentlemen, that his own cap was his. What is there about that cap, which admittedly was not picked up on the scene of the murder, that would drive him from truth? Do you believe Guerin?

Do you think a man who has risen high enough in the police department in the city of Brockton, a great police department, do you think a lieutenant of that department would on his oath commit the perjurious utterance of saying that was Sacco's cap and that he took it out of his house and that it is in the same condition now as then if that were a fabrication?

And Sacco denied it. Why, gentlemen of the jury? It is too obvious to need argument. The reason he denied it was because this cap that was picked up by——

Mr. Moore. If your Honor please, I will ask either the retraction of

the statement that the defendant denied that that was his hat or a reading of the record. My recollection of the record is that the defendant
stated in the first instance, that it was; in the second instance on press-
ing that he wasn't sure because he thought his cap was a little lighter.
Now, that is my recollection of the testimony. At no time did he say
positively that it was not his hat. Neither would he say positively that
it was or positively that it was not.

THE COURT. That is my recollection of the testimony. [2209]

MR. MOORE. Take an exception.

THE COURT. But it is for you gentlemen to determine what the
evidence was.

MR. KATZMANN. Gentlemen, I trust—I am grateful to Mr. Moore for
interrupting—I trust that in so important a case as a charge of murder
against two human beings, that I would not permit myself to stray a
thousandth part from the testimony as I recall it. I am not attempting
to repeat to you what has taken six weeks to utter before you word
for word. I am trying to sum up fairly a just summary of what they
have said, and call your attention and that of counsel for the defendant,
who did me the kindness of interrupting me, that [when] I finally left
the defendant Sacco he said, "No, that cap is too dirty. I have got 50
cents to buy a new cap whenever I need one."

And I ask you, gentlemen, if it is not a fair inference from that
statement, if I am now stating the evidence to you accurately, to say
that Sacco denied that was his cap. Those were the words that I had in
mind. I remembered the train of examination that my brother had
spoken of, although doubtless my memory is not as good as his, and I
remember at first he said he thought it was and secondly he began to
express a doubt; and will you ever forget, gentlemen, the amount of
time that he took on the stand examining that cap? And as I recall it,
his final utterance was, "No, that cap looks too dirty. I always had
50 cents to buy a new cap." Is that not the evidence, gentlemen, and
if that is the evidence, isn't it a denial of the ownership of that cap?

. . . . .

Then came the episode of trying the cap on. . . . He tried it on.
Then he put it on his head, and it rested there, and then he pulled it
down, and I submit to you gentlemen that that dark hat, which is the
hat of the man who killed Alessandro Berardelli—because the man who
killed Alessandro Berardelli went away bareheaded in that automobile—
fits the head of the defendant Sacco exactly the same as does the hat
that on the testimony of Guerin you would be warranted and should
find is his hat.

Don't take my word for that, gentlemen. It is too serious a matter, because it is absolutely condemnatory of this defendant. No, not absolutely, but it clinches on the top of all other circumstances. Some one of you who wears a 7-⅛, if that is the size of those caps, try them both on. There is the acid test for you, gentlemen. Don't take anybody's word. [2210] Don't take Sacco's or anybody else. Try the caps on yourself, and if they are not identically of the same size, then so find, so find, gentlemen.

·   ·   ·   ·   ·

You know as a matter of common sense, that in a little over two hours I can't justly and fairly treat evidence that has taken six weeks, or three weeks, the defendants' case, to go in. There must be scores of things, doubtless, properly that appeal to you as being more convincing than those I have argued to you. I am omitting them because I haven't the time to take them up. Don't you do so. Consider every particle of evidence in this case. Decide it upon all the evidence, and nothing short of it.

We come to the matter of the Commonwealth's case. . . . [2211]

·   ·   ·   ·   ·

. . . [T]here was the witness Pelser, a young man as I recall it, 22 years of age.

·   ·   ·   ·   ·

He falsified to the defense. He falsified to the Commonwealth and then it became necessary for us to show you, and we did show you, how it was and when it was we first learned that he knew anything of the actual shooting of Berardelli. His identification on the stand in direct examination of the defendant Sacco was positive. He was the nearest—if not the nearest, there could not have been anybody who could have been much [2212] nearer than he, and I think he was the nearest to the actual shooting of Berardelli.

·   ·   ·   ·   ·

[W]hen I examined the testimony of Barbara Liscomb last night, I found that the defendants themselves produced a witness who necessarily, absolutely confirmed Pelser in the vital part of his story that he was at the window and looked out and saw what he saw. Why, they are the only two people in the case who testify that the man down at the body of Berardelli pointed his revolver at the Rice & Hutchins factory. . . .

Confirmation through Barbara Liscomb of what he said. He was frank enough here, gentlemen, to own that he had twice falsified before to both sides, treating them equally and like, and he gave you his reason. . . . He is big enough and manly enough now to tell you of his prior falsehoods and his reasons for them. If you accept them, gentlemen, give such weight to his testimony as you say should be given.

And in weighing the evidence of the identifying witnesses of the Commonwealth and the rest of them, don't forget this, gentlemen. It is necessarily a human trait that when one man, or, worse still, two men are charged with first degree murder, it is much more of a human quality, [2213] a much more natural thing for us human beings to do to deny that they know anything that would take these men into a verdict of guilty than to say that they knew something that would condemn them. That is human nature, gentlemen.

And now let me speak of the quality generally of the identification by witnesses for either side. [2214]

. . . . .

They find fault, gentlemen, with Levangie, they say that Levangie is wrong in saying that Vanzetti was driving that car. I agree with them, gentlemen.

. . . . .

We cannot mold the testimony of witnesses, gentlemen. We have got to take them as they testify on their oaths, and we put Levangie on because necessarily he must have been there. He saw something.

. . . . .

And can't you reconcile it with the . . . probability that at that time Vanzetti was directly behind the driver in the quick glance this man Levangie had of the car going over when they were going up over the crossing? If you recall the [bullet] hole in the sign board right near Levangie, or not far from his shanty, will you have any difficulty in dealing with the testimony of Levangie? [2215]

. . . . .

You have looked at the face of Sacco for six long weeks, and is there a man of his countrymen—and I speak of that only because of their bearing certain pigmentary characteristics, dark hair and dark skin—is there a man of his nationality who has testified on either side of this case who approached him in physiognomy? Hasn't he a face, gentlemen of the jury, that once seen you would never forget?

But more than that, gentlemen, remember this in connection with the identification of every witness for the Commonwealth who have said, "That is the man," or, "I think that is the man," or, "I am sure that is the man," or, "He is the dead image of the man," and various phraseology that they used. . . . Two human lives had been taken, and those bystanders . . . who either had the courage to remain or could not get away, whatever be the fact, what would you expect them to do if they could do it? [2216]

Why, they would bend every effort they severally possessed to visualize and to remember the face of the occupants, or the faces of the occupants of that car. . . .

. . . . .

That is what Mary Splaine did, and they say she told in the lower court, "I will not positively say he is the man." Yes, she did say it, but she also said, "I will not say he is not the man." She gave you her explanation of why she said it, . . . that upon reflection she was positive, she was sure. . . . You cannot have looked on Mary Splaine, a smart business woman, . . . and have seen the truth shining like stars out of her young womanly eyes and believe for a moment that . . . [she] would dare, before a court of justice or before God . . . condemn Sacco to his death with a wilful lie. You cannot believe that, gentlemen . . . [2217]

Austin Reed, who saw them just before the turning point in the flight of the car, . . . went around to the station to see if either or any of the three men then under arrest was the man whose face he visualized and remembered, Vanzetti. [2218]

A clean-cut young fellow. Why in the name of common sense would he attempt to swear away the life of Vanzetti? What interest could Austin Reed have in saying it?

And then there is Lola Andrews. I have been in this office, gentlemen, for now more than 11 years. I cannot recall in that too long service for the Commonwealth that ever before I have laid eye or given ear to so convincing a witness as Lola Andrews. [2219]

. . . . .

Gentlemen, where was the car found? Where was the car found April 17th? In the wood in West Bridgewater near the poor farm not far from Elm Square, a mile or two, [from] where these defendants were on the night of May 5th. . . .

. . . . .

You don't find the car in Worcester. You don't find it in Pittsfield. You don't find it in South Boston, nor do you find it in Fall River. You find it in West Bridgewater, and the night these men were arrested, they were arrested within hailing distance of it. Can you put two and two together, gentlemen?

What killed Alessandro Berardelli? [2223]

. . . . .

. . . [T]his left-handed twist bullet, No. III, was fired by a Colt .32. Was it fired by this Colt .32? Some one of learned counsel for the defendant has said that it is coming to a pretty pass when the microscope is used to convict a man of murder. I say heaven speed the day when proof in any important case is dependent upon the magnifying glass and the scientist and is less dependent upon the untrained witness without the microscope. Those things can't be wrong in the hands of a skilled user of a microscope or a magnifying glass.

There are certain things I said to you about the cap that I don't ask you to take anybody's words about. Take the caps; put them on your own heads those of you who wear that size and let your fellows see it; a fair request to make and a fair use of the evidence when it is in your possession.

I say to you on this vital matter of the No. III bullet. . . . Take the three Winchester bullets that were fired by Capt. Van Amburgh at Lowell and take the seven United States Bullets that were fired by Mr. Burns at Lowell, and, lastly, take the barrel itself which we will unhitch for you, and determine the fact for yourself, for yourselves.

. . . . .

Take the glass, gentlemen, and examine them for yourselves. If you [2224] choose, take the word of nobody in that regard. Take the exhibits themselves. Can there be a fairer test than I ask you to submit yourselves to? [2225]

. . . . .

Now, passing hastily on to the question of the .38 revolver. . . .

. . . . .

Who knows best, referring to that same revolver, whether there is a new hammer in it or not[?] . . . [2229] Mr. Fitzmeyer, the gunsmith upstairs for 31 or 41 years, he said it was a new hammer put in that gun. Who knows more about it, the man who put the hammer in or James E. Burns; an expert user of firearms, a gunsmith for 41 years, or an expert who never saw the gun until he came into the court room?

. . . . .

Well, gentlemen, there were many crowns placed upon the head of James Bostock of Brockton by both counsel for the defense in their argument. . . . James Bostock . . . says on the Saturday before the murder he saw Berardelli show the gun, the man whom they say is a fine witness. [2230]

Mr. Moore. I beg your pardon, just one second. My recollection of the evidence is Bostock did not identify this gun. He said he saw simply a bright nickel gun. He made no effort to identify either as to calibre or as to make.

THE COURT. Gentlemen, you remember what the evidence is. You will, of course, apply it according to your remembrance of the evidence.

MR. KATZMANN. I say to you, gentlemen, my recollection of the evidence of Bostock in that particular is that he said . . . that the gun we produced was similar and answered the description of the gun and that he saw a gun in the possession of Berardelli on the Saturday before his death . . . [2231]

.   .   .   .   .

I want to say with the utmost good nature, gentlemen, when I listened to four hours of argument jointly, four hours and a half, on behalf of the defendants of these two learned gentlemen and after I heard misquotation after misquotation of the evidence, I knew that these two honorable gentlemen were giving the evidence as best they could remember it and I said to myself, "We have had six weeks long trial. These gentlemen are above misquoting the evidence and you 12 gentlemen will straighten it out and you will remember what it was." And I never arose from my chair to interrupt in argument. I realize that they are defending men on trial for their lives and I would not transgress and I have quoted you the evidence when they have interrupted before and I will quote it to you again. [2234]

.   .   .   .   .

Now, gentlemen, I have tried you beyond what I ought. I trust you will overlook it in a public servant who is seeking to do his duty and to do no more. If I had my way I would not have trespassed upon your time or your strength at all, but I have been sworn here to perform a duty to the people of this district.

.   .   .   .   .

Make a decision, gentlemen, this case can never be more ably tried in the interests of these defendants than it has been in this trial. They have had their day in court, and the Commonwealth has had its day in court. Both parties desire a final decision on this accusation. In reaching that decision the Commonwealth asks of you that you sweep aside any consideration of personal pity, which I grant you must feel for these defendants, or for the wife and child of one of them.

.   .   .   .   .

The question is one of fact, gentlemen, arrived at under the rules of law. It has been said to you that your decision will take away the lives of two men [2236] if it be that of guilty. Well, gentlemen, that is not so in one sense. You are not taking away the lives of the defendants by finding them guilty of a murder of which they are guilty. The law takes their lives away and not you. It is for you to say if they are guilty and you are done. You pronounce no sentence of death. . . . Gentlemen of the jury, do your duty. Do it like men. Stand together, you men of Norfolk. [2237]

. . . . . .

E. THE CHARGE TO THE JURY

[July 19, 1921]

THE COURT. Mr. Foreman and gentlemen of the jury—you may remain seated—the Commonwealth of Massachusetts called upon you to render a most important service. Although you knew that such service would be arduous, painful and tiresome, yet you, like the true soldier, responded to that call in the spirit of supreme American loyalty. There is no better word in the English language than "loyalty." For he who is loyal to God, to country, to his state and to his fellowmen, represents the highest and noblest type of true American citizenship, than which there is none grander in the entire world. You gentlemen have been put to the real test, and you have proven to the world, and particularly to the people of Norfolk County, that you truly represent such citizenship. For this loyalty, gentlemen, and for this magnificent service that you have rendered to your State and to your fellow men, I desire, however, in behalf of both to extend to each of you their profoundest thanks, gratitude, and appreciation.

The issues raised under these indictments are so many and varied, and the law applicable thereto being somewhat difficult of a clear understanding, the charge necessarily will require considerable time. [2239]

. . . . . .

————THE JUDGE then explained the difference between first and second degree murder.————

Murder in the first degree is the gravest offense known to the law. This is so because of the statutory penalty of death. The severity of the penalty is demanded, not in the spirit of revenge or of vengeance, but [2239] rather as punishment for the crime committed, and for the following reasons: first, because the life of a human being has been taken; and secondly, because the law seeks to protect and make safer the lives of all the people of the Commonwealth by deterring and preventing the further commission of similar crimes. This, then, being the law, gentlemen, it is of no consequence whether you and I believe it or not. It is the law of Massachusetts and has been for many generations past, and being such, it becomes your sacred and solemn duty, as well as mine, to obey it, and if we do otherwise, substitute in place of a government of laws, the arbitrary rule of men, and such substitution when carried to excess means the impairment, if not the destruction, of the American government and its various institutions, and may God forbid that the pure waters of such a Government, the grandest and noblest in the civilized world, should ever be polluted by streams made foul by the arbitrary rule of men; for according to the highest and best judgment and wisdom of men from the day that little band of Pilgrims landed at Plymouth Rock until this very hour, human life, liberty, and property could only be made safe and secure by a strict and faithful obedience to the laws of the land. . . . [2240]

Let me repeat to you what I said to another jury in a similar case: Let your eyes be blinded to every ray of sympathy or prejudice but let them ever be willing to receive the beautiful sunshine of truth, of reason, and sound judgment, and let your ears be deaf to every sound of public opinion or public clamor, if there be any, either in favor of or against these defendants. Let them always be listening for the sweet voices of conscience and of sacred and solemn duty efficiently and fearlessly performed. The law grants to every person the same rights and privileges, and imposes upon each corresponding duties, obligations, and responsibilities; for whoever is willing to accept the blessings of government should be perfectly willing to serve with fidelity that same government. [2241]

. . . . .

The Commonwealth must prove beyond reasonable doubt every fact or element necessary to prove the crime of murder. If the Commonwealth should fail to establish every fact that is essential to prove the crime of murder, then crime alleged has not been established beyond reasonable doubt. If, again, you should find some fact to be true that is essential to establish the crime of murder and which fact is consistent with innocence and inconsistent with guilt, then the Commonwealth has failed to prove the crime of murder as alleged.

At the very beginning of this subject, you must thoroughly understand that it means the doubt of a reasonable man who is earnestly seeking the truth. It does not mean the doubt of a man who is earnestly looking for doubts. It means such a doubt that exists in the mind of a juror after there has been, on his part, an honest and conscientious effort to ascertain the truth. It does not mean a doubt beyond all peradventure. Neither does it mean beyond all imaginary or possible doubt, because everything relating to human affairs and human evidence is open to some possible or imaginary doubt.

The law does not require proof so positive, so unerring and convincing that amounts to a mathematical or absolute certainty. You might obtain proof of that character in the exact sciences, but not in human investigations. [2243]

.   .   .   .   .

Identity, gentlemen, may be established by direct or by circumstantial evidence or by both. Direct evidence is evidence of personal observation by the witness of the criminal act itself. Circumstantial evidence depends upon the proof of circumstances or facts from which the ultimate fact or the crime itself is inferred. It has been said that circumstantial evidence alone should never be sufficient to establish the guilt of any defend- [2251] ant in any criminal case. Such a statement, gentlemen, is the result of ignorance rather than sound reason or mature judgment, for it has been truly said that crime would go unpunished to a very large extent without the aid of circumstantial evidence. Both kinds of testimony, gentlemen, may be at times irresistibly strong and at other times irresistibly weak. Therefore, each case must stand by itself. It is not the name, gentlemen, that you give to the evidence which should govern your conclusion, but rather it is the quality, the character, and the probative effect of such evidence independent of the name ascribed to it.

.   .   .   .   .

Therefore, in the eyes of the law there is no important distinction between circumstantial evidence and any other kind of evidence. It is the degree of proof that the evidence establishes; for, no matter what the evidence may be, it is necessary that that evidence should satisfy you of the guilt of these defendants so that you cannot come to any other reasonable conclusion than that they are guilty. [2252]

.   .   .   .   .

Now, the Commonwealth claims that there are several distinct pieces of testimony that must be considered upon the question of personal identification. Let us see what they are. First, that the fatal Winchester bullet, marked Exhibit III, which killed Berardelli, was fired through the barrel of the Colt automatic pistol found upon the defendant Sacco at the time of his arrest. If that is true, that is evidence tending to corroborate the testimony of the witnesses of the Commonwealth that the defendant Sacco was at South Braintree on the 15th day of April, 1920, and it was his pistol that fired the bullet that caused the death of Berardelli. To this effect the Commonwealth introduced the testimony of two witnesses, Messrs. Proctor and Van Amburgh. And on the other hand, the defendants offered testimony of two experts, Messrs. Burns and Fitzgerald, to the effect that the Sacco pistol did not fire the bullet that caused the death of Berardelli. [2254]

    .   .   .   .

Second, that the deceased Berardelli had a revolver, that immediately following his death none was found in his clothing, that Berardelli about three weeks before his death, in company with his wife, left said revolver with the Iver Johnson Company of Boston for the purpose of having a new spring put into it, that according to the foreman of the repair shop of Iver Johnson Company a new spring and hammer were put into an H. & R. revolver that had a repair tag number upon it of 94765, which number was given to the repair job by the person who took the revolver from Berardelli at the time it was left to be repaired; that on the Saturday night previous to the shooting some witness testified that a revolver in the hands of Berardelli,—he saw in the hands of Berardelli, was something similar to the one he had previously seen with Berardelli.

Now, the Commonwealth claims that if this revolver, found or taken from the defendant Vanzetti, was taken by him at the time of the killing of Berardelli, that is evidence tending to corroborate the witnesses of the Commonwealth that the defendant Vanzetti was in the bandit car and, therefore, was present at the time of the alleged shooting at South Braintree. You must therefore see that the new hammer and spring may become a very important feature in the identity of this revolver.

. . . [T]he defendants have offered testimony tending to prove that said revolver never was the property of Berardelli, but having passed through several hands it became the property of the defendant Vanzetti and that, according to the testimony of the two experts, the said Messrs. Burns and Fitzgerald, no new spring and hammer were put into said revolver by the employees of said Iver Johnson Company.

    .   .   .   .

Third, that there is evidence tending to prove that a cap was found [2255] near the body of Berardelli, that said cap was in general appearance and color like that worn by the defendant Sacco; and that the defendant Sacco was seen going away without any cap upon his head. Now, the Commonwealth claims that if this cap belonged to

Sacco it could not have been found near the dead body of Berardelli unless the defendant Sacco lost it at the time of said shooting. . . .

On the other hand, you should remember that the defendant Sacco and his wife both have testified that said cap never belonged to the defendant, that he never owned it, and if that is true, it should not be considered by you as evidence against him. Again, gentlemen, you have another controverted question of fact. What is the truth? . . .

There is another piece of testimony to which I specifically call your attention, because the Commonwealth claims that such testimony tends to prove, and in fact proves, a consciousness of guilt on the part of these defendants. [2256]

.   .   .   .   .

. . . [T]he law requires that there must be a causal connection or some probative relationship between the evidence tending to prove a consciousness of guilt and the crime charged in the indictments.

But the Commonwealth claims that all the evidence of the declarations, conduct and movements of the defendants while at the Johnson house, at subsequent times thereto and on subsequent occasions, tends to prove a consciousness of guilt of the murders of Berardelli and Parmenter. This is on the ground that the evidence is consistent only with the consciousness of having committed the crime of murder and inconsistent with any other theory. While, on the other hand, the defendants claim that if [2257] there was any consciousness of guilt at all it did not refer to the murders of Berardelli and Parmenter but to some punishment that they or their friends might receive for being slackers, which might include deportation, as well as some other form of punishment. [2258]

.   .   .   .   .

Now, then, the question you must determine is this: Did the defendants, in company with Orciana and Boda, leave the Johnson house because the automobile had no 1920 number plate on it, or because they were conscious of or became suspicious of what Mrs. Johnson did in the Bartlett house? If they left because they had no 1920 number plates upon the automobile, then you may say there was no consciousness of guilt in consequence of their sudden departure, but if they left because they were consciously guilty of what was being done by Mrs. Johnson in the Bartlett house, then you may say that is evidence tending to prove consciousness of guilt on their part.

But still, you must remember that such consciousness of guilt, if you find such consciousness of guilt, must relate to the murders of Berardelli and Parmenter and not to the fact that they and their friends were slackers and liable to be deported therefor or were even afraid that some kind of punishment might come to them.

. . . . .

The next question that you might consider would be what actually took place in the electric car and the automobile when the defendants were arrested and immediately following after that. Is the testimony of Officer Connolly true, in that Vanzetti put his hand in his hip pocket? . . . [2259]

. . . . .

I might say, further, it is not sufficient that the Officer Connolly thought either of the defendants were to draw a revolver by the manifestations made. The real question is as to the mental state of either and both defendants Vanzetti and Sacco at that time. Did either of them or both of them, as has been testified, have in their minds the desire and the purpose and intention of drawing and using a revolver upon either of the arresting officers? . . . [2260]

. . . . .

. . . [T]he Commonwealth claims that many statements were made by each of these defendants to prove a consciousness of guilt and that such consciousness of guilt, in connection with other established facts, proves consciousness of guilt of the murders of Berardelli and Parmenter.

Now, the law says that intentional false statements, deception and concealment of truth are evidences of consciousness of guilt and can be used against a defendant when, and only when, such consciousness relates to the crime charged in the indictment. That false statements were made by both of these defendants is admitted. This being true, you must deter- [2261] mine their purpose, object, and intent in making them. Did they know that Berardelli and Parmenter had been murdered? Did they realize and appreciate that they were being held in connection with these murders? Did they make false statements for the purpose of taking away suspicions from them of these murders? Did they knowingly make false statements as to their whereabouts on the day of the murders for the purpose of deceiving both Chief Stewart and District Attorney Katzmann and eventually for the ultimate purpose of establishing their innocence of the crimes charged?

. . . . .

[T]he defendants say that although said statements were false, yet they were not made for the purpose of deceiving Chief Stewart or District Attorney Katzmann in regard to any fact whatsoever that had any relationship to the murders of Berardelli and Parmenter, because they said they had no knowledge whatsoever at that time of the murders of Berardelli and Parmenter. . . . [T]hey . . . say that they made them to protect themselves and their friends from some kind of punishment, either by way of deportation because they were radicals, or because of their activities in the radical movement, or because of radical literature that they then had possession of. [2262]

. . . . . .

An alibi is always a question of fact. Therefore, all testimony which tends to show that the defendants were in another place at the time the murders were committed tends also to rebut the evidence that they were present at the time and place the murders were committed. If the evidence of an alibi rebuts evidence of the Commonwealth to such an extent that it leaves reasonable doubt in your minds as to the commission of the murders charged against these defendants, then you will return a verdict of not guilty.

On the other hand, if you find that the defendants, or either of them, committed the murders and the Commonwealth has satisfied you of such fact beyond reasonable doubt from all the evidence in these cases, including the evidence of an alibi, then you will return a verdict of guilty against both defendants or against such defendants as you may find guilty of such murders.

. . . . . .

I have now finished my charge. My duties are now at an end. I have tried to preside over the trial of these cases in a spirit of absolute fairness and impartiality to both sides. If I have failed in any respect you must not, gentlemen, in any manner fail in yours. I therefore now commit into [2263] your sacred keeping the decision of these cases. You will therefore take them with you into yonder jury room, the silent sanctuary where may the great Dispenser of Justice, wisdom and sound judgment preside over all your deliberations. Reflect long and well so that when you return, your verdict shall stand forth before the world as your judgment of truth and justice. Gentlemen, be just and fear not. Let all the end thou aimest at be thy country's, thy God's, and truth's.

I would like to see counsel just a moment.

[*Conference at bench between Court and counsel.*]

. . . . . .

THE COURT. I said in my charge that a new hammer and spring were put on the Berardelli revolver at the Iver Johnson place. Upon an examination of the record and upon suggestion of counsel for the defendants, I find that I was in error in that statement. The record shows there was only a new hammer put upon the revolver at the Iver Johnson place.

I also find I made this statement, and that was that the Saturday night previous to the murder one Bostock saw a revolver with Berardelli that was similar to the Berardelli revolver. It has been suggested that that is not consistent with the record. I am going to direct your attention to the record on that question; . . . you must be governed by that and not what I said. [2264] . . . [*To the jury*] You may go, gentlemen, until half past two.

AFTERNOON SESSION.   [*2:30* P.M.]

THE COURT. You may poll the jury, please, Mr. Clerk.

[*The jury are polled and both defendants answer "present."*]

THE COURT. Now, as I understand, gentlemen, you have agreed on the exhibits that are to go to the jury room. I want that you should be very careful to see that nothing goes excepting that which has been introduced in evidence and nothing should go excepting after there has been a thorough and careful examination by counsel for both defendants. . . . You may, therefore, gentlemen, now retire to your room with a view of reaching a verdict in these cases.

[*The jury retire from the courtroom.*]

THE COURT. If the Jury should call for a magnifying glass, the one that was used during the trial by counsel and by the jury, the Court in its discretion allows the same to be sent to the jury, over the objection of the defendants. . . .

[*The jury later sent for the magnifying glass, and the Court ordered it sent out, to which counsel for the defendants objected and exception duly noted.*]

EVENING SESSION.   [*7:30* P.M.]

THE COURT. Poll the jury, Mr. Clerk.

[*The jury are polled and both defendants answer "present."*]

THE COURT. If the jury is agreed, you may please take the verdict.

F. THE VERDICT

CLERK WORTHINGTON. Gentlemen of the jury, have you agreed upon your verdict? [2265]

THE FOREMAN. We have.

CLERK WORTHINGTON. Nicola Sacco.

DEFENDANT SACCO. Present.

[*Defendant Sacco stands up.*]

CLERK WORTHINGTON. Hold up your right hand. Mr. Foreman, look upon the prisoner. Prisoner, look upon the Foreman. What say you, Mr. Foreman, is the prisoner at the bar guilty or not guilty?

THE FOREMAN. Guilty.

CLERK WORTHINGTON. Guilty of murder?

THE FOREMAN. Murder.

CLERK WORTHINGTON. In the first degree?

THE FOREMAN. In the first degree.

CLERK WORTHINGTON. Upon each indictment?

THE FOREMAN. Yes, sir.

CLERK WORTHINGTON. Bartolomeo Vanzetti. Hold up your right hand. Look upon the Foreman. Mr. Foreman, look upon the prisoner. What say you, Mr. Foreman, is Bartolomeo guilty or not guilty of murder?

THE FOREMAN. Guilty.

CLERK WORTHINGTON. In the first degree, upon each indictment?

THE FOREMAN. In the first degree.

CLERK WORTHINGTON. Hearken to your verdicts as the Court has recorded them. You, gentlemen, upon your oath, say that Nicola Sacco and Bartolomeo Vanzetti is each guilty of murder in the first degree upon each indictment. So say you, Mr. Foreman? So, gentlemen, you all say?

THE JURY. We do, we do, we do.

THE COURT. [*To the jury*] I can add nothing to what I said this morning, gentlemen, except again to express to you the gratitude of the Commonwealth for the service that you have rendered. You may now go to your homes, from which you have been absent for nearly seven weeks. The Court will now adjourn.

DEFENDANT SACCO. They kill an innocent men. They kill two innocent men. . . .

[*The Court is adjourned.*] [2266]

3

SHOULD THERE BE A NEW TRIAL?

Sources used in this chapter: *The Sacco-Vanzetti Case: Transcript of the Record of the Trial of Nicola Sacco and Bartolomeo Vanzetti in the Courts of Massachusetts and Subsequent Proceedings, 1920-27,* Volumes IV and V; *The Letters of Sacco and Vanzetti,* edited by Marion Denman Frankfurter and Gardner Jackson; *Boston Herald;* and Dearborn (Mich.) *Independent.*

————FROM THE day the verdict of guilty was brought in, until the hour six years later when Sacco and Vanzetti were executed, their lawyers filed eight motions for a new trial—all of which were heard and denied by Judge Thayer. The first of these motions argued that the verdict was against the weight of the evidence. The purpose of each of the seven supplementary motions that followed was not to prove beyond reasonable doubt the innocence of the defendants, but to prove that newly discovered, highly significant evidence existed which, though it would not necessarily overturn the previous verdict, was sufficiently potent to deserve careful consideration in a new trial.

Our attention will be limited to only the most weighty of these: the 1st supplementary motion: the Ripley-Daly motion; the 2nd: the Gould motion; the 5th: the Proctor motion; and the 7th: the Medeiros motion—and the denials of each, first by Judge Thayer, then by the Supreme Judicial Court of Massachusetts to which each of the above motions was appealed.

Judge Thayer denied the first motion on Dec. 24, 1921. He reviewed some of the issues of the case and explained that he had no right to interfere with the verdict unless he could show that the jurors had committed obvious errors in judgment or had acted in bad faith. He wrote in conclusion:————

I cannot—as I must if I disturb these verdicts—announce to the world that these twelve jurors violated the sanctity of their oaths, threw to the four winds of bias and prejudice their honor, judgment, reason, and conscience, and thereby abused the solemn trust reposed in them by the law as well as by the Court. And all for what purpose? To take away the lives of two human beings created by their own God. . . .

If I am in error in my judgment as to the sufficiency of the evidence to warrant a conviction or if I have committed any error at any time that might operate in any manner to the prejudice of either or both of these defendants, the Supreme Judicial Court will make correction in due time; and if that Court shall find such error, nobody will welcome the correction more gladly than will I. But until that time comes, so far as these motions are concerned, the verdicts of the jury must stand. Therefore the motions for new trials in both cases for the reasons herein given are hereby denied.

WEBSTER THAYER,
Justice of the Superior Court. [5563]

————NO ATTEMPT was made to appeal from this decision, but even before this motion was denied, the 1st supplementary motion was filed on Nov. 8, 1921. It dealt with conduct by Walter H. Ripley, foreman of the jury, which the defense claimed was prejudicial to the defendants. Probably the most weighty item in the 1st motion was an affidavit appended to it on Sept. 30, 1923, and signed by William H. Daly, an intimate friend of Ripley's for 38 years. In the affidavit, Daly swore that on May 31, 1921, he met Ripley who was then on his way to serve on the Sacco-Vanzetti jury. Here is Daly's version of their discussion of the case:————

. . . [T]he affiant [Daly] said that he did not believe that they were guilty; that it was not reasonable to suppose that a man would go and rob a factory where he had worked, was well known, and in broad daylight, and thereupon the said Ripley said to the affiant "Damn them, they ought to hang them anyway." [3580]

.   .   .   .   .

————TEN DAYS after this affidavit was signed, Ripley suddenly died. When Judge Thayer denied the Ripley-Daly motion, Oct. 1, 1924, the Daly affidavit was not referred to.

The Gould motion was filed on May 4, 1922. Roy E. Gould, an itinerant peddler of razor sharpening paste, swore in his affidavit that he was following Parmenter and Berardelli up Pearl Street in order to be on hand to sell paste to the men in the factory after they were paid. Before Gould caught up with the paymaster and his guard, the hold-up occurred and the bandit car began its getaway. It passed within ten feet of him, Gould said, and as it did, the bandit next to the driver shot at Gould. The bullet passed through his overcoat without injuring him. As he stood in the street after the shooting, Gould gave his name and address to a policeman, a fact that the defense supported with an affidavit by the policeman. Gould, however, was not interviewed by the police or prosecutor nor asked to testify. In the statement he made for the defense a year after the trial, Gould describes the man who shot at him and compares him to Sacco, swearing that:—

. . . Sacco's eyebrows are not as heavy as the eyebrows of the man that affiant saw in said automobile and that the eyes of Sacco have not the same piercing quality as the eyes of the man that affiant saw, and that Sacco has not as high cheek-bones as the man that affiant saw, and that his features are not as sharp as the features of the man that affiant saw, and that Sacco appears to be older, heavier and broader through the shoulders than the man affiant saw.

That the affiant is flat and unqualified in his statement that the man that he saw at South Braintree on April 15, 1920, at or about the hour of three o'clock in the afternoon riding in the bandit car, front seat, on the right-hand side of the driver, is not the man that he saw in the Dedham County Jail and who was pointed out to him as Nicola Sacco.

That while affiant has not seen Bartolomeo Vanzetti personally, he has seen three distinct photographs of him and that he in no sense resembles the man affiant saw at South Braintree on April 15th, 1920.

This affidavit is made freely and voluntarily and not for any reward received or promised, and affiant is willing to testify as to these facts if the defendants or either of them are given a new trial herein. [3505]

————IN DENYING the Gould motion, Oct. 1, 1924, Judge Thayer again reviewed what he felt were the salient points in the case. He dismissed Gould in short order:————

The affiant never saw Sacco, according to his affidavit, from April 15, 1920, the day of the murder, until November 10, 1921, when he went to Dedham jail at the request of Mr. Moore. In other words, the affiant must have carried a correct mental photograph in his mind of Sacco for practically eighteen months, when he only had a glance in which to take this photograph on the day of the murder.

To set aside a verdict on evidence of this character would be to deprive, in my judgment, the Commonwealth of its rights without reason or justification. [3513]

In the first place, this evidence only means the addition of one more eye witness to the passing of the bandit automobile. This, therefore, would simply mean one more piece of evidence of the same kind and directed to the same end, and in my judgment, would have no effect whatever upon the verdicts. For these verdicts did not rest, in my judgment, upon the testimony of the eye witnesses; for the defendants, as it was, called more witnesses than the Commonwealth who testified that neither of the defendants were in the bandit car.

The evidence that convicted these defendants was circumstantial and was evidence that is known in law as "consciousness of guilt." This evidence, corroborated as it was by the eye witnesses, was responsible for these verdicts of guilty. The supreme judicial court has said that the trial judge in passing judgment on motions for new trials should take into consideration "the strength or weakness of the evidence upon which the verdicts were returned." On this account I have again reviewed and considered the evidence with great care and solicitude. [3514]

————IN HIS review of the evidence, Judge Thayer emphasized the testimony of the officers who arrested Sacco and Vanzetti:————

The two police officers who arrested the defendants on the electric car that runs from West Bridgewater to Brockton on the night of May 5th gave testimony that tended to prove that Vanzetti reached for his hip pocket, and one of the officers testified that he said to him, "Keep your hands on your lap or you will get into trouble"; . . . Sacco reached his hand to put under his overcoat and he (the officer) told him to keep his hands outside of his clothes and on his lap; . . . [3518]

.   .   .   .   .   .

Both of the defendants denied this testimony of the officers *in toto*, but that denial did not settle this question, for the jury had a right to believe the officers and if they did, then this evidence is entitled to great weight and consideration. It cannot be brushed aside by the mere wave of the hand, for the jury had a right to determine the reason why these defendants carried upon the night in question loaded guns, and they also had a right to determine that radicalism had nothing to do with their carrying these guns and that radicalism had nothing to do with their attempt to use these guns upon the officers. The defendants have made no claim to that effect, because it is their claim that there was no such attempt on their part. I have referred to it for the purpose of showing that the jury had a right to eliminate radicalism as a reason for either carrying the loaded guns as well as their attempted use of them upon the officers.

.   .   .   .   .   .

In the determination of this motion, or any other in which new trials have been denied, if I have erred in my judgment (and I fully realize that I am human), let me express the assurance that the supreme judicial court of this Commonwealth in due time will correct such error. Therefore, for the reasons herein given, and others not herein specifically mentioned, the motion of the defendants for a new trial, based upon the Gould affidavit, should be and the same is herein and hereby denied.

WEBSTER THAYER,
Justice of the Superior Court. [3527]

————IN HIS charge to the jury, Judge Thayer stated that Captain Proctor of the State Police had testified "to the effect" that bullet III, "which had killed Berardelli, was fired through the barrel of the Colt automatic pistol found upon the defendant Sacco at the time of his arrest." [2254] Part of the 5th supplementary motion for a new trial was an affidavit obtained in October 1923 by William G. Thompson, an eminent and conservative member of the Massachusetts bar who in 1924 became the chief counsel for both defendants upon the withdrawal from the case of Moore and the McAnarney brothers.————

Affidavit of William H. Proctor [3641]

. . . . .

I was associated with the prosecution of the defendants in the case, and I had in my custody for a considerable time the Colt automatic pistol taken from the defendant Sacco at the time of his arrest. . . .

. . . . .

I also had in my custody and made examination of from time to time, with great care, the bullets said to have been taken from the body of Berardelli, all except one of which were, as I testified at the trial, fired from a pistol which was not a Colt automatic pistol. One of them was, as I then testified and still believe, fired from a Colt automatic pistol of .32 calibre.

During the preparation for the trial, my attention was repeatedly called by the District Attorney and his assistants to the question: whether I could find any evidence which would justify the opinion that the particular bullet taken from the body of Berardelli, which came from a Colt automatic pistol, came from the particular Colt automatic pistol taken from Sacco. I used every means available to me for forming an opinion on this subject. I conducted, with Captain Van Amburgh, certain tests at Lowell, about which I testified, consisting in firing certain cartridges through Sacco's pistol. At no time was I able to find any evidence whatever which tended to convince me that the particular model bullet found in Berardelli's body, which came from a Colt automatic pistol, which I think was numbered III and had some other exhibit number, came from Sacco's pistol and I so informed the District Attorney and his assistant before the trial. This bullet was what is commonly called a full metalpatch bullet and although I repeatedly talked over with Captain Van Amburgh the scratch or scratches which he claimed tended to identify this bullet as one that must have gone through Sacco's pistol, his statements concerning the identifying marks seemed to me entirely unconvincing.

At the trial, the District Attorney did not ask me whether I had found any evidence that the so-called mortal bullet which I have referred to as number III passed through Sacco's pistol, nor was I asked that question on cross-examination. The District Attorney desired to ask me that question, but I had repeatedly told him that if he did I should be obliged to answer in the negative; consequently, he put to me this question: Q. Have you an opinion as to whether bullet number III was fired from the Colt automatic which is in evidence? To which I answered, "I have." He then proceeded. Q. And what is your opinion? A. My opinion is that it is consistent with being fired by that pistol.

That is still my opinion for the reason that bullet number III, in my judgment, passed through some Colt automatic pistol, but I do not intend by that answer to imply that I had found any evidence that the so-called mortal bullet had passed through this particular Colt automatic pistol, and the District Attorney well knew that I did not so intend and framed his [3642] question accordingly. Had I been asked the direct question: whether I had found any affirmative evidence whatever that this so-called mortal bullet had passed through this particular Sacco's pistol, I should have answered then, as I do now without hesitation, in the negative.

WILLIAM H. PROCTOR [3643]

————MR. KATZMANN offered an affidavit in reply:————

I, Frederick G. Katzmann, being first duly sworn, on oath, depose and say, that I have read the affidavit of Capt. William H. Proctor dated October 20, 1923; . . . that prior to his testifying, Captain Proctor told me that he was prepared to testify that the mortal bullet was consistent with having been fired from the Sacco pistol; that I did not repeatedly ask him whether he had found any evidence that the mortal bullet had passed through the Sacco pistol, nor did he repeatedly tell me that if I did ask him that question he would be obliged to reply in the negative.

FREDERICK G. KATZMANN
Dedham, Mass., Oct. 31, 1923. [3681]

————MR. WILLIAMS gave a more detailed account in his affidavit:——

[*Oct. 30, 1923*]

I first met Captain William H. Proctor during the trial of these cases at Dedham. . . . I asked him if he could tell in what pistol this so-called mortal bullet was fired, and he said that he could not although the marks upon it were consistent with its having been fired in the Sacco pistol. He said that all he could do was to determine the width of the landmarks upon the bullet. His attention was not repeatedly called to the question, whether he could find any evidence which would justify the opinion that this bullet came from the Sacco pistol. I conducted the direct examination of Captain Proctor at the trial and asked him the question quoted in his affidavit, "Have you an opinion as to whether bullet number III was fired from the Colt automatic which is in evidence?"

This question was suggested by Captain Proctor himself as best calculated to give him an opportunity to tell what opinion he had respecting the mortal bullet and its connection with the Sacco pistol. His answer in court was the same answer he had given me personally before.

HAROLD P. WILLIAMS [3682]

————ON OCT. 1, 1924, Judge Thayer denied the Proctor motion:——

MOTION FOR NEW TRIAL

DECISION ON AFFIDAVIT OF WILLIAM H. PROCTOR

The Proctor affidavit, upon which a motion for a new trial is based, is a most unusual one. This is so because the then District Attorney of Norfolk County is charged with unprofessional conduct, in that he "framed" certain questions with a view of obtaining testimony from Captain Proctor that he (the District Attorney) knew was not true and which was prejudicial or might be prejudicial to the defendants.

. . . . . .

Now, let us examine the questions and answers carefully, to see if the charges made are consistent with the facts:

Questions and Answers

Q. [*By Mr. Williams*] Have you an opinion as to whether bullet number III was fired from the Colt automatic which is in evidence?

MR. McANARNEY. Will you please repeat that question?

The question was repeated as follows:

Q. Have you an opinion as to whether bullet number III was fired from the Colt automatic which is in evidence? *A.* I have.

Q. What is your opinion? *A.* My opinion is that it is consistent with being fired from that pistol.

In my judgment, the questions propounded by Mr. Williams were clearly put, fairly expressed, and easily understood; they have been so commonly used by experienced trial lawyers throughout the Commonwealth for so many years that they have become almost stereotyped questions. It cannot be said that Captain Proctor did not have time to fully understand and appreciate the full meaning of the questions propounded to him, because the first one was put twice to him before he answered.

Let us now carefully consider the questions and answers by applying to them the usual tests of ascertaining facts. Were any of these questions "framed" by Mr. Williams on account of any unworthy or improper motive? Study the fairness of the questions propounded by Mr. Williams, with the view of determining whether or not Captain Proctor did not have the fullest opportunity to express his honest opinion. Is there any hidden mystery or unworthy concealed motive in the first question, which is as follows: "Have you an opinion as to whether bullet number III was fired from the Colt automatic which is in evidence?" Bullet No. III was the mortal bullet, and the only Colt automatic which was in evidence was the Sacco pistol.

Is there anything about that question that any man who has been a member of the State Police for over thirty years could not easily and [3699] readily understand, if he was then in full possession of his mental faculties and was desirous of expressing his true opinion? Was there any power under the sun that could have prevented him from expressing his honest conviction at that time?

Now, what was his answer to the question which was as follows:

"Have you an opinion as to whether bullet number III was fired from the Colt automatic which is in evidence?" His answer was: "I have." So now it is absolutely certain that Captain Proctor had then formed an opinion on that question.

Now, let us consider the next question, which was as follows: "And what is your opinion?" Is there anything unfair or improper in that question? By that question, did not Mr. Williams invite Captain Proctor to state his true opinion at that time?

In the first place, let us inquire what was Captain Proctor's answer to that question. It was as follows: "*A*. My opinion is that it is consistent with being fired through *that pistol*." Certainly there is no ambiguity, doubt, or uncertainty in that answer.

Captain Proctor now says that had he been asked if he found any affirmative evidence that the mortal bullet passed through the Sacco pistol, he would have answered then "as I do now, without hesitation, in the negative." As I said before, it is not a question of how he would answer at the time he signed the affidavit, but what did he in fact and' truth answer at the trial, and what did he then mean.

My next inquiry is this: To test the accuracy of the statement of Captain Proctor, let me make the inquiry: When Mr. Williams asked him for his opinion, in reply to the question whether the bullet number III (the mortal bullet) was fired from the Colt automatic in evidence, why did he not answer that it was his opinion that the mortal bullet did not pass through the Sacco pistol? For no witness who ever went upon the witness stand had a better opportunity to express his true opinion than did Captain Proctor at that time.

Again, if Captain Proctor found no facts in his examination that would warrant the opinion that the mortal bullet did pass through the Sacco pistol, if he was then desirous of expressing his true opinion, why did he then use the expression that it was "consistent with it." The word "consistent" was selected by Captain Proctor and not by Mr. Williams.

Again, I ask, if Captain Proctor found no facts that caused him to believe that the mortal bullet passed through the Sacco pistol, why, when he had a perfect opportunity so to do, did he not say that his opinion was then, as it is now, that it was not *consistent* with it? Can it be possible that Captain Proctor's mental condition was in such a state at the time of trial that the words "consistent with" and "inconsistent with" had the same meaning to him?

In other words, it must be too plain for discussion that one cannot very well have an opinion that it was consistent with the mortal bullet having passed through the Sacco pistol and at the same time be inconsistent with it. [3700]

Again I am asked to believe that when Captain Proctor testified in court to the effect that when he said it was consistent with being fired through the Sacco pistol, he intended to mean that it might have been fired through any .32 calibre Colt automatic, and that was all.

Now, let us throw the searchlight of careful investigation on that statement. If it is true, why after searching through his vocabulary of expressions did he select, of his own volition, the words "that pistol"? For, it must be remembered that the only pistol at that time that he had been offered in evidence was the Sacco pistol; therefore, I must find that the use of those words "that pistol" can apply to only *one pistol*, and *that pistol* was Sacco's pistol.

Now, let us proceed further with this inquiry, with the further object of ascertaining what was then the real situation. Counsel for the motion, with great earnestness and force, argued that the true interpretation of this affidavit is as follows: that the District Attorney, knowing that Captain Proctor honestly believed that the mortal bullet was not fired through the Sacco pistol, by prearrangement with Captain Proctor prevailed on him to compromise the truth, in that Captain Proctor should testify that it was his opinion that it was consistent with its having been fired through the Sacco pistol. In other words, that Captain Proctor, by prearrangement (which means intentional) compromised the truth with the District Attorney by his (Captain Proctor's) testifying knowingly to something that was false.

I do not believe that the interpretation of counsel for the motion is the true one. Neither do I believe that Captain Proctor would like this interpretation, for if it is true it places him in the very unfortunate position of testifying intentionally to something that was false. Knowing Captain Proctor as I do, I do not take any stock whatsoever in this interpretation; neither do I think that Captain Proctor would like to either. If I did, I feel that I would be doing a tremendous injustice to him, and this, under no circumstances, will I do. I have referred to this matter for the purpose of showing its absurdity and the length to which counsel, in their over-enthusiasm during heated discussion, will sometimes go; for this conclusion, like all other conclusions, becomes illogical, unreasonable, and unsound when not constructed on the solid foundation of established facts and truth.

Now, let us see what Captain Proctor did intend to say when he testified, and what was the probative effect of his testimony. Captain Proctor was not at the time of trial a most impressive witness. . . .

[3701] With his limited knowledge, Captain Proctor did not testify that the mortal bullet did pass through Sacco's pistol, but that from his examination of the facts it was simply consistent with it.

Now, what did *his* examination reveal? He satisfied himself from his investigation so that he testified positively that the mortal bullet passed through a .32 calibre Colt automatic pistol. This was one step toward establishing the identity of the bullet that passed through the Sacco pistol, and it was a very important one. . . . This is a long way from saying that it was his opinion that in fact it did pass through the Sacco pistol.

Now, let us ascertain how counsel on both sides interpreted this opinion of Captain Proctor now under consideration. I have taken the pains to examine the record. I found that counsel for defendants, in cross examination of Captain Proctor, were so well satisfied with its lack of probative weight, that he was not asked a single question as to the passing of the mortal bullet through the Sacco pistol. . . .

Again, although it was claimed in argument by counsel for the defendants that the District Attorney fraudulently "framed" a question to Captain Proctor because of his standing at the head of the State Police, yet the record shows a clear refutation of the imputation because it shows that the District Attorney himself, regarding Captain Proctor's testimony as of little weight, did not, in his final argument which consumed nearly four hours, once call Captain Proctor by name.

Again, it was argued that the court understood that Captain Proctor testified to the effect that the mortal bullet was fired through the Sacco pistol. This is another interpretation of counsel that I do not agree with. Of course, the Court referred to this matter in the following language: "to this effect, the Commonwealth introduced the testimony of two experts, Messrs. Proctor and Van Amburgh; on the other hand, the defendants offered the testimony of two experts, Messrs. Burns and Fitzgerald; to the effect that the Sacco pistol did not fire the bullet that caused the death of Berardelli."

It is not the duty of the Court, in charging a jury, to deal with the weight and probative effect of testimony of witnesses. The statute expressly forbids the Court so to do. And, furthermore, it was clearly the duty of the Court to say, referring to the testimony of Captain Proctor, that there [3702] was some testimony notwithstanding its frailty that tended to prove this fact in question, for Captain Proctor did testify that some Colt .32 calibre automatic fired the fatal bullet. Again, he testified at least to one measurement that corroborated the testimony of Captain Van Amburgh, who testified that he was of the opinion the fatal bullet was fired through the Sacco pistol. From these facts Captain Proctor testified that he was of the opinion the fatal bullet was fired through the Sacco pistol. From these facts Captain Proctor testified that it was his opinion that it was consistent with it. Therefore, it was a mere statement to the jury of the testimony of Captain Proctor that tended to prove a certain proposition; but, so far as proving it is concerned, that was clearly within the province of the jury.

FINDING OF FACTS

I sincerely hope that I have not dealt unkindly or unfairly in what I have said concerning this affidavit. I fully appreciate the fact that age had left its heavy burden upon this man's shoulders, after a great many years of honorable service to the Commonwealth. But it must be remembered that it was his affidavit that has made it very distasteful and unpleasant to me in determining the merits of this motion. For it must also be remembered that it was he who charged the District Attorney, Mr. Katzmann, and his then assistant, Mr. Harold P. Williams, with misconduct in their respective offices, which misconduct assailed their honor, their integrity, and their solemn obligation that they were then under to the Commonwealth, to the defendants and to the Court; for it must ever be borne in mind that their honor, reputation and high standing at the bar were dear and precious to them. . . . [T]hey have a perfect right to ask that their accuser shall furnish evidence against them that is clear, satisfactory, and convincing. Metaphysical argument and illogical conclusions based thereon by skilful counsel should never prevail against pure logic that is based upon established facts.

. . . . .

COUNTER-AFFIDAVITS

With my findings of facts, it is unnecessary for me to state at length and in detail the contents of the counter-affidavits of Messrs. Katzmann and Williams,—they are clear and convincing. I cannot, however, close this phase of the matter without saying that I carefully watched the conduct of both Messrs. Katzmann and Williams in the trial of these cases [3703] for nearly seven weeks, and I never observed anything on their part but what was consistent with the highest standard of professional conduct.

Decision

For the reasons hereinbefore given and others not herein specifically mentioned, I find that the defendants have not established, by a fair preponderance of the evidence, any of the material allegations in the so-called Proctor affidavits which would warrant me in granting a new trial. Therefore, exercising every authority vested in me by law that relates to the granting of motions for new trials, I decline to grant this motion for a new trial on the Proctor affidavit, and the same is herein and hereby denied.

WEBSTER THAYER,
Justice of the Superior Court. [3704]

————DURING their seven years in jail, Sacco and Vanzetti wrote many letters, a number of which were published in *The Letters of Sacco and Vanzetti*. The editors of these letters did not correct any errors in spelling or grammar. It should also be noted that the author's name is not given at the end of most of these letters. The two letters below were written by Sacco to Mrs. Cerise Jack of Sharon, Mass., who gave Sacco English lessons during the winter of 1923-24.[1]————

December 6, 1923. Dedham Jail

MY DEAR MRS. JACK:

I can not the scritto in my poor English the joyful that is manifest in a soul of the reclus when he receivid a visit from e friend who he believe in her or in him to find the sincere brotherly affection. To say Mrs. Jack that I was very how glad to see you last night.

Dante, Mrs. Jack, hi is always in my heart and hi always my dear and lovely boy; many a time I did believe that hi will ben promising boy yes because hi alwas was my dear comradship and I could read in [11] is brite eyes and tru of his little intelligent head the better day. I remember when wi youst live in South Stoughton Mass in our little sweet home and frequently in evening Rosina,[2] Dante and I, we youst go see a frend about a fifteen minute wolk from my house and bey away going to the my friend house hi always surpriset me bey aske me a such heard question that some time it was impesseble for me to explain. So wi youst remain there a few hour and when was about nine ten o'clock we youst going back home and Dante in that time of

---

[1] From *The Letters of Sacco and Vanzetti*, edited by Marion Denman Frankfurter and Gardner Jackson, copyright 1928, 1956 by the Viking Press, Inc., New York.

[2] Rosina is Mrs. Sacco.

hour hi was always sleeping, so I youst bring him always in my arm away to home; some time Rosina she youst halp me to carry him and in that same time she youst get Dante in her arm both us we youst give him a warm kisses on is rosy face. Those day Mrs. Jack they was a some happy day. . . . [12]

March 15, 1924. *Dedham Jail*

MY DEAR FRIEND MRS. JACK:

Wednesday night I went to sleep with idea to write you at first thing in morning but when I was into bed I begen to turn this way an the other way and I was try my best to sleep. So after while I fall sleep, enddid I do not know how long I been sleep when I was up again with a terrible dream . . . terrible I said yes, but beauty at same time, and here way it is. The dream it was develope in one place in mine camp of Pennsylvania state, and here it was a big large number of laborers in strike for better wages and the masses of workers they was impatient tired of long waiting, because the bos who own the col mine there threw out of the house a big number people, of poor mother and child and for the moment they were living under the tent in one concentration camp. But here the poor mother they was not pacific yet, because they know that they would soon send the soldiers to chase the mother out of the camp. [18]

And so the big masse of the workers they was in complete revolt from the cruelty the bos of the mine. In this camp they were two or three speakers and every one of them was used a kind and warm word for the freedom of the people. While the immensity of the work masses they were applauding the speakers, the soldiers comes with bayonet gun for chase the crowd, but after word they find out they was wrong because every one of the strikers they stand still like one man. And so the fight it was beginning, and while the fight was begin I jump upon a little hill in meddle of the crowd and I begin to say, Friend and comrade and brotherhood, not one of us is going to move a step, and who will try to move it will be vile and coward, here the fight is to go to finish. So I turn over towards the soldiers and I said, Brothers you will not fire on your own brothers just because they tell you to fire, no brothers, remember that everyone of us we have mother and child, and you know that we fight for freedom which is your freedom. We want one fatherland, one sole, one house, and better bread. So while I was finish to say that last word one of the soldiers fire towards me and the ball past through my heart, and while I was fall on ground with my right hand close to my heart I awake up with sweet dream!

So when I was awake I had my right hand still tightly upon my heart
like if it was hold back the speed of the beating of my heart. . . . [19]

————AFTER the first five motions had been denied by Judge Thayer,
Mr. Thompson appealed to the Supreme Judicial Court of Massachusetts. Unlike some courts of review, such as the New York Court of
Appeals or the English Court of Criminal Appeal, the Massachusetts
court did not have the power to review the evidence and to decide
whether the jury, as reasonable men, should have voted for conviction. Instead of retrying the guilt or innocence of the defendants, the
Massachusetts court reviewed the conduct of the trial judge; it dealt
with such questions of law as errors arising from wrongful admission
of evidence and technical errors in the judge's charge.

On May 12, 1926, the five justices of the Supreme Judicial Court
rendered their opinion on the appeal for a new trial. In effect, this
35,000 word decision found that Judge Thayer had conducted the
trial with discretion and without raising any questions of law that
could be disputed by the upper court.

Of the Daly affidavit the court ruled:————————————————

. . . [B]efore being sworn as a juror, it must be assumed that
Ripley had answered in the negative the statutory questions put by
the judge in his preliminary examination, whether he had expressed
or formed an opinion, or was sensible of any bias or prejudice. [4350]

————IN respect to the Proctor motion the court held:————————

The credibility of the affiant Proctor . . . was for the judge, who,
among other things, expressly found that neither the district attorney
nor his assistant intentionally solicited an ambiguous answer to the
questions under consideration for the purpose of obtaining a conviction. The burden was on the defendants to establish wilful misconduct
of the prosecuting officers by a fair preponderance of the evidence
and the conclusion of the judge that this burden had not been sustained cannot as matter of law be set aside by us. . . . [4357]

————THE COURT held that Judge Thayer's denial of the Gould motion was entirely within his discretion and raised no question of law.

While these appeals were pending, Sacco was confined to the Dedham jail. Celestino Medeiros, (sometimes spelled "Madeiros") a young
Portuguese hoodlum, was confined to the same jail while his lawyers
appealed his conviction for a holdup murder. On November 18, 1925,
Medeiros gave a jail runner a copy of a magazine with the request that

it be delivered to Sacco. In the magazine Sacco discovered the following note: "I hear by confess to being in the south Braintree shoe company crime and Sacco and Vanzetti was not in said crime."

The defense hurried into action obtaining affidavits from Medeiros and the underworld figures whom he implicated in the South Braintree holdup. The Medeiros motion was placed before Judge Thayer on May 26, 1926. Medeiros' affidavit gives his recollection of the holdup:

On April 15, 1920, I was picked up at about 4 A.M. at my boarding house, 181 North Main Street, Providence, by four Italians who came in a Hudson 5-passenger open touring car.

. . . . .

We went from Providence to Randolph, where we changed to a Buick car brought there by another Italian. We left the Hudson car in the woods and took it again after we did the job, leaving the Buick in the woods in charge of one man, who drove it off to another part of the woods, as I understood.

After we did the job at South Braintree and changed back into the Hudson car at Randolph, we drove very fast through Randolph, and were seen by a boy named Thomas and his sister. His father lives on a street that I think is called Oak Street, and is in the window metal business or something of that kind. I became acquainted with him four years later when I went to live in Randolph with Weeks on the same street. Thomas told me one day in conversation that he saw the car that did the South Braintree job going through Randolph very fast.

When we started we went from Providence first to Boston and then back to Providence, and then back to South Braintree, getting there about noon. We spent some time in a "speakeasy" in South Braintree two or three miles from the place of the crime, leaving the car in the yard of the house. When we went to Boston we went to South Boston and stopped in Andrews Square. I stayed in the car. The others went into a saloon to get information, as they told me, about the money that was to be sent to South Braintree.

I had never been to South Braintree before. These four men persuaded me to go with them two or three nights before when I was talking with them in a saloon in Providence. The saloon was also a pool-room near my boarding house. They talked like professionals. They said they had done lots of jobs of this kind. They had been engaged in robbing freight cars in Providence. Two were young men from 20 to 25 years old, one was about 40, the other about 35. All wore caps. I was then 18 years old. I do not remember whether they were shaved or not. Two of them did the shooting—the oldest one and another. They were left on the street. The arrangement was that they should meet me in a Providence saloon the next night to divide the money. I went there but they did not come.

I sat on the back seat of the automobile. I had a Colt .38 calibre auto- [4417] matic but did not use it. I was told that I was there to help hold back the crowd in case they made a rush. The curtains on the car were flapping. I do not remember whether there was any shotgun or rifle in the car or not.

These men talked a lot about New York. As soon as I got enough money I went to New York and also to Chicago hoping to find them in cabarets spending the money, but I never found them.

They had been stealing silk, shoes, cotton, etc., from freight cars and sending it to New York. Two of them lived on South Main Street and two on North Main Street, in lodging houses. I had known them three or four months. The old man was called Mike. Another one was called Williams or Bill. I don't remember what the others were called.

The money that they took from the men in South Braintree was in a black bag, I think.

I was scared to death when I heard the shooting begin.

Both cars had Massachusetts numbers.

The names of these men don't amount to anything. They change them whenever they want to. When they are driven out of New York they come to Providence. I haven't any idea where they are now. I have never seen any of them since.

Sacco and Vanzetti had nothing to do with this job. . . . It was entirely put up by the oldest of the Italians in Providence.

I read this statement and it is true.

CELESTINO F. MEDEIROS

I know the last names of the gang but I refuse to tell who they are.

CELESTINO F. MEDEIROS [4418]

Affidavit of James F. Weeks

My name is James F. Weeks. I am making this affidavit in the State Prison at Charlestown, to which I have been sentenced for life for murder in the second degree in connection with the attempted robbery of the Wrentham National Bank.

I have known Celestino Medeiros for about six years. I and a man named Bedard, who is also serving a sentence of life imprisonment in the State Prison, were associated with Medeiros in the attempted robbery of the Wrentham National Bank. The Wrentham Bank crime occurred [4400] on a day in the first week in November, 1924; I think it was November 1. It was on a Saturday. Shortly before this crime Medeiros and I were in a bar-room or "speakeasy" at the corner of Southampton Street and Dorchester Avenue in Andrews Square, South Boston, for the purpose of arranging some of the details, and Medeiros remarked to me that it was strange that he should be in this very same bar-room that he had visited four years before when he was in the South Braintree job. At that time he also told me that he and the gang that were with him in the South Braintree job came to this saloon early in the morning from Providence, R.I., to get information about the payroll that they were going to rob. He did not tell me the name of the man in the saloon that gave the information, or where the tip came from.

One night in the summer of 1924 I was at the Bluebird Inn in Seekonk, Mass., which was run by a man named Barney Monterio and a woman named Mary Boice. It was a roadhouse and a disorderly house. A girl named Tessie had recently been brought there, and a gang drove up in a motor car, consisting of a man known as Bibber Barone and some others. Medeiros was employed there at that time as a bouncer. Bibber Barone demanded the girl, saying that she was his. Medeiros stood on the porch and Barone was on the grass in front, and Medeiros told Barone that he and his gang had double-crossed him once on a job, and that he might forgive them for that, but if they took the girl he would bump them all, and that it would be sure death. They left, as they knew that Medeiros was handy with his gun.

Medeiros often told me about the South Braintree job. He said that it was arranged by the Joe Morell gang. The members of the gang as Medeiros mentioned them to me, and I knew independently, were the following: the Morell or Morelli brothers, namely, Michael (commonly called Mike), Joseph (commonly called Joe), Patsy (whose real name was Pasquale), Fred (commonly called Butsy), and Frank. There was also a man commonly called Bill. Whether he was one of the Morell brothers, or whether Bill was another name for Bibber Barone, I do not know. I know that Bibber Barone was a member of the gang, and Medeiros has also mentioned his name several times to me. Medeiros often told me that this entire gang was a gang of thieves, and I know it myself. Their headquarters were Providence, and they did most of their stealing in Providence, shipping the goods to New

York, but sometimes they were in New York themselves. Medeiros told me that Joe was the boss of the gang. [4401]

Medeiros told me that at one time several years before the South Braintree job a man called Gyp the Blood was a member of the gang. . . .

Medeiros gave me the names of at least four of the gang who were in the South Braintree job. I am quite sure that the names he gave me were Mike, Joe, Bill, and Butsy. I have an impression that he also mentioned Frank, but I am not sure of that. I think he did not mention the name of Patsy as being in that job.

Medeiros also told me that some of these Morells had been arrested some months before the South Braintree job for stealing from freight cars in Providence, but were out on bail.

When we were talking about what cars we should use in the Wrentham Bank job he told me that he wanted a Hudson car to get away with and did not want a Buick; that he had had enough of the Buick in the South Braintree job. In preparation for the Wrentham job we had stolen a Buick car in Pawtucket, and we afterwards stole a Hudson open car in Pawtucket. . . .

Medeiros told me that a Hudson car was used in the South Braintree job as well as a Buick. He said that after the South Braintree job Joe Morell had promised to give him his share of the job, but that he had double-crossed him, and he (Medeiros) never got a cent out of it, and that he tried for a long time to find Morell to get his share.

Medeiros lived with me for a time at Randolph. I lived on a road leading off Oak Street, called Cedar Road; and Medeiros has told me several times that as they went along Oak Street after the South Braintree job they went so fast that he couldn't have noticed my side street, called Cedar Road. Cedar Road is a little beyond the house of Thomas Driver. I know that Medeiros came to know young Thomas Driver later.

I know Joe Morell myself. I helped him once steal a load of whiskey out of a warehouse on Smith Hill, Providence, and after the job was over he told me that it was vinegar and wouldn't give me anything. [4402]

. . . . .

Joe and his gang worked on tips. Who gave them the tip for the South Braintree job I never heard.

I think that Bibber Barone was convicted of freight car robberies. I also think that some years ago Gyp the Blood served in the Rhode Island State Prison at Cranston, and that Barone was sent to Atlanta.

Mike and Frank Morell followed the races and bet on them and on baseball games, and always had plenty of money. . . .

In October, 1924, Medeiros shot a woman in the North End of Boston. He had lived with her in Providence on Wickendon Street near Fox Point, I think.

Medeiros often talked with me about the Sacco and Vanzetti case. He said, "Those men have plenty of money to get out with"; but he also said that if they ever got convicted, he would come to the front before he would see them go to the chair.

I have made this statement to Mr. Thompson voluntarily, and upon the advice of the Deputy Warden to tell the truth. I know that Sacco and Vanzetti had nothing whatever to do with the South Braintree payroll robbery. It is well known and has long been well known among a certain crowd who did that job. Before I made this statement I was informed and believed that Medeiros had handed to Sacco in the Dedham Jail a paper confessing that he was in the South Braintree job. . . .

JAMES F. WEEKS [4403]

————JUDGE THAYER'S denial of the Medeiros motion was based chiefly on his low opinion of Medeiros' credibility. He said of him:——

Madeiros is, without doubt, a crook, a thief, a robber, a liar, a rum-runner, a "bouncer" in a house of ill-fame, a smuggler, and a man who has been convicted and sentenced to death for the murder of one Carpenter, who was cashier of the Wrentham Bank. An affidavit from a man of this type must be examined and scrutinized with the greatest pos- [4726] sible care, caution, and judgment before the verdict of a jury approved by the Supreme Judicial Court of this Commonwealth is set aside. [4727]

.   .   .   .   .

If Madeiros' statement of fear is true, why did the Morelli Gang desire to take a timid young man with them, on a fully-planned and intentional murder job? For the evidence conclusively established the fact that the deceased were shot down at sight and were not given even a chance. This Morelli Gang was a gang of thieves and bootleggers, of mature years and large experience in crime. There were in their gang eight or nine, which would seem to be a sufficient number without calling upon a timid young man whom they had known but a short time, to go with them on an intentional murder job. Joe Morelli and others of the Morelli Gang, who have signed affidavits, have affirmed that they never knew Madeiros in their lives. Even though they are criminals, there would seem to be a semblance of truth to be attached to their statements, because there is no affidavit from any police officer or anybody else whose word would be considered reliable who affirmed that they ever saw with their own eyes Madeiros in the company of any of the Morelli Gang. [4739]

. . . . . .

. . . As far as this Court is concerned, the only question involved is, whether or not the verdicts of the jury, that have been affirmed by the Supreme Judicial Court of this Commonwealth, should be set aside on the Confession of Madeiros. . . . But this Court, if his natural feelings of humanity were stretched to the limit, cannot find as a fact that Madeiros told the truth. This being so, his duty is unmistakeably plain. Therefore, this Court, exercising every authority vested in it by the law of this Commonwealth in the granting of motions for new trials on newly-discovered evidence, denies these motions for new trials that are based upon the Confession of Madeiros and all other affidavits filed in connection therewith. . . .

WEBSTER THAYER,
October 22nd, 1926.   *Justice of the Superior Court.* [4777]

———THE EDITORIAL below, which appeared in the *Boston Herald* on Oct. 26, 1926, won its author, F. Lauriston Bullard, a Pulitzer Prize.

WE SUBMIT—

In our opinion Nicola Sacco and Bartolomeo Vanzetti ought not to be executed on the warrant of the verdict returned by a jury on July 14, 1921. We do not know whether these men are guilty or not. We have no sympathy with the half-baked views which they profess. But as months have merged into years and the great debate over this case has continued, our doubts have solidified slowly into convictions, and reluctantly we have found ourselves compelled to reverse our original judgment. We hope the supreme judicial court will grant a new trial on the basis of the new evidence not yet examined in open court. We hope the Governor will grant another reprieve to Celestino Madeiros so that his confession may be canvassed in open court. We hope, in case our supreme bench finds itself unable legally to authorize a new trial, that our Governor will call to his aid a commission of disinterested men of the highest intelligence and character to make an independent investigation in his behalf, and that the Governor himself at first hand will participate in that examination, if, as a last resort, it shall be undertaken.

We have read the full decision in which Judge Webster Thayer, who presided at the original trial, renders his decision against the application for a new trial, and we submit that it carries the tone of the advocate rather than the arbitrator. At the outset he refers to "the verdict of a jury approved by the supreme court of this commonwealth" and later he repeats that sentence. We respectfully submit that the supreme court never approved that verdict. What the court did is stated in its own words thus: "We have examined carefully all the exceptions in so far as argued, and finding no error the verdicts are to stand." The supreme court did not vindicate the verdict. The court certified that, whether the verdict was right or wrong, the trial judge performed his duty under the law in a legal manner. The supreme court overruled a bill of exceptions but expressed no judgment whatever as to the validity of the verdict or the guilt of the defendants. Judge Thayer knows this, yet allows himself to refer to the verdict as "approved by the supreme court."

.   .   .   .   .

Now as to Madeiros: A criminal with a bad record, true, and under sentence of death. But the government relied in part on one of his confessions to convict him of a murder. His evidence was accepted against himself when his own life was at stake. His evidence now is offered in behalf of two other men whose lives also are at stake. We submit that Madeiros should be placed on the stand in open court, facing a jury and a judge, and subjected to examination and cross-examination. He may be lying, but the criterion here is not what a judge may think about it but what a jury might think about it. The question is—Would the new evidence be a real factor with a jury in reaching a decision?

We submit that doubt is cast on the verdict of the jury by the important affidavit made after the trial by Capt. W. H. Proctor of the state police. On the stand, testifying as an expert, his evidence was understood by the jury and the judge to be that the fatal bullet issued from Sacco's pistol. Careful examination of the record discloses curious facts. Capt. Proctor did not here reply to direct questions. His affidavit states what the record implies, that a device was fixed up in advance for dodging direct answer to a direct question. His replies were understood to mean that he believed the bullet came from that weapon. He allowed that impression to go abroad. But his affidavit contradicts that testimony. Now when the supreme court dealt with that point it expressed no opinion as to whether or not an "ambiguous answer" had been arranged to "obtain a conviction." The court ruled only that the trial judge had decided that no such prearrangement had been made, and that the supreme court could not "as matter of law" set aside the ruling of the trial judge.

For these and other reasons we hope that the resources of our laws will prove adequate to obtain a new trial. Let it be remembered that the new trial is asked for on the basis of evidence never before the supreme court previously. The court has ruled on exceptions to the old trial, never on all evidence for a new one. If on a new trial the defendants shall again be found guilty, we shall be infinitely better off than if we proceed to execution on the basis of the trial already held; the shadow of doubt, which abides in the minds of large numbers of patient investigators of this whole case, will have been removed. And if on second trial Sacco and Vanzetti should be declared guiltless, everybody would rejoice that no monstrous injustice shall have been done. We submit these views with no reference whatever to the personality of the defendants, and without allusion now to that atmosphere of radicalism of which we heard so much in 1921. [12]

————MUCH MORE than Sacco, Vanzetti used the leisure time in prison to read and write. His writing included fiction, autobiography, and translation, as well as numerous articles and letters. The following two letters are from *The Letters of Sacco and Vanzetti*, edited by Marion Denman Frankfurter and Gardner Jackson, copyright 1928, 1956 by The Viking Press, Inc., New York. They were written by Vanzetti to Leonard Abbott, an anarchist friend in New York, and Mrs. Maude Pettyjohn of Dayton, Wash.————

November 25, 1926. Charlestown Prison

DEAR FRIEND ABBOTT:

Your letter of November 23rd reached me yesterday evening. . . .

You said, dear Abbott, that the Russian Revolution "has dethroned one class to put another in charge." I don't believe, in fact I am positive, that that was not done in Russia—that it is impossible to be done either in Russia or elsewhere. In Russia, this happened: The Czarism was destroyed by a revolution; part of [213] the owners were expropriated; a party took the power, stopped the continuation of expropriation and appropriated to itself that part of the social wealth which had already been expropriated by the people. From that moment the revolution began its regression and a few leaders of a small party became the only and real rulers of Russia. They were immediately compelled to form a national army, and built a policy worse than the Czars' one; to uphold a new church, not better than the old one; and, given the conditions, to be more reactionary and tyrannic than the dethroned autocracy itself. Moreover, to hold their power and stop the natural evolving of the revolution, the few leaders of the small party, now in the government, were compelled to take in their service the officials of the Czar army and police, the burocrat, the bourgeois, and to repress and suppress all the people, workers and revolutionist who disagree with them.

So that it is now experimentally, historically proved what the "damn fool anarchist" are saying from a half a century at least: The proletariat cannot become a ruling class; it can dethrone the actual ruler and place its leaders in their place, but in so doing the revolution would be in vain and the workers exploited and oppressed as before, if not worse.

In fact, the outcome of the Russian Revolution, under the Bolsheviki Leaders' dictatorship, is an increased perfectioned exploitation of the proletariat, reached, achieved through the great and scientific industry. [214]   .   .   .   .   .

December 11, 1926. *Charlestown Prison*

My dear Friend: [217]

.   .   .   .   .   .

To believe that hope, faith, optimism, confidence, are good to the individual, is part of the race wisdom; an historical experience. So we all are most grateful and appreciative of your motherly incitation to them.

Yet, life, happiness, health and goodness depend from things which are what and as they are, and not what and as we believe or hope them to be. So that wrong faith, absurd hope, unfounded optimism and confidence are or may be fatal or at least very deleterious to the individual, in spite of their real help to him as animators. For they mislead us and when we face evil, cannot help us.

I believe better, to try and look the reality straight in its face, eyes into eyes. The question is not to shift from barren reality by any dreams or auto-suggestion. It is: 1st—Not to let ourselves be overwhelmed by the adversity, scared by black prospects, but face them as bravely as possible. 2nd—Try to fight them with all our force. To destroy bad realities, to create good ones, lo! that makes gods out of men and women.

It is for such reason that I indict all the new and all religions. They dope the people so to eternate slavery, unequality, exploitations, crimes, vices and death. The new religions are not better than the old ones for this. . . . By these criterion I came to understand the phylosophy of "free will" and that of "determinism." According to the latter, none is guilty. The former is more wrong and deleterious than the latter, and it explains the mercilessness of the law, the dishonesty of the State, the ferocity monstrous of the churches, and the immorality of the pure moralists. The latter, [221] too, has its weakness and bad consequences. It tends to weaken the human will, to incline its believers to an idle fatalism, to self-indulgence and irresponsibility in a way, for if things cannot be otherwise than how they are, or go otherwise than how they go, if we are what external factors determine, you can see the consequence of such thinking. As for me, I believe to a certain extent in both, as limited and changeable phenomenum interdependent, and dependant from some higher phenomenism. So, I have no ultimate word on them and I remain a Voluntarist. [222]

. . . . .

————THE EDITORIAL below appeared in the Dearborn (Mich.) *Independent* on Dec. 11, 1926. Although this paper was published by Henry Ford and frequently reflected his views, there is reason to believe that Ford, long an opponent of capital punishment, would not have endorsed the position taken in this editorial.————

GOVERNMENT BY BOMB

Partisans of Nicola Sacco and Bartolomeo Vanzetti, under sentence of death for murder, are attempting to persuade Governor Fuller of Massachusetts to pardon them by the classic argument of the bomb. The highest courts of Massachusetts have decided that they were granted a fair trial. The presiding judge has declared likewise, and has refused to open the case. The accused men have enjoyed a stay of execution for five years while eminent attorneys have argued the case on every conceivable technicality in the hope of finding a flaw in the verdict. The defendants have been afforded every opportunity before the law to prove their innocence. And the law has adjudged them guilty.

But because Sacco and Vanzetti happen to be members of a revolutionary party a great hue and cry is raised in their behalf. Charges of "persecution" fill the air. Demands for their freedom are made by radical organizations and newspapers throughout the land. Nor is this all. Bombs are exploded in front of United States embassies the world over. The homes of witnesses who testified against Sacco and Vanzetti are blown to atoms. The judge and jury who tried them are victims of retaliatory acts. Governor Fuller, visiting in Paris, is threatened with death unless he accedes to the demands. Substitution of the bomb for ordered law is a dangerous experiment. [11]

————THE FOLLOWING letter from Vanzetti to Alice Stone Blackwell of Boston is from *The Letters of Sacco and Vanzetti*, edited by Marion Denman Frankfurter and Gardner Jackson, copyright 1928, 1956 by The Viking Press, Inc., New York.————

January 10, 1927. *Charlestown Prison*
Dear Comrade Blackwell:
I know perfectly well that within four months, Massachusetts will be ready to burn me. I know that the magistrature first, then the State, can do with me what they please and choose. . . . That Massachusetts is predetermined to deny me the last right, and to kill me in one way or another, I am positive of it.

So every hope to get reparation and freedom has been killed in me by each and all the words and deeds [230] of Massachusetts' black gowned, puritanic, cold-blooded murderers. On the first day of the 1927, I formulated the wish, that I may get out within this year, no matter if alive or dead. And I hope with all my force that this will come true. By it, I do not mean suicide.

Very often I turn around my mind's eyes to see, contemplate and study the world even and mankind. The spectacle is extremely repugnant and heart tearing. At it, one does not know if to love or if to hate, if to sympathize or if to despise humanity.

Things are going from bad to worse. War in China, Nicaragua, revolution in Java, Mexico, Brazil; the Balkans on foot of war; France and Italy mobilizing one against the other; England, United States, France and Japan in a crazy rivalry of armament; South America and United States in danger of war; Italy under the fascist dictatorship; Russia under the Bolsheviki one; scandals, corruption, crimes, diseases, degeneration, greed, hatred, unconsciousness, prejudices, and insanity sweeping the earth. I wonder how it all will end. . . . [231]

. . . "Equality is the condition sine qua non of justice." The justice and the injustice have a common source; the man's respect of himself and of the dignity of the human person. If from these two loves and respects innate in man, follow plans and deeds of equalities in production and distribution, consideration and rights, that is justice. If we, because of these loves and respects are led to establish privileges for us and those whom we love more at the expense of other, that is injustice.

The destiny of man on earth, is poverty. To live little, to work hard, to always learn; the passion for the justice and the philosophy, to sustain and abstain,—such is our destiny. We have war because we are not sufficiently heroic for a life which does not need war. [232]

. . . . .

————WILLIAM G. THOMPSON appealed Judge Thayer's denial of the Medeiros motion to the Supreme Judicial Court on Jan. 27-8, 1927. Part of the defendants' brief was this comparison of the Medeiros-Morelli and Sacco-Vanzetti hypotheses as explanations of the South Braintree crime.————————————————————————————

	Medeiros-Morelli	Sacco-Vanzetti
Character of accused.	Typical gangsters and gunmen of the worst type.	One of them an industrious workman with a family and a savings bank deposit, and no previous criminal record. The other a fish peddler never before his arrest accused of crime. Both unpopular as pacifists and extreme radicals.
Motive.	Desperate need of funds for lawyer and bail before trial for serious Federal offence. Source of income through robbing freight cars blocked by U. S. Marshal and R. R. police.	Robbery for private gain alleged. No claim or evidence that either defendant ever received or had any part of the stolen money.
Opportunity to plan crime.	Had been repeatedly stealing large shipments from *Slater and Morrill* and *Rice and Hutchins* of *South Braintree* after a member of the gang had "spotted" them in that place.	None alleged.
Accusation by confederate. [4791]	Direct testimony of participant.	None.
Identification by others.	Opportunity restricted, but Joe, Mancini, and Benkosky identified from photographs by Government as well as defense witnesses. No available photographs of Mike or Frank. Undoubted resemblance of Joe Morelli to Sacco in many particulars.	Some identification of Sacco; very slight of Vanzetti at the scene of the murder. Identifications open not only to doubt, but to the gravest suspicion owing to unprecedented manner of displaying these defendants, previous identifications of other criminals by same witnesses, changes in stories, suppression of testimony, manifestly impossible details such as the man identified as Vanzetti using "clear and unmistakable English," and the man identified as Sacco having an unusually large hand.

Alibi.	Full of contradictions as to Morellis. None by Medeiros.	Testified to by many reputable witnesses.
Consciousness of guilt.		Alleged motion to draw gun on officer—contradicted.
	Falsehoods consistent with nothing but consciousness of guilt of crime charged. Confession by Medeiros.	Falsehoods explained by terror felt by radicals and draft evaders at time of persecution of "reds" two days after murder or suicide of a friend while in the custody of Department of Justice officials.
Bullets.	One fired from pistol of type owned by Joe Morelli (Colt .32), and five from type owned by Mancini ("Star" or "Steyr," 765 mm.).	One only claimed to have been fired by weapon of Sacco, and none by Vanzetti. Sharp disagreement of experts, but if real opinion of one of the Government's experts had been known at the time of the trial he would have proved a *defence witness.* [4792]
Other Corroborative Matter.	Morellis were American-born and could have used "clear and unmistakable" English. *Every member of the murder party accounted for.* Unwillingness of Morelli lawyer to state anything tending to implicate his former clients in the South Braintree murders.	Testimony shows that cap claimed to be Sacco's was *not* identified by Kelley, and effort to connect Vanzetti's popular make of revolver with Berardelli's supported by most remote type of evidence, including confused records of gunshop offered by an ex-agent (unrevealed) of the Department of Justice. Does not account for other members of the party.
Stolen Money.	Medeiros' possession of $2,800 immediately thereafter (about his "split" of the total sum stolen).	None. On the contrary, when arrested, Sacco and Vanzetti, supposed to be in possession of over $15,000, and ex-hypothesi, to be accomplished automobile thieves, were using street cars after an unsuccessful attempt to borrow a friend's six-year-old Overland.
Attitude of Authorities.	Seriously offer statements and affidavits of Morellis denying participation in crime. Declined request of defendant's counsel to interview *all witnesses* jointly to avoid vulgar contest of affidavits. Declined to investigate.	Anti-Red excitement capitalized; highly prejudicial cross-examination as to draft evasion and anarchistic opinions and associations; patriotic speeches and charge by Judge to jury; . . . suppression of testimony favorable to defence; intentionally misleading testimony of expert on vital points. [4793]

————IN AFFIRMING Judge Thayer's denial of the Medeiros motion, the justices of the Supreme Judicial Court on April 5, 1927, wrote:————

An impartial, intelligent and honest judge would be justified in finding that the confession gains no persuasive force from the credibility of Medeiros; that the facts relied upon by the defendants in confirmation, if true, go no further than to furnish basis for a contention that he and some members of the Morelli gang of criminals took part in the murder at South Braintree, but fall far short of furnishing adequate proofs of their guilt or of establishing reasonable doubt of the guilt of the defendants. [Therefore] . . . a new trial is not necessary to prevent a failure of justice. [4893]

4

THE SENTENCE

Sources used in this chapter: *The Sacco-Vanzetti Case: Transcript of the Record of the Trial of Nicola Sacco and Bartolomeo Vanzetti in the Courts of Massachusetts and Subsequent Proceedings, 1920-27*, Volume V.

————THE DEFENSE had exhausted all possible means of obtaining a new trial in the Massachusetts courts. Katzmann's successor as district attorney of Norfolk County, therefore, appeared before Judge Thayer to ask that the Sacco-Vanzetti case be forthwith ended.————

COMMONWEALTH OF MASSACHUSETTS

Superior Criminal Court
Thayer, J.

COMMONWEALTH

v.

NICOLA SACCO

AND

BARTOLOMEO VANZETTI

Present:

WINFIELD M. WILBAR, District Attorney
WM. P. KELLY, Ass't. District Attorney
DUDLEY P. RANNEY, Ass't. District Attorney for the Commonwealth.

WILLIAM G. THOMPSON, Esq.,
HERBERT B. EHRMANN, Esq., for the Defendants.

Dedham, Massachusetts,
Saturday, April 9, 1927.
10 A.M.

•   •   •   •   •

MR. WILBAR. It appears by the record of this Court, if your Honor please, that on indictment No. 5545, Commonwealth vs. Nicola Sacco and Bartolomeo Vanzetti that these defendants stand convicted of murder in the first degree. The records are clear at the present time, and I therefore move the Court for the imposition of sentence. . . .

CLERK WORTHINGTON. Nicola Sacco, have you anything to say why sentence of death should not be passed upon you? [4895]

Statement by Nicola Sacco

Yes, sir. I am not an orator. It is not very familiar with me the English language, and as I know, as my friend has told me, my comrade Vanzetti will speak more long, so I thought to give him the chance.

I never know, never heard, even read in history anything so cruel as this Court. After seven years prosecuting they still consider us guilty. And these gentle people here are arrayed with us in this court today.

I know the sentence will be between two class, the oppressed class and the rich class, and there will be always collision between one and the other. We fraternize the people with the books, with the literature. You persecute the people, tyrannize over them, and kill them. We try the education of people always. You try to put a path between us and some other nationality that hates each other. That is why I am here today on this bench, for having been the oppressed class. Well, you are the oppressor.

You know it, Judge,—you know all my life, you know why I have been here, and after seven years that you have been persecuting me and my poor wife, and you still today sentence us to death. I would like to tell all my life, but what is the use? You know all about what I say before, and my friend—that is, my comrade—will be talking, because he is more familiar with the language, and I will give him a chance. My comrade, the man kind, the kind man to all the children, you sentence him two times, in the Bridgewater case and the Dedham case, connected with me, and you know he is innocent. You forget all the population that has been with us for seven years, to sympathize and give us all their energy and all their kindness. You do not care for them. Among that peoples and the comrades and the working class there is a big legion of intellectual people which have been with us for seven years, but to not commit the iniquitous sentence, but still the Court goes ahead. And I think I thank you all, you peoples, my comrades who have been with me for seven years, with the Sacco-Vanzetti case, and I will give my friend a chance.

I forgot one thing which my comrade remember me. As I said before, Judge Thayer know all my life, and he know that I am never
been guilty, never,—not yesterday nor today nor forever.

CLERK WORTHINGTON. Bartolomeo Vanzetti, have you anything to
say why sentence of death should not be passed upon you?

Statement by Bartolomeo Vanzetti

Yes. What I say is that I am innocent, not only of the Braintree
crime, but also of the Bridgewater crime. That I am not only innocent
of these two crimes, but in all my life I have never stole and I have
never [4896] killed and I have never spilled blood. That is what I
want to say. And it is not all. Not only am I innocent of these two
crimes, not only in all my life I have never stole, never killed, never
spilled blood, but I have struggled all my life, since I began to reason,
to eliminate crime from the earth.

Everybody that knows these two arms knows very well that I did
not need to go in between the street and kill a man to take the money.
I can live with my two arms and live well. But besides that, I can live
even without work with my arm for other people. I have had plenty
of chance to live independently and to live what the world conceives
to be a higher life than not to gain our bread with the sweat of our
brow.

My father in Italy is in a good condition. I could have come back
in Italy and he would have welcomed me every time with open arms.
Even if I come back there with not a cent in my pocket, my father
could have give me a possession, not to work but to make business, or
to oversee upon the land that he owns. He has wrote me many letters
in that sense, and other well to do relatives have wrote me many letters
in that sense that I can produce.

Well, I want to reach a little point farther, and it is this,—that not
only have I not been trying to steal in Bridgewater, not only have I
not been in Braintree to steal and kill and have never steal or kill or
spilt blood in all my life, not only have I struggled hard against crimes,
but I have refused myself the commodity or glory of life, the pride of
life of a good position, because in my consideration it is not right to
exploit man. I have refused to go in business because I understand that
business is a speculation on profit upon certain people that must depend upon the business man, and I do not consider that that is right
and therefore I refuse to do that.

Now, I should say that I am not only innocent of all these things, not only have I never committed a real crime in my life—though some sins but not crimes—not only have I struggled all my life to eliminate crimes, the crimes that the official law and the official moral condemns, but also the crime that the official moral and the official law sanctions and sanctifies,—the exploitation and the oppression of the man by the man, and if there is a reason why I am here as a guilty man, if there is a reason why you in a few minutes can doom me, it is this reason and none else. [4897]

. . . . .

You see it is seven years that we are in jail. What we have suffered during these seven years no human tongue can say, and yet you see me before you, not trembling, you see me looking you in your eyes straight, not blushing, nor changing color, not ashamed or in fear.

Eugene Debs say that not even a dog—something like that—not even a dog that kill the chickens would have been found guilty by American jury with the evidence that the Commonwealth have produced against us. I say that not even a leprous dog would have his appeal refused two times by the Supreme Court of Massachusetts—not even a leprous dog.

They have given a new trial to Madeiros for the reason that the Judge had either forgot or omitted to tell the jury that they should consider the man innocent until found guilty in the court, or something of that sort. That man has confessed, and the court give him another trial. We have proved that there could not have been another Judge on the face of the earth more prejudiced and more cruel than you have been against us. We have proven that. Still they refuse the new trial. We know, and you know in your heart, that you have been against us from the very beginning, before you see us. [4898] Before you see us you already know that we were radicals, that we were underdogs, that we were the enemy of the institution that you can believe in good faith in their goodness—I don't want to condemn that —and that it was easy on the time of the first trial to get a verdict of guiltiness.

We know that you have spoke yourself and have spoke your hostility against us, and your despisement against us with friends of yours on the train, at the University Club of Boston, on the Golf Club of Worcester, Massachusetts. I am sure that if the people who know all what you say against us would have the civil courage to take the stand, maybe your Honor—I am sorry to say this because you are an old man, and I have an old father—but maybe you would be beside us in good justice at this time. [4899]

.   .   .   .   .

This is what I say: I would not wish to a dog or to a snake, to the most low and misfortunate creature of the earth—I would not wish to any of them what I have had to suffer for things that I am not guilty of. But my conviction is that I have suffered for things that I am guilty of. I am suffering because I am a radical and indeed I am a radical; I have suffered because I was an Italian, and indeed I am an Italian; I have suffered more for my family and for my beloved than for myself; but I am so convinced to be right that if you could execute me two times, and if I could be reborn two other times, I would live again to do what I have done already.

I have finished. Thank you.

THE COURT. Under the law of Massachusetts the jury says whether a defendant is guilty or innocent. The Court has absolutely nothing to do with that question. The law of Massachusetts provides that a Judge cannot deal in any way with the facts. As far as he can go under our law is to state the evidence.

During the trial many exceptions were taken. Those exceptions were taken to the Supreme Judicial Court. That Court, after examining the entire record, after examining all the exceptions,—that Court in its final words said, "The verdicts of the jury should stand; exceptions overruled." That being true, there is only one thing that this Court can do. It is not a matter of discretion. It is a matter of statutory requirement, and that being true there is only one duty that now devolves upon this Court, and that is to pronounce the sentences.

First, the Court pronounces sentence upon Nicola Sacco. It is considered and ordered by the Court that you, Nicola Sacco, suffer the punishment of death by the passage of a current of electricity through your body within the week beginning on Sunday, the tenth day of July, in the year of our Lord, one thousand, nine hundred and twenty-seven. This is the sentence of the law.

It is considered and ordered by the Court that you, Bartolomeo Vanzetti——

MR. VANZETTI. Wait a minute, please, your Honor. May I speak for a minute with my lawyer, Mr. Thompson?

MR. THOMPSON. I do not know what he wants to say.

THE COURT. I think I should pronounce the sentence.—Bartolomeo Vanzetti, suffer the punishment of death——

MR. SACCO. You know I am innocent. That is the same words I pronounced seven years ago. You condemn two innocent men.

THE COURT. ——by the passage of a current of electricity through your body within the week beginning on Sunday, the tenth day of July, in the year of our Lord, one thousand nine hundred and twenty-seven. This is the sentence of the law.

We will now take a recess.

[*At 11:00 A.M., the Court adjourned without day.*[1]] [4905]

---

[1] To adjourn "without day," or *sine die*, is to adjourn without fixing a day for a future meeting.

5

LAST EFFORTS: April 10–August 23, 1927

Sources used in this chapter: *The Letters of Sacco and Vanzetti*, edited by Marion Denman Frankfurter and Gardner Jackson; *The Sacco-Vanzetti Case: Transcript of the Record of the Trial of Nicola Sacco and Bartolomeo Vanzetti in the Courts of Massachusetts and Subsequent Proceedings, 1920-27*, Volume V; New York *World*; *The Saturday Review* (London).

————THE PACE of events which had been so leisurely, even indolent, quickened with the imposition of the sentence. Less than a month after the sentencing, a petition for clemency was filed with the governor, who in turn undertook a study of the case and appointed a committee to advise him. The seventh and last supplementary motion for a new trial, this time on the grounds of the prejudice of Judge Thayer, was filed in mid-summer and promptly denied by Judge Thayer. And later in August there were some unsuccessful, last-minute attempts to enter the Federal courts.

The petition for executive clemency consisted chiefly of a statement by Vanzetti urging a fresh examination of the whole case. He presented no new arguments or evidence. Sacco refused to sign the statement because he felt the state was determined to execute them and that further delays might do irreparable damage to his wife.

————VANZETTI in the following letter to Mary Donovan of the Sacco-Vanzetti Defense Committee explains how he felt about the petition to the Governor. The letter is from *The Letters of Sacco and Vanzetti*, edited by Marion Denman Frankfurter and Gardner Jackson, copyright 1928, 1956 by The Viking Press, Inc., New York.————

May 3, 1927. Dedham Jail

DEAR MARY:

This afternoon Aldino, Amleto, Milio and Rosa[1] were here with

———
[1] Aldino Felicani, founder of the Defense Committee; Amleto Fabbri, secretary of the Defense Committee in 1925-26; Milo Rossi, a friend; and Rosa Sacco.

Messrs. Thompson and Ehrmann for the last correction and signatures of the petition to the Governor. It is to me legally splendid and passable as to principles. Yet Nick refused to sign it in spite of all the reasons and argumentations of all. Amleto went away alone, weeping silently. It is two weeks that I am hammering this matter with him [Sacco]. I got tired and hopeless. These seven years have told their tale on him, and it seems useless to reason with him. I am wholly disconcert of this plight, for I hate to disagree between us in this important and public matter. I hope his emotions will change his mind for to-morrow, and that some comrade from the [254] Defense Committee will come back tomorrow for a last effort to obtain his signature. . . .

In a way, Nick is right, there are all the reasons for mistrust, pessimism, and scorn for further appeals after so many vain ones. Were the defense entitled to carry our case to the executive without our petition to the Governor, I too would have preferred to not appeal personally. But our signature to the petition being necessary; having after all, no right to scorn a man whose heart and bent towards the case we know not, and in consideration to those who wish our appeal to him, I toiled hard to edit the appeal and signed it, and I believe without incoherence or wrong. . . .

Meanwhile, be brave, steady, and have all the little care of yourself, as possible. We are beaten, yes; but not yet lost—we may still win. . . . [255]

————LATE IN April, 1927, Vanzetti was interviewed in prison by Philip D. Stong, a reporter for the North American Newspaper Alliance. During the interview Stong took shorthand notes on the margin of a newspaper. One of the direct quotations which he transcribed from Vanzetti's conversation, and which subsequently appeared in a feature story on May 13, 1927, in the New York *World*, has become the most famous statement from or about the Sacco-Vanzetti case:—

"If it had not been for these thing," says Vanzetti, "I might have live out my life, talking at street corners to scorning men. I might have die, unmarked, unknown, a failure. Now we are not a failure. This is our career and our triumph. Never in our full life can we hope to do such work for tolerance, for joostice, for man's onderstanding of man, as now we do by an accident.

"Our words—our lives—our pains—nothing! The taking of our lives —lives of a good shoemaker and a poor fish peddler—all! That last moment belong to us—that agony is our triumph!" [15]

————IN A REVIEW of the British edition of *The Letters of Sacco and Vanzetti*, Edward Shanks, writing in the English weekly, *The Saturday Review*, expresses doubt that Vanzetti ever uttered the above statement, which Shanks feels "will bear comparison to Lincoln's Gettysburg Address." Stong defended the authenticity of the statement in a letter published in *The Saturday Review*, May 11, 1929.————

Against the charge of ingenious journalism, brought against those paragraphs, I must enter a regretful denial. I cannot write that well. It seems to me that the internal evidence of that interview is sufficient to convince any honourably disposed person of its authenticity. The change of number in the pronoun was beautifully characteristic of Vanzetti. "I" unmarked, unknown, a failure—but "Our" career, triumph, work for tolerance and justice. [638]

I must confess to contributing the exclamation marks in the next paragraph. It would have been better to have left those out, for Vanzetti did not actually use them. He was not making a speech, or delivering dying words, or anything of the sort.

. . . . .

My one day's investigation of the case had convinced me that guilty or innocent, Sacco and Vanzetti were sure to be executed. With the certainty of their innocence, this knowledge became almost intolerable. I suppose that I must have let my deathbed cheerfulness droop for a moment—Vanzetti caught some expression, and he said what I have written very quietly, simply to comfort me. . . . [639]

————ON JUNE 1, Governor Fuller announced the appointment of President Abbott Lawrence Lowell of Harvard, President Samuel W. Stratton of the Massachusetts Institute of Technology, and Judge Robert Grant to an Advisory Committee which would make a rapid, impartial review of the trial record and would summon before it certain principals of the case. Among those interviewed were Judge Thayer, Prosecutor Katzmann, and eleven of the jurors. No record of what occurred at these interviews was released by the committee.

The available minutes of the proceedings of this committee do not possess the completeness or reliability of the minutes of the trial. The women who transcribed the proceedings were not court stenographers nor were they instructed to take down all of the colloquies between the Committee and various participants. It is true that some new evidence was unearthed as a result of the hearings, notably testimony by newspapermen and others who had observed Judge Thayer allegedly making remarks highly prejudicial to the defendants, and testimony

by Brockton Police Chief Jeremiah Gallivan that he had torn the
lining of the cap found at the murder scene in a search for marks of
identification. But because of the manner in which the hearings were
recorded, their quasi-legal status, and the relative lack of new evidence
they unearthed, little use will be made here of the Advisory Committee Report. This is not to say, however, that it is not a significant as
well as a highly interesting document.

After conducting hearings from July 1 to July 21, the Advisory
Committee presented its Report to the Governor on July 27. Its investigation was guided, the committee said, by three questions: Was
the trial fair? Are the accused entitled to a new trial? Are the accused
guilty of murder?

In respect to the first question, lawyers for the defense argued before the committee that the state of mind and conduct of Judge
Thayer made a fair trial impossible. Affidavits were produced alleging
that Judge Thayer in private conversations had referred to Sacco and
Vanzetti as "anarchistic bastards," and had remarked of his charge to
the jury, "I think that will hold them." Of the appeals Judge Thayer
was alleged to have said, "Let them appeal and see how far they will
get." (The above three quotes from the "Defendants' Brief" before
the Governor's Advisory Hearing appear on p. 5350 of the *Transcript
of the Record*.)

The following excerpt is from an outline of the argument of "Defendants' Brief" before the Advisory Committee:————————

(2) As Judge Thayer gave no reason for his denial of the motion of
both defendants, several times repeated, to separate the cases, and subsequently ruled that unless a stipulation was made eliminating all evidence of good character of both defendants he would permit questions
to be asked tending to show that Vanzetti had required to prove an
alibi in another criminal case, it may be fairly presumed that his
prejudice entered into this disastrous combination of rulings.

(3) The result of his prejudicial cross-examination of Kelley was to
make the cap an important exhibit in the case.

(4) The result of his cross-examination of Kurlansky must have been
to discredit him with the jury.

. . . . . .

(6) His rulings permitting the prejudicial cross-examination of Sacco
of course injured the defendants.

(7) His overemphasis in his charge (not subject to exception) on
the subject of consciousness of guilt must have prejudiced the defendants.

(8) His denial of the Ripley motion, the Proctor motion, the Gould

motion and the Medeiros motion, may well have been influenced by
his prejudice. This becomes all the more apparent when we consider
his confused reasoning in the Proctor, Gould, and Medeiros motions.
. . . [5354]

————THE COMMITTEE'S Report concluded its discussion of Judge
Thayer's alleged prejudice with this statement:————————

It has been said that while the acts and language of the Judge, as
they appear in the stenographic report seem to be correct, yet his attitude and emphasis conveyed a different impression. But the jury do
not think so. They state that the judge tried the case fairly; that they
perceived no bias; and indeed some of them went so far as to say that
they did not know, when they [5378k] entered the jury room to consider their verdict, whether he considered the defendants innocent or
guilty. . . .
Affidavits were presented to the Committee and witnesses were
heard to the effect that the Judge, during and after the trial, had experienced his opinion of guilt in vigorous terms. Prejudice means an
opinion or sentiment before the trial. That a judge should form an
opinion as the evidence comes in is inevitable. . . . From all that has
come to us we are forced to conclude that the Judge was indiscreet
in conversation with outsiders during the trial. He ought not to have
talked about the case off the bench, and doing so was a grave breach
of official decorum. . . . [But] such indiscretions in conversation did
not affect his conduct of the trial or the opinions of the jury, who
indeed, so stated to the Committee. [5378 l]

.   .   .   .   .

To summarize, therefore, what has been said: The Committee have
seen no evidence sufficient to make them believe that the trial was unfair. On the contrary, they are of the opinion that the Judge endeavored, and endeavored successfully, to secure for the defendants a fair
trial; that the District Attorney was not in any way guilty of unprofessional behavior, that he conducted the prosecution vigorously but
not improperly . . . [5378n]

————WHILE he waited for the Governor to announce his decision,
Vanzetti read, worked on his translation of Proudhon, and wrote
letters. The following letter is addressed to Mrs. Elizabeth Glendower
Evans of Brookline, Mass., a socially prominent, wealthy supporter of
the Sacco-Vanzetti Defense Committee. The letter is from *The Letters
of Sacco and Vanzetti*, edited by Marion Denman Frankfurter and

June 22, 1927. *Dedham Jail*

DEAR, DEAR FRIEND MRS. EVANS:

It was good of you to write me such a good and beautiful letter as yours of last, amid the troubles and botherings of a beginning at a summer house. [285]

. . . . .

The two volumes of *The Rise of American Civilization* came with your letter. . . . Well, I reached page 136, first volume, reading almost exclusively at bedtime after 9 o'clock, when the nearest of the two electric lamps is extinted. Then I sit on the end of my bed, place a pillow against the wall, a blanket on my shoulder, and in the corner of my room beside the window, I enjoy that history at the light of one lamp, managing to avoid the window's bars shadows. [286]

. . . . .

Maybe I am wrong and unjust in my judgment of this work, because I know just its beginning now. And my criticism, it may be acid, does not mean that I am not greatly enjoying and learning from the book. I read it in the light of Proudhon; and to my mind, contrary but learned doctrines are salutary. The only great trouble is that Massachusetts' hanger may not give me time to finish the lecture. All the rest is O.K.

I noticed that, in the beginning, the authors affirm that though the economical factor is very dominant it is not alone in history; but they fail badly in showing the other historical factor. . . .

. . . I belong to those anty-marxist socialist who affirm that though economy be a base of life it is not the only, and maybe neither the greatest of the historical factor. Proudhon declare that the cause prima of all war, strife and revolution is pauperism—which is not poverty— that poverty, work, sobriety, study and the steadfast passion of phylosophy (search of the truth) is the destiny of men in earth. Whereas we seek dominion, idleness, materialism, and [287] hence our misery; the war will destroy mankind if we will not be heroic enough to destroy war in its causes and in ourselves. And what pages he wrote— pages that make you think of a titanic—of a forehead large as the State Prison cursed dome. . . .

Well, when my traduction of Proudhon *Peace & War* will be published by Vanguard, I send you a copy if—if—if Fuller will give me his *beneplacido* instead of its contrary. . . .

Is this double investigation going to be another mockery? spitting on our faces? sponge of vinager and bitterness on the top of a lance? the last stubbing between our ribles? Alas I have been treated by all so meaningly and bestially, that I can trust no one of the other side of the barricade—though knowing to be wrong.

The light is gone, I am closing this letter to go to prepare my corner for the reading of your American History. Good night, dear Mrs. Evans, and be well. [288]

————WITHOUT waiting for the Governor's decision, Sacco, convinced that death was at hand, wrote a farewell letter to his seven-year-old daughter, Ines. It is from *The Letters of Sacco and Vanzetti,* edited by Marion Denman Frankfurter and Gardner Jackson, copyright 1928, 1956 by The Viking Press, Inc., New York.————

July 19, 1927. *Charlestown State Prison*

MY DEAR INES:

I would like that you should understand what I am going to say to you, and I wish I could write you so plain, for I long so much to have you hear all the heart-beat eagerness of your father, for I love you so much as you are the dearest little beloved one.

It is quite hard indeed to make you understand in your young age, but I am going to try from the bottom of my heart to make you understand how dear you are to your father's soul. If I cannot succeed in doing that, I know that you will save this letter and read it over in future years to come and you will see and feel the same heart-beat affection as your father feels in writing it to you.

I will bring with me your little and so dearest letter and carry it right under my heart to the last day of my life. When I die, it will be buried with your father who loves you so much, as I do also your brother Dante and holy dear mother.

You don't know Ines, how dear and great your letter was to your father. It is the most golden present that you could have given to me or that I could have wished for in these sad days.

It was the greatest treasure and sweetness in my struggling life that I could have lived with you and your brother Dante and your mother in a neat little farm, and learn all your sincere words and tender affection. Then in the summer-time to be sitting with you in the home nest under the oak tree shade—be- [67] ginning to teach you of life and how to read and write, to see you running, laughing, crying and singing through the verdent fields picking the wild flowers here and there from one tree to another, and from the clear, vivid stream to your mother's embrace.

The same I have wished to see for other poor girls, and their brothers, happy with their mother and father as I dreamed for us—but it was not so and the nightmare of the lower classes saddened very badly your father's soul.

For the things of beauty and of good in this life, mother nature gave to us all, for the conquest and the joy of liberty. The men of this dying old society, they brutally have pulled me away from the embrace of your brother and your poor mother. But, in spite of all, the free spirit of your father's faith still survives, and I have lived for it and for the dream that some day I would have come back to life, to the embrace of your dear mother, among our friends and comrades again, but woe is me!

I know that you are good and surely you love your mother, Dante and all the beloved ones—and I am sure that you love me also a little, for I love you much and then so much. You do not know Ines, how often I think of you every day. You are in my heart, in my vision, in every angle of this sad walled cell, in the sky and everywhere my gaze rests.

Meantime, give my best paternal greetings to all the friends and comrades, and doubly so to our beloved ones. Love and kisses to your brother and mother. [68]

With the most affectionate kiss and ineffable caress from him who loves you so much that he constantly thinks of you. Best warm greetings from Bartolo to you all.

YOUR FATHER [69]

————AFTER reading the Advisory Committee's Report, Governor Fuller issued a statement on August 3 which ended with these words:

This task of review has been a laborious one and I am proud to be associated in this public service with clear-eyed witnesses, unafraid to tell the truth, and with jurors who discharged their obligations in accordance with their convictions and oaths.

As a result of my investigation, I find no sufficient justification for executive intervention.

I believe with the jury, that these men, Sacco and Vanzetti, were guilty, and that they had a fair trial. I furthermore believe that there was no justifiable reason for giving them a new trial. [5378]

————THE LAST attempt to obtain a new trial by means of filing a motion in the Massachusetts courts was made on August 6. The basis for the motion was Judge Thayer's alleged prejudice; many of the affidavits presented to the Advisory Committee served as supporting evidence. To the dismay of the defense, Judge Thayer was assigned to hear the motion, but probably any other judge would have ruled, as he did, that according to Massachusetts law no motion for a new trial can be heard after sentence has been imposed. The Supreme Judicial Court in a decision announced on August 19, supported Judge Thayer's refusal to consider the motion. The case of *Commonwealth v. Sacco and Vanzetti* was closed in the courts of Massachusetts.

————THE EXECUTION was scheduled for shortly after midnight on August 10-11. During the evening of the 10th, the defendants were dressed in specially prepared clothing that would readily conduct electricity, hair was shaved from their heads where the electrodes of the electric chair would be attached, and Mrs. Sacco and Miss Vanzetti were officially notified that the defendants' bodies would be available for embalming on the morning of the 11th. Thirty-six minutes before the time set for the execution, Governor Fuller postponed the execution until midnight, August 22, ". . . to afford the courts an opportunity to complete the consideration of the proceedings now pending." Among the preparations for death made by Sacco and Vanzetti during the next twelve days, was the writing of several farewell letters. Sacco wrote the following letter to Dante, his thirteen-year-old son. It appears in *The Letters of Sacco and Vanzetti*, edited by Marion Denman Frankfurter and Gardner Jackson, copyright 1928, 1956 by The Viking Press, Inc., New York.————

August 18, 1927. *Charlestown State Prison*

MY DEAR SON AND COMPANION:

Since the day I saw you last I had always the idea to write you this letter, but the length of my hunger strike and the thought I might not be able to explain myself, made me put it off all this time.

The other day, I ended my hunger strike and just as soon as I did that I thought of you to write to you, but I find that I did not have enough strength and I cannot finish it at one time. However, I want to get it down in any way before they take us again to the death-house, because it is my conviction that just as soon as the court refuses a new trial to us they will take us there. And between Friday and Monday, if nothing happens, they will electrocute us right after midnight, on August 22nd. Therefore, here I am, right with you with love and with open heart as ever I was yesterday.

I never thought that our inseparable life could be [70] separated, but the thought of seven dolorous years makes it seem it did come, but then it has not changed really the unrest and the heart-beat of affection. That has remained as it was. More. I say that our ineffable affection reciprocal, is today more than any other time, of course. That is not only a great deal but it is grand because you can see the real brotherly love, not only in joy but also and more in the struggle of suffering. Remember this, Dante. We have demonstrated this, and modesty apart, we are proud of it.

Much we have suffered during this long Calvary. We protest today as we protested yesterday. We protest always for our freedom.

.   .   .   .   .

Well, my dear boy, after your mother had talked to me so much and I had dreamed of you day and night, how joyful it was to see you at last. To have talked with you like we used to in the days—in those days. Much I told you on that visit and more I wanted to say, but I saw that you will remain the same affectionate boy, faithful to your mother who [71] loves you so much, and I did not want to hurt your sensibilities any longer, because I am sure that you will continue to be the same boy and remember what I have told you. I knew that and what here I am going to tell you will touch your sensibilities, but don't cry, Dante, because many tears have been wasted, as your mother's have been wasted for seven years, and never did any good. So, Son, instead of crying, be strong, so as to be able to comfort your mother, and when you want to distract your mother from the discouraging soulness, I will tell you what I used to do. To take her for a long walk in the quiet country, gathering wild flowers here and there, resting under the shade of trees, between the harmony of the vivid stream and the gentle tranquility of the mothernature, and I am sure that she will enjoy this very much, as you surely would be happy for it. But remember always, Dante, in the play of happiness, don't you use all for yourself only, but down yourself just one step, at your side and help the weak ones that cry for help, help the prosecuted and the victim, because that are your better friends; they are the comrades that fight and fall as your father and Bartolo fought and fell yesterday for the conquest of the joy of freedom for all and the poor workers. In this struggle of life you will find more love and you will be loved. [72]

.   .   .   .   .

Much I thought of you when I was lying in the death house—the singing, the kind tender voices of the children from the playground, where there was all the life and the joy of liberty—just one step from the wall which contains the buried agony of three buried souls. It would remind me so often of you and your sister Ines, and I wish I could see you every moment. But I feel better that you did not come to the death-house so that you could not see the horrible picture of three lying in agony waiting to be electrocuted, because I do not know what effect it would have on your young age. But then, in another way if you were not so sensitive it would be very useful to you tomorrow when you could use this horrible memory to hold up to the world the shame of the country in this cruel perse- [73] cution and unjust death. Yes, Dante, they can crucify our bodies today as they are doing, but they cannot destroy our ideas, that will remain for the youth of the future to come.

Dante, when I said three human lives buried, I meant to say that with us there is another young man by the name of Celestino Madeiros that is to be electrocuted at the same time with us. He has been twice before in that horrible death-house, that should be destroyed with the hammers of real progress—that horrible house that will shame forever the future of the citizens of Massachusetts. They should destroy that house and put up a factory or school, to teach many of the hundreds of the poor orphan boys of the world.

Dante, I say once more to love and be nearest to your mother and the beloved ones in these sad days, and I am sure that with your brave heart and kind goodness they will feel less discomfort. And you will also not forget to love me a little for I do—O, Sonny! thinking so much and so often of you.

Best fraternal greetings to all the beloved ones, love and kisses to your little Ines and mother. Most hearty affectionate embrace.

Your Father and Companion [74]

————THE LETTER below appeared in *The Sacco-Vanzetti Defense Committee Bulletin*, Vol. I, No. 18. It is undated; apparently it was published in September, 1927.————

August 21, 1927. *From the Death House of Massachusetts State Prison*

Dear Friends and Comrades of the
    Sacco-Vanzetti Defense Committee:
After tomorrow mid-night, we will be executed, save a new staying

of the execution by either the United States Supreme Court or by Governor Alvan T. Fuller.

We have no hope. This morning, our brave defender and friend Michael Angelo Musmanno was here from his return from Washington, and told us he would come back this afternoon if he would have time for it. Also Rosa and Luigi were here this morning, and they too, promised us to return this afternoon. But now it is 5:30 P.M. and no one returned yet. This tells us that there is no good news for us, for, if so, some of you would have hurried to bring them to us. It almost tells us that all your efforts have failed and that you are spending these remaining few hours in desperate and hopeless efforts to evitate our execution. In a word, we feel lost! Therefore, we decided to write this letter to you to express our gratitude and admiration for all what you have done in our defense during these seven years, four months, and eleven days of struggle.

That we lost and have to die does not diminish our appreciation and gratitude for your great solidarity with us and our families.

Friends and Comrades, now that the tragedy of this trial is at an end, be all as of one heart. Only two of us will die. Our ideal, you our comrades, will live by millions; we have won, but not vanquished. Just treasure our suffering, our sorrow, our mistakes, our defeats, our passion for future battles and for the great emancipation.

Be all as of one heart in this blackest hour of our tragedy. And have heart.

Salute for us all the friends and comrades of the earth.

We embrace you all, and bid you all our extreme good-bye with our hearts filled with love and affection. Now and ever, long life to you all, long life to Liberty. Yours in life and death,

BARTOLOMEO VANZETTI
NICOLA SACCO [6]

August 21, 1927. *From the Death House of Massachusetts State Prison*

MY DEAR DANTE:

I still hope, and we will fight until the last moment, to revindicate our right to live and to be free, but all the forces of the State and of the money and reaction are deadly against us because we are libertarians or anarchists.

I write little of this because you are now and yet too young to understand these things and other things of which I would like to reason with you.

But, if you do well, you will grow and understand your father's and my case and your father's and my principles, for which we will soon be put to death.

I tell you now that all that I know of your father, [321] he is not a criminal, but one of the bravest men I ever knew. Some day you will understand what I am about to tell you. That your father has sacrificed everything dear and sacred to the human heart and soul for his fate in liberty and justice for all. That day you will be proud of your father, and if you come brave enough, you will take his place in the struggle between tyranny and liberty and you will vindicate . . . [our] names and our blood.

.   .   .   .   .

I would like you to also remember me as a comrade and friend to your father, your mother and Ines, . . . and you, and I assure you that neither have I been a criminal, that I have committed no robbery and no murder, but only fought modestily to abolish crimes from among mankind and for the liberty of all. [322]

.   .   .   .   .

Remember, Dante, remember always these things; we are not criminals; they convicted us on a frame-up; they denied us a new trial; and if we will be executed after seven years, four months and seventeen days of unspeakable tortures and wrong, it is for what I have already told you; because we were for the poor and against the exploitation and oppression of the man by the man.

The documents of our case, which you and other ones will collect and preserve, will prove to you that your father, your mother, Ines, my family and I have sacrified by and to a State Reason of the American Plutocratic reaction.

The day will come when you will understand the atrocious cause of the above written words, in all its fullness. Then you will honor us.

Now, Dante, be brave and good always. I embrace you.

P. S. I left the copy of *An American Bible* to your mother now, for she will like to read it, and she will give it to you when you will be bigger and able to understand it. Keep it for remembrance. It will also

testify to you how good and generous Mrs. Gertrude Winslow has
been with us all. Good-bye, Dante.

BARTOLOMEO [323]

————EARLY in August while the last attempts were being made in the
Massachusetts courts, counsel for defense sought to enter the case in
the Federal courts. Three writs of *habeas corpus* were presented to
three United States judges. Because such a writ cannot be issued by
a Federal court to state authorities unless a violation of Federal law or
the Constitution is established, the lawyers for Sacco and Vanzetti
based their petition on an alleged violation of the Fourteenth Amendment. Excerpts from that petition (which was presented on August
10 first to Justice Holmes of the United States Supreme Court and
then to Judge George W. Anderson of the Circuit Court of Appeals
of the First Circuit and on August 19 to Judge James M. Morton of
the United States District Court for the District of Massachusetts) are
given below followed by Holmes' memorandum denying the petition.

Your petitioners, Nicola Sacco and Bartolomeo Vanzetti, . . . respectfully represent that their imprisonment and restraint . . . is without due process of law and is in violation of the Fourteenth Amendment to the Constitution of the United States of America, by reason
of the fact that the proceedings whereby your petitioners have been
convicted of murder in the first degree, their motions for a new trial
denied, and sentence of execution for said crime imposed upon them
in the courts of the Commonwealth of Massachusetts have not constituted such a judicial determination of their guilt as to be due process
of law within the meaning of the Fourteenth Amendment . . . inasmuch as, the honorable Webster Thayer, a judge of the Superior Court
of said Commonwealth, who presided over the jury trial . . . and
made numerous material discretionary rulings . . . adverse to your
petitioners and prejudicial to them, . . . was so prejudiced against
the defendants and their counsel from the time of the beginning of
the trial . . . [until] the said Thayer made his last ruling adverse to
the defendants that the defendants have never had a judicial consideration by the said [5527] Thayer during the trial or afterwards of
questions materially involving their lives and liberty, as is shown by
certain affidavits . . . annexed hereto . . . [These are principally affidavits obtained during the Advisory Committee hearings and sworn
to by newspapermen and others who attended the trial.] [5528]

•   •   •   •   •

Your petitioners further say that under the law of the Commonwealth of Massachusetts the decision of the said Judge Webster
Thayer, in so far as it is a decision upon a question of fact, is final
and not reviewable by any tribunal within said Commonwealth, and
that said practice . . . is a denial of that due process of law guaranteed by the Fourteenth Amendment. . . .

. . . . . .

THAT THEREFORE unless the execution can be stayed by virtue of
process from the Courts of the United States of America your petitioners will be deprived of their lives without due process of law and
will be executed at or after midnight on Monday, August twenty-
second, 1927, in violation of the laws and of the Fourteenth Amendment to the Constitution of the United States. [5529]

WHEREFORE to be relieved of said unlawful detention, imprisonment
and impending execution, your petitioners pray that a writ of habeas
corpus, directed to . . . William Hendry, Warden of the Charlestown
State Prison, may issue in this behalf so that your petitioners may be
forthwith brought before this Court to do, submit to and receive what
the law may direct, and that the Court order a stay of said execution
until such time as the constitutional questions raised herein can be fully
determined by the Courts of the United States.

(Signed) BARTOLOMEO VANZETTI
NICOLA SACCO
by ARTHUR D. HILL, Atty. [5531]

Memorandum of Mr. Justice Holmes

This petition was presented to me this tenth day of August, 1927,
and was argued by counsel for the petitioners. I am unable to find in
the petition or affidavits, as I understand them, any facts that would
warrant my issuing the writ. I have no authority to issue it unless it
appears that the Court had no jurisdiction of the case in a real sense so
that no more than the form of a court was there. But I cannot think
that prejudice on the part of a presiding judge however strong would
deprive the Court of jurisdiction, that is of legal power to decide the
case, and in my opinion nothing short of a want of legal power to
decide the case authorizes me to interfere in this summary way with
the proceedings of the State Court.

(Signed) OLIVER WENDELL HOLMES
Associate Justice Supreme Court
of the United States [5532]

————ONLY TWO mass circulation daily newspapers in the United States argued vigorously for a new trial throughout 1926 and 1927: The *Post-Dispatch* in St. Louis and *The World* in New York. The *Post-Dispatch* was more militant than *The World*, but the latter became progressively more active as the date of the execution approached. On August 19, three days before the execution, *The World* printed the following full-page editorial, which was probably written by its chief editorial writer, Walter Lippmann.————

DOUBT THAT WILL NOT DOWN

Although the courts have yet to rule on all phases of the Sacco-Vanzetti case, we respectfully remind the Governor of Massachusetts once more that nothing which has been decided by the courts or by his Advisory Committee automatically fixes the sentence of death as the only possible conclusion. The exaction of the death penalty is not finally a judicial question, but a question of public policy which has to be settled within the discretion of the Executive. The jury at the original trial brought in a verdict of guilty. The presiding judge at that trial has repeatedly denied motions for a new trial. The Appellate Courts have decided that the rulings of this judge were according to law. The Advisory Committee concluded that the two men are guilty. But no one has yet passed finally on the question as to whether the highest interests of the State demand that the two men be executed or that they be imprisoned for life. That is a question for the Governor, which he must decide not on the basis of whether he thinks the men are guilty but on the basis of whether he thinks, given all the circumstances, that an irrevocable sentence of death is wise.

*   *   *   *   *

Gov. Fuller has stated publicly in another connection that he regards the death penalty as the one form of punishment most calculated to deter the professional criminal. With that opinion we for our part are in sympathy, and it is not our practice in clear cases of premeditated murder to plead for clemency. But because we share Gov. Fuller's opinion as to the theory of capital punishment we recognize that certain conditions must be fulfilled before the exaction of the penalty can have the deterrent effect which it ought to have. There must be no doubt in the minds of the community that the condemned had an absolutely unprejudiced trial. There must be no doubt that the condemned is guilty beyond a reasonable doubt. Above all, the circumstances must be such that the condemned dies in the role of a convicted criminal, and not in the role of a martyr.

These elemental conditions have not been fulfilled, we submit, in the case of Sacco and Vanzetti. There remains in the minds of uncounted multitudes the gravest doubt as to whether they have had an absolutely unprejudiced trial on all the available evidence. This doubt, far from being reduced, has been augmented by the finding of the Advisory Committee that the presiding judge, who was also the reviewing judge, committed a grave breach of official decorum. The inquiry by the committee, which we were among the first to recognize as disinterested in its purposes, has plainly failed to carry conviction. There can be no question, therefore, that if Sacco and Vanzetti die on Monday night multitudes will regard their death not as a just penalty for a brutal crime but as a martyrdom. No one who believes in the deterrent effect of the death penalty can say that such an execution is calculated to produce the effect for which it is designed.

*   *   *   *   *

We recognize perfectly well that no government can with self-respect yield to the clamor of ignorance and sentimentality and partisanship. We realize perfectly well how much more difficult it is for the Governor to commute these sentences in the face of organized threats and of sporadic outrages. It will take greatness of mind and heart for the Governor and his Council to choose the wiser course. It will take that kind of greatness which lifts men above the passions of the moment, makes them impervious to the threats of their enemies and the outcry of their own partisans, and arms them with a resolution to take that course which the sober judgment of history will vindicate.

If Gov. Fuller commutes these sentences the Communists and Anarchists will shout that they coerced him. They will make the most of it for a day, a week, a month. The extremists on the other side will call him a weakling, and sneer. They will make the most of it for a day, a week, a month. But in the meantime moderate and disinterested opinion, which is never very talkative, will mobilize behind him and will recognize that he did a wise and a brave thing which can have no other result in the long run than to protect the prestige of the State and to deepen the confidence of the people in its wisdom.

Therefore we plead with the Governor to see this matter in the light not of to-day and to-morrow but of the years to come. We plead with him to stay the execution because it will defeat the only purpose for which the death penalty can be exacted. We plead with him to remember that, however certain he may be in his own mind that the two men are guilty, no such certainty exists in the minds of his fellow-citizens. They are in doubt. They are troubled. We feel sure we speak for a multitude whose loyalty and disinterestedness are beyond all question when we say that the guilt of Sacco and Vanzetti has not been proved beyond a reasonable doubt.

* * * * *

————AFTER discussing some of the doubts raised by the testimony concerning Sacco's and Vanzetti's guns, the editorial turns to Sacco's cap. ————

To the question of Sacco's cap the Lowell committee attaches great importance. To the same point great importance was attached by the prosecution at the original trial. For when the prosecuting attorney summed up his case he said to the jury of this cap:

It is absolutely condemnatory of this defendant. No, not absolutely, but it clinches on top of all the other circumstances.

Now the Lowell committee itself says, reviewing "the chief circumstances" in the case against Sacco:

A cap is found on the ground near the body of the man he is accused of killing which bears a resemblance in color and general appearance to those he was in the habit of wearing, and when tried on in court it fitted—that is, his head was the size of one of the men who did the shooting.

Let us see.

The question of identifying this cap as one of Sacco's caps came up three times in the trial, and only three. It came up once more in testimony before the Lowell committee. Anything the Lowell committee knows about this cap, anything anybody knows about this cap, must be drawn from these four sources. For there is no other evidence, and never has been.

First, the three references to the cap during the trial:

Mrs. Sacco, wife of the defendant, takes the stand. The prosecuting attorney asks her (Record, p. 1085) if her husband ever had a cap like this cap that was found at the murder scene. She says:

My husband never wore caps with anything around for his ears, never, because he never liked it and because, besides that, never, he never wore them because he don't look good in them, positively.

The prosecuting attorney goes on to point out marks on the cap and holes in the lining (Record, p. 1085).

Q. Did you ever see a mark like this (*indicating*), you might or might not, but did you ever see a hole like that (*indicating*) in your husband's cap?

A. Not that I remember. I never seen holes in my husband's cap like that.

This ends Mrs. Sacco's evidence about the cap.

* * * * *

Then there is Sacco himself on the witness-stand. His attorney asks him (Record, p. 908) if this is his cap. He answers, "No, sir." His attorney asks him (Record, p. 909) if he ever had a cap of any color made in the form of this cap with a fur lining, and he answers, "Never in my life." He is asked to try the cap on (Record, p. 909), does try it on, and says, "Could not go in. My size is 7-⅛." He is asked (Record, p. 909) if he knows anything about the history of this cap, and replies, "No, sir."

Then the prosecuting attorney takes Sacco for cross-examination. He is asked again to try putting the cap on (Record, p. 978), tries putting it on, and the following passage occurs in the testimony:

A. Can't go in.

Q. Can't go in?

A. No.

Q. Try and pull it down in back and see if it can't go in?

A. Oh, but it is too tight.

The prosecuting attorney goes on to point out holes in the lining of the cap. He establishes the fact (Record, p. 979) that Sacco was in the habit of hanging his own cap on a nail in the factory where he worked. But when he asks Sacco (Record, p. 979) if his own cap had a hole in it Sacco replies that he is "pretty sure" it didn't. And this ends Sacco's evidence about the cap.

Now, it can be said that neither Sacco nor his wife would be anxious to help the State prove its case. This is manifestly true. But the point is that if the Lowell committee believes it has found evidence that this cap was Sacco's, and that it fitted Sacco's head, it cannot have in mind Sacco's evidence or his wife's evidence; for if that evidence proves anything it proves that the cap was not Sacco's and did *not* fit his head.

The committee, therefore, must have some other evidence in mind. There is only one other piece of evidence for it to have in mind. For in the whole course of the trial only one other witness was ever questioned about identifying this cap as Sacco's. This witness was George T. Kelley, superintendent of the factory in which Sacco worked.

Kelley takes the stand. He is asked by the prosecuting attorney (Record, p. 449) if he has ever noticed anything in respect to the cap that Sacco wears. He replies, "Nothing more than coming in to work and hanging it up on a nail." He is shown the cap found at the murder scene and asked (Record, p. 450) if this cap is like the one worn by Sacco. He replies:

> The only thing I could say about that cap, Mr. Williams, from hanging up on a nail in the distance, it was similar in color. As far as details are concerned, I could not say it was.

He is asked (Record, p. 450) if he ever saw a tear in the lining of Sacco's cap. He answers, "No, sir." He is again asked (Record, p. 452) if the cap found at the murder scene is "alike in appearance to the cap worn by Sacco," and again replies, "In color only." The following colloquy then occurs:

> The Court—That is not responsive to the question. I wish you would answer it, if you can.
>
> The Witness—I can't answer it when I don't know right down in my heart that that is the cap.
>
> The Court—I don't want you to. I want you should answer according to what is in your heart.
>
> The Witness—General appearance, that is all I can say. I never saw that cap so close in my life as I do now.

Later in the trial Kelley is recalled to the witness-stand by the defense and in the course of cross-examination is asked this question (Record, p. 1046) by the prosecuting attorney: "Did you realize the importance if your testimony identified that cap as Sacco's cap?"

To which Kelley answers:

"I did not think I had identified it, Mr. Katzmann."

*   *   *   *   *

The cap appears once more, in the testimony of one Jeremiah F. Gallivan, Chief of Police of South Braintree, before the Lowell committee. Gallivan testifies that the holes in the lining of the cap found at the murder scene—the holes which the prosecution had attempted to prove were made by the nail where Sacco hung his cap—had been made by the police themselves in an effort to find some identification mark: the lining being intact at the time of the delivery of the cap to Gallivan.

This is the end of the cap. And we are left with the extraordinary conclusion:

That the Lowell committee has decided that the cap found at the murder scene was Sacco's cap, on the basis of—

1. Mrs. Sacco's denial of the fact.

2. Sacco's denial of the fact, and his statement that he could not pull the cap down on his head.

3. Kelley's testimony that Sacco's cap, which he had only seen "hanging up on a nail in the distance," was like the murder cap "in color only," in "general appearance."

Kelley denied that he had identified the cap.

Then who did identify it?

Who satisfied the Lowell committee so completely regarding the identity of this cap that the Lowell committee is ready to use this cap as one of the six links that justify Sacco's execution?

When there is no other evidence in the record it is no wonder that thoughtful men are puzzled.

*   *   *   *   *

From the foregoing it can be seen that the evidence is far from conclusive. And no undue weight should be attached to it on the theory that our criminal system does not make mistakes. It makes many mistakes. In the well-authenticated records of criminal proceedings in this country there are a great number of cases which cast the gravest doubt upon all evidence which rests on snap identification, the testimony of rifle experts and such things. Dozens of cases are known where the evidence seemed conclusive, where juries convicted and where subsequent events proved that the accused was innocent.

.   .   .   .   .

The Sacco-Vanzetti case is clouded and obscure. It is full of doubt. The fairness of the trial raises doubt. The evidence raises doubt. The inadequate review of the evidence raises doubt. The Governor's inquiry has not appeased these doubts. The report of his Advisory Committee has not settled these doubts. Everywhere there is doubt so deep, so pervasive, so unsettling, that it cannot be denied and it cannot be ignored. No man, we submit, should be put to death where so much doubt exists.

The real solution of this case would be a new trial before a new judge under new conditions. Fervently we hope that the Supreme Judicial Court of Massachusetts will decide that under the law such a new trial can be held. But if it does not, then to the Governor, to his

Council and to the friends of justice in Massachusetts we make this plea:

Stay the execution. Wait. The honor of an American Commonwealth is in your hands. Listen, and do not put an irrevocable end upon a case that is so full of doubt. It is human to err, and it is possible in the sight of God that the whole truth is not yet known.

*   *   *   *   *

————WITH TWO days left before the day of execution, defense lawyers made their last legal move: they petitioned Justice Holmes for writs of *certiorari* from the United States Supreme Court. This request for the Supreme Court to review the judgment of the court that convicted Sacco and Vanzetti was denied by Justice Holmes and, two days later, by Justice Stone in the following memoranda:————

This is a case of a crime charged under state laws and tried by a State Court. I have absolutely no authority as a Judge of the United States to meddle with it. If the proceedings were void in a legal sense, as when the forms of a trial are gone through in a Court surrounded and invaded by an infuriated mob ready to lynch prisoner, counsel, and jury if there is not a prompt conviction, in such a case no doubt I might issue a *habeas corpus*—not because I was a Judge of the United States, but simply as anyone having authority to issue the writ might do so, on the ground that a void proceeding was no warrant for the detention of the accused. No one who knows anything of the law would hold that the trial of Sacco and Vanzetti was a void proceeding. They might argue that it was voidable and ought to be set aside by those having power to do it, but until set aside, the proceeding must stand. That is the difference between void and voidable—and I have no power to set the proceeding aside—that, subject to the exception that I shall mention, rests wholly with the State. I have received many letters from people who seem to suppose that I have a general discretion to see that justice is done. They are written with the confidence that sometimes goes with ignorance of the law. Of course, as I have said, I have no such power. The relation of the United States and the Courts of the United States to the States and the Courts of the States is a very delicate matter that has occupied the thoughts of statesmen and judges for a hundred years and can not be disposed of by a summary statement that justice requires me to cut red tape and to intervene. Far stronger cases than this have arisen with regard to the blacks when the Supreme Court has denied its power.

A State decision may be set aside by the Supreme Court of the

United States—not by a single Justice of that Court—if the record of the case shows that the Constitution has been infringed in specific ways. An application for a writ of *certiorari* has been filed on the ground that the record shows such an infringement; and the writ of *habeas corpus* having been denied, I am asked to grant a stay of execution until that application can be considered by the full Court. I assume that under the Statute my power extends to this case although I am not free from doubt. But it is a power rarely exercised and I should not be doing my duty if I exercised it unless I thought that there was a reasonable chance that the Court would entertain the application and ultimately reverse the judgment. This I can not bring myself to believe. The essential fact of record that is relied upon is that the question of Judge Thayer's prejudice, raised and it is said discovered only after the trial and verdict, was left to Judge Thayer and not to another Judge. But as I put it to counsel, if the Constitution of Massachusetts had provided that a trial before a single Judge should be final, without appeal, it would have been consistent with the Constitution of the United States. In such a case there would be no remedy for prejudice on the part of the Judge except Executive Clemency. Massachusetts has done more than that. I see nothing in the Constitution warranting a complaint that it has not done more still.

It is asked how it would be if the Judge were subsequently shown to have been corruptly interested or insane. I will not attempt to decide at what point a judgment might be held to be absolutely void on these grounds. It is perfectly plain that, although strong language is used in the present application, the judgment was not void even if I interpret the affidavits as proving all that the petitioners think they prove—which is somewhat more than I have drawn from them. I do not consider that I am at liberty to deal with this case differently from the way in which I should treat one that excited no public interest and that was less powerfully presented. I cannot say that I have a doubt, and therefore I must deny the stay. But although I must act on my convictions, I do so without prejudice to an application to another of the Justices which I should be very glad to see made, as I am far from saying that I think counsel was not warranted in presenting the question raised in the application by this and the previous writ.

(Signed) OLIVER WENDELL HOLMES
Justice Supreme Court of
the United States

August 20, 1927.

Memorandum of Mr. Justice Stone

Application considered and denied without prejudice to application to any other justice. I concur in the view expressed by Justice Holmes as to the merits of the application and action of counsel in presenting it. [5517]

6

THE EXECUTION

Source used in this chapter: *The New York Times.*

————ON THE NIGHT of the execution of Sacco and Vanzetti, mobs stoned United States embassies in several European and South American countries and thousands of workers struck in France, Italy, and the United States. In Boston heavily armed police patrolled outside of Charlestown Prison in trucks, cars, boats, and on foot and horseback. Inside the prison one reporter, an Associated Press man, was permitted to witness the execution. Using the detail supplied by the A.P. man, Louis Stark sent the following dispatch to *The New York Times.*————

CHARLESTOWN STATE PRISON, MASSACHUSETTS, TUESDAY, AUGUST 23— Nicola Sacco and Bartolomeo Vanzetti died in the electric chair this morning, carrying out the sentence imposed on them for the South Braintree murders of April 15, 1920.

Sacco marched to the death chair at 12:11 and was pronounced lifeless at 12:19.

Vanzetti entered the execution room at 12:20 and was declared dead at 12:26.

To the last they protested their innocence, and the efforts of many who believed them guiltless proved futile, although they fought a legal and extralegal battle unprecedented in the history of American jurisprudence.

With them died Celestino F. Madeiros, the young Portuguese, who won seven respites when he "confessed" that he was present at the time of the South Braintree murder and that Sacco and Vanzetti were not with him. He died for the murder of a bank cashier.

The six years' legal battle on behalf of the condemned men was still on as they were walking to the chair and after the current had been applied, for a lawyer was on the way by airplane to ask Federal Judge George W. Anderson in Williamstown for a writ of *habeas corpus*.

The men walked to the chair without the company of clergy. Father Michael J. Murphy, Prison Chaplain, waited until a minute before twelve and then left the prison.

Sacco cried, "Long live anarchy!" as the prison guards strapped him into the chair and applied the electrodes. He added a plea that his family be cared for.

Vanzetti at the last made a short address, declaring his innocence.

Madeiros walked to the chair in a semistupor caused by overeating. He shrugged his shoulders and made no farewell statement.

Warden William Hendry was almost overcome by the execution of the two men, especially that of Vanzetti, who shook his hand warmly and thanked him for all his kindnesses.

The Warden was barely able to whisper the solemn formula required by law:

"Under the law I now pronounce you dead, the sentence of the court having been legally carried out."

The words were not heard by the official witnesses. [1]

. . . . .

The witnesses walked through the prison and entered the death house with the Warden. They took their places, and then Madeiros was escorted into the chamber. He walked without support, attended by two guards, one at each side. He was strapped in the chair at 12:03 and at 12:09 he was pronounced dead.

. . . . .

Sacco, whose cell was next to that of Madeiros, was the next. A guard opened his door. Sacco was ready. His face was pale from his long confinement. Without a word he took his place between his guards. Walking slowly but steadily he traversed the seventeen steps into the death chamber. He required no support and sat down in the chair. As the guards were finishing their work, Sacco cried out in Italian: "Long live anarchy!"

In English he shouted:

"Farewell my wife and child, and all my friends!"

He has two children, Dante, fourteen, and Inez, six, but his difficulty in speaking English and the excitement of the occasion were responsible for the slip.

"Good evening, gentlemen," he said jerkily. Then came his last words:

"Farewell, Mother."

Warden Hendry waited until Sacco apparently was satisfied that there was no more to say. Then he gave the signal. Sacco was pronounced dead at 12:19:02.

Vanzetti's door was opened. He, too, was calm. He shook hands with the two guards and kept step with them. He had four more steps to the death chair than Sacco. On entering the chamber he spoke to the Warden, shaking hands and saying:

"I want to thank you for everything you have done for me, Warden."

Vanzetti spoke in English. His voice was calm throughout. There was not the slightest tremor or quaver.

Then, addressing the witnesses, he said:

"I wish to tell you that I am innocent, and that I never committed any crime but sometimes some sin."

They were almost the same words he addressed to Judge Webster Thayer in the Dedham courtroom last April when he was sentenced to die during the week of April 10, the sentence having been deferred because the Governor's Advisory Commission was working on the case.

"I thank you for everything you have done for me," he went on, calmly and slowly. "I am innocent of all crime, not only this, but all. I am an innocent man."

Then he spoke his last words:

"I wish to forgive some people for what they are doing to me."

Vanzetti stepped into the chamber at 12:20:30. At 12:26:55 he was declared dead.

Before midnight Warden Hendry told reporters how he broke the news to Sacco and Vanzetti.

"I simply told them it was my very painful duty to convey to them the information that they were going to die shortly after midnight," he said. "I told them that their lawyers had informed me that they had done all they could and had failed."

Father Michael J. Murphy, Prison Chaplain, again offered the men his services, but they refused his offer of the last rites.

.   .   .   .   .   .

The police broke up a meeting of nearly five hundred Italians in Salem Street, in the North end, as midnight approached. They threatened to hold a demonstration in front of the Bunker Hill Monument, and also threatened to hold a protest meeting before the State House and on the Common.

Mounted police charged a crowd of several thousand that gathered just outside the roped-off area surrounding the jail at the hour of execution. Two hundred Sacco and Vanzetti sympathizers had congregated in Thompson Square to join a parade out to Bunker Hill. Po-

licemen afoot were unable to control the excited crowd. The charge
of the mounted police drove men, women, and children back in a
wave. Several persons were crushed. Two women were arrested,
charged with sauntering and loitering.

More than one thousand cars were blocked in a traffic jam along
Main Street, obstructing the passage of pedestrians and police. The
street became a tangled mass of automobiles and other vehicles. There
was a terrific din as policemen shouted orders, the ironshod hoofs of
their mounts clattered over pavements and hundreds of automobilists
shouted their sirens continuously.

Charlestown Prison was armed and garrisoned as if to withstand a
siege. Machine guns, gas and tear bombs, not to mention pistols and
riot guns, constituted the armament, and to man it were five hundred
patrolmen, detectives, and state constables besides the usual prison
guard.

A weird and martial picture was presented when motion-picture
photographers held aloft flaming calcium torches, lighting up a passing
detail of mounted state police with a ghastly flicker and silhouetting
their silent figures against the grim gray of the prison walls.

Mrs. Rose Sacco and Miss Luigia Vanzetti called three times at the
death house during the day. Their last visit was at seven o'clock in
the evening, when they remained five minutes and departed weeping.
Gardner Jackson and Aldini Felicani of the Defense Committee, who
accompanied the women, arranged with Warden Hendry for the transfer of their bodies to the relatives.

Mrs. Sacco and Miss Vanzetti arrived at the prison for the first time
in the day at eleven A.M. Dr. Joseph I. MacLaughlin, the prison physician, was in the death house at the time and Vanzetti introduced his
sister to him. The two women were downcast. They pressed their
faces close to the heavily barred cell doors under the eyes of the
guards.

An hour passed, and the interview ended with tearful farewells.
Farewell embraces were not permitted. There were handclasps and
faces were pressed to the cell doors. The bars are an inch thick and
an inch apart and heavily meshed.

Madeiros at noon seemed quite calm and smoked many cigarettes.
Vanzetti worked on a letter to his father. Sacco paced up and down
his cell. But when Michael A. Musmanno of defense counsel called
on Sacco and Vanzetti at 2:30 P.M. he found them depressed and ready
for death. They told him they were convinced no power on earth
would save them. Sacco begged to see his wife again. Vanzetti re-

gretted that his sister had come from Italy to be with him in his last moments of agony. He was sorry that her last memory of him would be clouded with knowledge of the gray prison, the death cell, and the electric chair.

At 3:10 P.M. the two women returned to the death house in an automobile driven by Miss Edith Jackson of New Haven. Mrs. Sacco, who has always presented a tearless and composed face to the public, wept for the first time as she approached the gate. Miss Vanzetti's arm supported her as the two passed into the death house for the second time in the day. They greeted the men through the wire mesh and remained an hour. Sacco spoke of his children and Vanzetti of his old home in Italy. The women were weeping as they stepped into the automobile.

William G. Thompson, former counsel of Sacco and Vanzetti, called then late in the day. Mr. Thompson had returned from his summer home at South Tamworth, New Hampshire, at the request of Vanzetti and visited both men at the death house. He spent nearly an hour there. When he left he said that Sacco and Vanzetti had reasserted that they were absolutely innocent of the South Braintree murders. He declared also that there was no truth in the report that he had been offered an opportunity to inspect the files of the Department of Justice and had refused.

The conversation with Vanzetti, said Mr. Thompson, was partly on the man's political and philosophical beliefs. He declined to discuss the report of Governor Fuller or that of the Advisory Commission other than to say that, having read both documents with care, he found nothing in them which altered his opinion "that these two men are innocent and their trial was in a very real sense unfair." [2]

.　.　.　.　.

7

REPERCUSSIONS: 1927–1957

Sources used in this chapter: *Outlook; U.S.A.* by John Dos Passos; *Massachusetts Laws of 1939;* New Bedford (Mass.) *Standard-Times; The Legacy of Sacco and Vanzetti* by G. Louis Joughin and Edmund M. Morgan; and *St. Louis Post-Dispatch.*

————THE FLOOD of journalism that rose during the last months of the case rapidly ebbed during the following year and was succeeded by writing of a different sort. Poets, novelists and playwrights with their slower reaction times, replaced the reporters and editorial writers. Upton Sinclair, half reporter and half novelist, was one of the first to react with *Boston* (1928), a two-volume novel about the case. The verse, which appeared during the case and shortly after the execution, was hardly memorable in spite of the fact that two anthologies of it were published in 1927. Edna St. Vincent Millay wrote what is probably the most widely known poem about the Sacco-Vanzetti case, "Justice Denied in Massachusetts," but her poetic essay, "Fear," is regarded by many as her most effective utterance on the subject. It is reprinted below in its entirety as it appeared in *Outlook*, November 9, 1927.[1]————

FEAR

There are two names you would not have me mention, for you are sick of the sound of them. All men must die, you say, and these men have died, and would that their names might die with them; would that their names were as names written in the sands, you say, to be dissipated by the next incoming tide! For you long to return to your gracious world of a year ago, where people had pretty manners and did not raise their voices; where people whom you knew, whom you had entertained in your houses, did not shout and weep and walk the streets vulgarly carrying banners, because two quite inconsequential people, two men who could not even speak good English, were about

---

[1] First published in *Outlook*, copyright © 1927 by Edna St. Vincent Millay.

to be put forever out of mischief's way. *Do* let us forget, you say; after all, what *does* it matter?

You are right; it does not matter very much. In a world more beautiful than this it would have mattered more. On the surface of a Christianity already so spotted and defaced by the crimes of the Church this stain does not show very dark. In a freedom already so riddled and gashed by the crimes of the state this ugly rent is with difficulty to be distinguished at all.

And you are right; it is well to forget that men die. So far we have devised no way to defeat death, or to outwit him, or to buy him over. At any moment the cloud may split above us and the golden spear of death leap at the heart; at any moment the earth crack and the hand of death reach up from the abyss to grasp our ankles; at any moment the wind rise and sweep the roofs from our houses, making one dust of our ceilings and ourselves. And if not, we shall die soon, anyhow. It is well to forget that this is so.

But that man before his time, wantonly and without sorrow, is thrust from the light of the sun into the darkness of the grave by his brother's blindness or fear it is well to remember, at least until it has been shown to the satisfaction of all that this too is beyond our power to change.

*   *   *

Two months ago, in Massachusetts, these men whom I do not name were efficiently despatched out of the sunlight into the darkness of the grave. The executions of the death sentence upon them went forward without interference; there were no violent demonstrations. Whatever of agitation there was has steadily decreased since that night. Today things are very quiet. From time to time some small newspaper remarks editorially that the hysteria which swept the country has abated, and congratulates its readers upon having escaped disintegration. Aside from this there is little comment. The general opinion is that the affair has pretty well blown over. And the world sleeps easy on its pillow.

Yet if all is quiet today, it is more for this reason than for any other; that though you sit in the same room with a man you cannot hear his thoughts. And the tumult is in the mind; [293] the shouting and rioting are in the thinking mind. Nothing has abated; nothing has changed; nothing is forgotten. It is as if the two months which have elapsed were but the drawing of a breath. In very truth, for those who sat in silence on that night of the 22nd of August, waiting for news from the prison, and in silence when the news came, it is still the night of the 22nd of August, for there has been no dawn.

I do not call these men by name, for I know how nervous and irritable you become at the sight of these names on the printed page; how your cheek flushes and you cluck with exasperation; how you turn to your family with words on your tongue which in former days you would not have used at all—"vipers, vermin, filth." This is because you were just dozing off nicely again after the shocking uproar of two months ago, and do not wish to be disturbed. You are as cross as an old dog asleep on the hearth if I shake you and try to get you out into the rainy wind. This is because what you most want out of life is not to be disturbed. You wish to lie peacefully asleep for a few years yet, and then to lie peacefully dead.

If you should rouse yourself for a moment and look about you at the world, you would be troubled, I think, and feel less peaceful and secure, seeing how it is possible for a man as innocent as yourself of any crime to be cast into prison and be killed. For whether or not these men whom I do not name were guilty of the crime of murder, it was not for murder that they died. The crime for which they died was the crime of breathing upon the frosty window and looking out.

"These Anarchists!" you say; "shall I never hear the last of them?"

Indeed, I fear it will be some time before you hear the last of them. I do not mean by this what you think I mean. I do not mean that plotting mischief is afoot, that thousands of people hitherto gentle and retired are now grimly engaged in fashioning engines of death to plant beneath the State House floor. This is not what I mean, although you will say it is what I meant.

*   *   *

It is of your children I was thinking, your young sons and daughters, your grandsons and granddaughters, these young people with whom you have already so much difficulty, because as you say, they have so few illusions. How often already have they not stood looking at you coldly while with warm cheek and faltering accent you presented your pretty concepts: duty, honor, courage, purity, sacrifice—those fragile dolls of yours, that are always dressed for summer, no matter what the sky?

Your children heard you discussing the case in question. "Anarchists, murderers, Anarchists, Anarchists." This was your discussion of the case. They looked at you, yawned, and left the room.

Their minds are dark to you. But they are busy. Out of your sight they read, they ponder, they work things out. In your presence they often sit in a not too respectful silence, interrupting suddenly your placid remarks by their brisk utterance of some untidy truth never mentioned in your house before.

They are frankly occupied chiefly with the real business of life, which, as everybody knows, is having your own way, and getting as much as possible for as little as possible. It is you who have taught them this angular truth, you have failed only in that you have not been able to impart to them as well the ruffles and passementerie with which you are accustomed to adorn it. They were just beginning to look about them at life when war broke out and surrounded them with death. They know how important it is to have a good time while you can; in the next war it is they who will be taken.

As for their illusions, well, they have seen you at war, and they are beginning to understand why you went to war; they have seen you engaged in many another dubious and embarrassing activity; and now they have seen this. They who have been chidden time and again for having so little softness in them see now their parents, for all their gentle voices and courteous ways, more hard, more unscrupulous, more relentless, than themselves in their most iron moods. It is from these children, I fear, that you are likely to hear again on the subject, though not in so many words.

But, you say, what we did was done for the good of the country, to protect its honor, its institutions, the glory of its flag.

What is this honor, that a breath can tarnish? This glory, that a whisper can bring it low? What are these noble institutions, that a wind from any quarter can set to trembling like towers of jelly?

You do not know exactly what they are. For you do not live with them. They are not trees to shade you, water to quench your thirst. They are golden coins, hidden under the mattress [294] in a very soiled wallet. The only pleasure they afford you is the rapturous dread lest some one may be taking them away. And some one is taking them away. But not the one you think.

Unkindness, hypocrisy, and greed—these are the forces that shall bring us low and enslave our children. Yet we quarter their troops in our houses without a murmur. We show them where the treasure is hid. But they know it already.

This is the way you look at it: These men were Anarchists, and they are well out of the way; you are fortunate to have escaped destruction at their hands; they were probably murderers; but, in any case, they are well out of the way. It was that word Anarchist which brought them to the chair; that word, and your ignorance of its meaning.

* * *

For you do not at all know what an Anarchist is. And all through this trial in which the word Anarchist has played such an important part you have not even looked up the word in the dictionary, your position being that, in the first place, you know quite well enough, and, in the second place, you would think shame to know.

An Anarchist, you insist, is a man who makes bombs and puts them under the State House, and that is that. On the contrary, that is by no means that. The person you have in mind is not an Anarchist, he is a bomber. You will find him everywhere—among Anarchists, among Fascists, among dry-law enforcers, among Modernists, among Fundamentalists, and freely distributed throughout the Ku Klux Klan. He is that person who, when he does not like a thing, lynches it, tars and feathers it, lays a curse upon it, or puts a bomb under it. His name is legion, and you will find him in every party.

An Anarchist, according to the dictionary, is a person who believes that human beings are naturally good, and that if left to themselves they would, by mutual agreement, govern themselves much better and much more peaceably than they are being governed now by a government based on violence. An interesting theory. Nonsense, of course, because man is not naturally good; man is naturally cruel, selfish and vain, and what he would be if left to his own devices it is horrible to contemplate. Still, it is an interesting concept, very idealistic, very pretty.

Of those who hold with the theory of Anarchism, the dictionary further tells us, there is one group whose members "occasionally resort to an act of violence against representatives of oppression to express a protest against, or to draw public attention to, existing social wrongs." (It is in this group that your bombers are happy and at home.) But "generally speaking," says the dictionary, "Anarchism repudiates violent methods, and hopes for a gradual evolution towards its goal."

* * *

Ah, you will say, but these men belonged to the violent group!

Their history would indicate otherwise. Up to the time of their detention for the crime for which they were later sentenced to die no slightest act of violence had ever been attributed to either of them. There are those who would have given much to be able to bring to light against them such an act of violence, and were unable to do so; it is to the counsel for the prosecution that I refer. "Throughout the entire trial" (I quote the uncontested statement of one who was in a position to know the facts)—"not one word of testimony was introduced against their character for honesty, peace, and good order."

I am going into this in some detail because I find it interesting. You, I fear, find it not only uninteresting, but vaguely and uncomfortably obscene. Yet, after all, you have very plentifully had your say on the subject—that action of yours, you know, that spoke so much louder than any words.

These men were castaways upon our shore, and we, an ignorant and savage tribe, have put them to death because their speech and their manners were different from our own and because to the untutored mind that which is strange is in its infancy ludicrous, but in its prime evil, dangerous, and to be done away with.

These men were put to death because they made you nervous; and your children know it. The minds of your children are like clear pools, reflecting faithfully whatever passes on the bank; whereas in the pool of your own mind, whenever an alien image bends above, a fish of terror leaps to meet it, shattering its reflection.

* * *

I am free to say these things because I am not an Anarchist, although you will say that I am. It is unreasonable to you that a person should go to any trouble in behalf of another person unless the two are members of the same family, or of the same fraternity, or, at the re- [295] motest of the same political party. As regards yourself and the man who lives next door to you, you wish him well, but not so very well. Even if he is a member of the same church as yourself, you do not wish him so inordinately well. Whereas if he does not belong to the same church as yourself, and if, in addition, he does things a little out of the ordinary, such as walk in the street without a hat, you do not wish him well at all. In any case, as regards your neighbor and yourself, although you have no desire to see his house burn down or his children killed in a motor accident, a most modest worldly success will do very well for him, as far as you are concerned. For these and other reasons sufficiently naive and self-revealing, you take it as a matter of course that, of the many persons involved in the recent agitation in Boston, those who were not in the ring for what they could get out of it were revolutionists of the most flagrant dye. It is impossible for you to conceive that men could weep in public and women permit themselves to be thrown in jail because (as it seemed to them) the blue hem of Justice was being dragged in the mire. In the world in which you live Justice is a woman of stone above a courthouse door.

As I said before, I am not sufficiently idealistic to share the political opinions of these men with whose fate I am concerned. It is impossible for me to be an Anarchist, for I do not believe in the essential goodness of man; man is quite patently, to my sight, the worm of the Moody and Sankey hymns. Except for this fact, I should of course think twice before writing as I do. For, although I was born in this country, and am possessed of that simple right of the citizen to hold any opinions he may hold, yet to avail one's self of this right and express opinions contrary to the opinions of the majority may become, as we have lately seen, a folly punishable by the extreme correction. For surely you are not still insisting that these two poor wretches were put to death solely for the crime of murder? You and I both know that we must be careful, not only what we do, but also what we say, and even what we think, if we would not have one day our sleep brutally broken in upon and ourselves rudely forced to enter a place where we do not at all wish to go. And surely you will not deny that, if you would remain undisturbed, it is more important to be on the side of the established order of things than to be innocent of even the grossest crime?

As I said before, I dare say these things because I am not an Anarchist; but I dare say them for another reason, too; because my personal physical freedom, my power to go in and out when I choose, my personal life even, is no longer quite as important to me as it once was. Death even, that outrageous intrusion, appears to me at moments, and more especially when I think of what happened in Boston two months ago, death appears to me somewhat as a darkened room, in which one might rest one's battered temples out of the world's way, leaving the sweeping of the crossings to those who still think it important that the crossings be swept. As if indeed it mattered the least bit in the world whether the crossings be clean or foul, when of all the people passing to and from there in the course of an eight-hour day not one out of ten thousand has a spark of true courage in his heart, or any love at all, beyond the love of a cat for the fire, for any earthly creature other than himself. The world, the physical world, and that once was all in all to me, has at moments such as these no road through a wood, no stretch of shore, that can bring me comfort. The beauty of these things can no longer at such moments make up to me at all for the ugliness of man, his cruelty, his greed, his lying face. [310]

————AFTER the poets had spoken, the Sacco-Vanzetti case was taken up by the playwrights. Maxwell Anderson wrote *Gods of the Lightning* (1928) and *Winterset* (1935) about the case, although only the latter play is of the first order. *The Male Animal* (1939) by James Thurber and Elliott Nugent is a witty play, but its only connection with the Sacco-Vanzetti case is tenuous. The central character is a professor whose job is threatened if he goes through with his plan to read his class Vanzetti's statement to Philip Stong beginning, "If it had not been for these thing . . ."

Probably the most effective literary use of the Sacco-Vanzetti case appears in eight novels published between 1927 and 1946, all of which make extensive use of it. Two of these are outstanding: *Boston* and John Dos Passos' *U.S.A.* (New York, 1937). What most commends *Boston* is the remarkable care with which Sinclair has compiled a perceptive and responsible historical record of the case. Dos Passos' use of the case is more indirect yet more fundamental. As an active worker for the Sacco-Vanzetti Defense Committee, he became deeply involved in the case. During the months in which he worked in Boston writing press releases, addressing meetings, marching in picket lines— and getting arrested for his efforts—Dos Passos developed the conception of American society that is the framework of his great novel, *U.S.A.* Little mention is made of Sacco and Vanzetti in *U.S.A.*, yet the conception of "the two nations" which evolves in the passage below is the central image of the novel.————

THE CAMERA EYE (50)[2]

they have clubbed us off the streets   they are stronger   they are rich   they hire and fire the politicians the newspapereditors the old judges the small men with reputations the collegepresidents the wardheelers (listen businessmen collegepresidents judges America [461] will not forget her betrayers) they hire the men with guns   the uniforms the policecars the patrolwagons

all right you have won   you will kill the brave men our friends tonight

there is nothing left to do   we are beaten   we the beaten crowd together in these old dingy schoolrooms on Salem Street   shuffle up and down the gritty creaking stairs sit hunched with bowed heads on

———
[2] Reprinted from John Dos Passos, *U.S.A.* (New York, 1937: Houghton Mifflin Co.), by permission of the author.

benches and hear the old words of the haters of oppression made new
in sweat and agony tonight

our work is over   the scribbled phrases   the nights typing releases
the smell of the printshop the sharp reek of newprinted leaflets   the
rush for Western Union stringing words into wires the search for
stinging words to make you feel who are your oppressors America.

America our nation has been beaten by strangers who have turned
our language inside out who have taken the clean words our fathers
spoke and made them slimy and foul

their hired men sit on the judge's bench they sit back with their feet
on the tables under the dome of the State House they are ignorant of
our beliefs they have the dollars the guns the armed forces the power-
plants

they have built the electricchair and hired the executioner to throw
the switch

all right we are two nations

America our nation has been beaten by strangers who [462] have
bought the laws and fenced off the meadows and cut down the woods
for pulp and turned our pleasant cities into slums and sweated the
wealth out of our people and when they want to they hire the executioner to throw the switch

but do they know that the old words of the immigrants are being re-
newed in blood and agony tonight do they know that the old American
speech of the haters of oppression is new tonight in the mouth of an
old woman from Pittsburgh of a husky boilermaker from Frisco who
hopped freights clear from the Coast to come here in the mouth of a
Back Bay socialworker in the mouth of an Italian printer of a hobo
from Arkansas   the language of the beaten nation is not forgotten in
our ears tonight

the men in the deathhouse made the old words new before they
died

*If it had not been for these things, I might have lived out my life
talking at streetcorners to scorning men. I might have died unknown,
unmarked, a failure. This is our career and our triumph. Never in our
full life can we hope to do such work for tolerance, for justice, for
man's understanding of man as now we do by an accident.*

now their work is over   the immigrants haters of oppression lie
quiet in black suits in the little undertaking parlor in the North End
the city is quiet   the men of [463] the conquering nation are not to
be seen on the streets

they have won why are they scared to be seen on the streets? on

the streets you see only the downcast faces of the beaten   the streets
belong to the beaten nation   all the way to the cemetery where the
bodies of the immigrants are to be burned   we line the curbs in the
drizzling rain we crowd the wet sidewalks elbow to elbow silent pale
looking with scared eyes at the coffins
  we stand defeated America [464]

————NOR WAS the Sacco-Vanzetti case lacking in legal repercussions,
although these were quite delayed. In 1939 the Massachusetts state
legislature enacted in Chapter 341 of the *Laws of 1939* the following:

.   .   .   .   .

In a capital case the entry in the supreme judicial court shall transfer
to that court the whole case for its consideration of the law and the
evidence, and the court may order a new trial if satisfied that the
verdict was against the law or the weight of the evidence, or because
of newly discovered evidence, or for any other reason that justice may
require.

.   .   .   .   .

————HOW HAD the passage of time affected the surviving members
of the Sacco-Vanzetti jury? Had the world-wide controversy provoked by the jury's decision altered the thinking of any of the jurymen? To find the answers to these questions a reporter on the New
Bedford (Mass.) *Standard-Times* interviewed the surviving members of the Sacco-Vanzetti jury in 1950. Excerpts from his story of
November 12, 1950, appear below.————

.   .   .   .   .

Most important reason for discussing anew the Sacco-Vanzetti case
. . . is that the most authentic and qualified source of information
never has been tapped—until now. That source is . . . —THE JURY.
  Where better to find an answer to the claim that Sacco and Vanzetti were convicted in a hysterically anti-radical period of U. S. history of a crime they did not commit? Who else survives who heard
every syllable of evidence, sized up every witness and can say what
evidence counted most in reaching the verdict?
  The answer would seem to be obvious. Yet in all the years since the
trial, none of the so-called experts, be they columnists, authors or
rostrum "liberals," none ever took the trouble to inquire into the jury.
Until The *Standard-Times* traced down these jurors and recorded their

opinion, they never had been consulted since Sacco and Vanzetti were executed.

. . . . . .

Here is what the seven known survivors of the Sacco-Vanzetti jury told The *Standard-Times* about their memorable verdict:

THE VERDICT OF GUILTY was in accordance with the evidence, was a just verdict, and they would vote the same way today.

THE TRIAL JUDGE was eminently fair, indicated no inkling of prejudice, if he had any, to the jury, and his memory has been inexcusably sullied by defenders of Sacco and Vanzetti.

THE SO-CALLED RADICALISM of the defendants played absolutely no part in the verdict. In fact, the jury is astounded still at the charge to the contrary, and amazed the trial ever became a worldwide cause celebre on that basis.

From children of the four jurors known to be dead, it was learned that their juror-parents shared the sentiments of the survivors.

It can be stated, then, that at least 10 jurors, having heard the evidence, seen the witnesses and lived through fanfare since the trial, have no reason to regret their decision and encountered no evidence that would persuade them the trial and verdict of Sacco and Vanzetti was anything but just. Ripley died too soon after the trial to be included in this category and, as pointed out, the other juror, if he is living, cannot be located.

. . . . . .

Is it not remarkable that none of the so-called experts on the case has consulted this jury or sought to measure the qualifications of the members?

AUTHORS NEVER MET JURORS

In 1949, author Philip Duffield Stong wrote in *The Aspirin Age* of the Sacco-Vanzetti case. His comment on the jury: "A dozen Yankees who had decided on the guilt of the accused before they took their seats."

According to the surviving jurors, Stong is a liar. Before making his incredibly sweeping statement, did Stong take the trouble to meet any of the jurors? He did not.

Does the Sacco-Vanzetti jury fit the condemnation of it by Supreme Court Justice Felix Frankfurter? The latter, in 1921 a Harvard Law School professor, long was articulate in the Sacco-Vanzetti cause. He has written magazine articles alleging a miscarriage of justice by the jury, and also a book. In *The Atlantic* of March 1927, he had this to say:

"In view of the temper of the times, the nature of the accusation, the opinions of the accused, the tactics of the prosecution and the conduct of the judge, no wonder the men of Norfolk convicted Sacco and Vanzetti."

In his book, *Case of Sacco and Vanzetti*, Frankfurter wrote there was no wonder the jury voted for conviction, with its "solidarity against the alien, the indignation against the two draft-dodgers." They had been inflamed by a "riot of political passion and patriotic sentiment," he wrote.

Justice Frankfurter is, more than anybody else, responsible for the widely-accepted belief Sacco and Vanzetti were convicted as radicals, not murderers. He never met or talked to the jurors he said were unfit. He has never tried to.

RECENT BOOK FOLLOWS LINE

Latest book published on the case, *The Legacy of Sacco and Vanzetti*, by Harvard Law School Prof. Edmund M. Morgan and G. Louis Joughin, teacher at New York's New School for Social Research, declares there was a "heavy accumulation of proof that the majority of Americans in 1921 were not well suited for service on a jury trying social undesirables."

Proof of the validity of such a statement would depend on the character of the Sacco-Vanzetti jury. Did the authors of *The Legacy* ever call upon any single member of the jury to see whether their blanket repudiation could be substantiated in the particular case they wrote so hotly about? No juror ever met either author of *The Legacy*.

The law school professor and the sociology teacher refer to the jury as "weak," with it "inevitable that the quality of the verdict should be tainted. A sick society makes sick decisions. The men of Norfolk constituted a jury whose ideals were cognate with their verdict."

Strong words, which neither author, nor any of their predecessor-sympathizers ever made the slightest effort to check for authenticity. They damned the jurymen and let it go at that.

Let us turn to the jury, for evidence of whether they were "weak," "passion-inflamed" and mind-made-up before and during the trial.

ASTOUNDING MEMORY

Most articulate survivor of the tribunal is Mr. Dever. His memory is astounding. Perhaps the fact he became a lawyer after the trial served to impress the details of the case in his mind. Nevertheless, his ability to carry on a narrative account of what transpired, never pausing over a name no matter how obscure, is extraordinary. Mr. Dever's recollections are so fluid, the listener is returned 29 years to the hot June days in the courtroom.

'DEFENDANTS' MAN'

"Funny thing, [too], I was a defendants' man. I say that in all honesty and sincerity. I was a defendants' man all the way through the trial. I don't mean I was determined to vote for their innocence regardless, but I was going to find them not guilty unless the facts proved otherwise, to my definite satisfaction.

"You are the first person formally to ask me anything about the trial. And I'll tell you something I don't think anybody knows.

"When we first left the courtroom for deliberations, I had the feeling that most everybody felt Sacco and Vanzetti were guilty. But I clung to the theory I began the trial with, that we should give them every opportunity. So I suggested, after a brief spell, that we have an informal ballot, nothing binding, just something to get a sample of opinion. My hope was that the ballot would inspire a thorough review of what we had heard and seen.

"Well, that informal ballot was 10-2 for conviction with me one of the two. And just what I hoped would transpire, did. We started discussing things, reviewed the very important evidence about the bullets and everybody had a chance to speak his piece.

"There never was any argument, though. We just were convinced Sacco and Vanzetti had done what the prosecution had charged them with."

How about the enduring charge that the defendants' radicalism was the basis for the finding of guilt by the jury?

"That had nothing whatsoever to do with it," Mr. Dever replied. "Absolutely nothing. The question never came up. I think every juror will tell you that.

"The only thing we considered in the jury room was whether the defendants were guilty as charged by the prosecution in the indictments, or, as I would have expressed it before becoming a lawyer, whether Sacco and Vanzetti did what they were accused of or whether they did not.

RADICALISM TALK 'ABSURD'

"I can repeat it over and over again. That talk of radicalism is absurd. Radicalism had nothing whatsoever to do with it."

.   .   .   .   .

"I was impressed by one aspect of the trial especially," he [John Ganley] recalled. "That was that Judge Thayer was absolutely fearless and absolutely on the level. He was trying to do his job thoroughly and not leaning either way.

"At the final showdown, when the jury was reaching its verdict, there were no objectors. It was 'Guilty.' Nobody had to put up an argument at all. Every member of the jury thought they were guilty.

"The more I've seen and heard, even after the trial, the more I am convinced they were guilty."

Identification testimony made a strong impression on Mr. Ganley at the trial. He recalled that of Reed, the Medfield [sic] railroad crossing tender, who, the juror said, "was given two bawlouts by somebody in the bandit auto for having the gates down," and got "two good looks" at some of the occupants. He identified Vanzetti as an occupant.

TESTIMONY STILL FRESH

Also comparatively fresh in Mr. Ganley's memory was the testimony of Bostock, a machinist, who said he passed two swarthy foreigners of Italian extraction leaning on the Rice and Hutchins fence a moment before the shooting, and the testimony of Mary Splaine, who was at work nearby, and identified Sacco as one of the killers. She saw the shooting from a window 60 feet from the scene.

"It was an entirely just verdict," summed up Mr. Ganley.

Juror King, very much alive at 64, had something in common with Sacco. Both were shoe workers.

Testimony on the bullets stands out in Mr. King's recollection of the evidence. He remembers also his impression that Judge Thayer was "very fair. Every day he cautioned us to remember these men are innocent until proved guilty. He told us to keep our minds open. Repeatedly, repeatedly, he emphasized fairness.

"Anybody who says Sacco and Vanzetti were convicted because they were radicals and not on the evidence is all wet. Propaganda about their being radicals and being framed on the charges did not reach me before the trial. I was just a man in the street, minding my own business.

"As jurors, such talk did not concern us. We felt the defense put the radical element in the trial to hide the issue of murder. During the whole trial, the defense was conducted on the basis of the defendants' being persecuted radicals. It must have consumed at least half of the time.

"My associations with the jury were very fine. They were a bunch of fine men, none of them vindictive. . . ."

·   ·   ·   ·   ·

More reticent about commenting on the trial than any of the other jurors, George A. Gerard of Stoughton says his memory is none too good. He thinks the verdict was entirely fair but that the "case is best forgotten."

"The outstanding thing about that trial was the judge. You can quote me on that. The fairest judge I ever saw or heard of.

"Who are these people who keep bringing up the case and com- [12] plaining about the verdict? If they say the country was witch-hunting those days it must have escaped me. I don't remember all the radical talk. I always thought it was propaganda only."

·   ·   ·   ·   ·

[Frank Marden's] . . . clearest impression from the trial is "the outstanding fairness of Judge Thayer. He was fair to the other side, too, fair all around." He also recalls "the fairness of Mr. Katzmann. He didn't seem to be trying to put anything over on the defense."

Considering the evidence, Mr. Marden was impressed by identification witnesses, particularly Pelser . . . and the bullet testimony. He made the observation all trial witnesses were not in agreement, but added, "In the case of life and death of a man I think people will testify as best they can.

"I never have had a bit of reason to think the trial was anything but fair. I don't think we jurors thought of the defendants in any way except as two persons accused of murder.

'JURY OF ONE MIND'

"The jury got along fine. I remember that when we went out we had a smoke, talked about something else for a few minutes and gradually brought up the subject. Every one was of the same mind, the same opinion, that Sacco and Vanzetti were guilty."

·   ·   ·   ·   ·

LAST JUROR PICKED

The last juror chosen, [Seward Parker] thought it a "very fair trial by a good judge and heard by a good bunch of fellows. There never was a nicer crowd of men than that jury.

"I can't understand why the trial went around the world. They talk of Reds being involved in it, somehow. There never was a mention of Red in the courtroom or among the jury. I've been in hopes lots of times they would forget that trial, but it looks as if those so-called sympathizers will forever be bringing it up. I never could see where the idea of prejudice was picked up.

"Why should we want to pick up two Reds and try to convict them of murder? We did not know if they were Reds and we did not care.

"To my mind, and I really think this, the judge tried to help the defendants. He was square with us, too."

Recalling the evidence that impressed him most, Mr. Parker said, "The bullets, of course. That testimony and evidence on it sticks in your mind. You can't depend on the witnesses. But the bullets, there was no getting around that evidence." [13]

. . . . .

A later era recognizes the grave threat to democratic processes that the fact distorted, or omitted, can be. It is no compliment to American justice and fair play that for these many years the Sacco-Vanzetti jury has been damned in books written without even knowledge of whether its members were alive or dead to respond.

Time continues, of course, its inexorable inroad on the small band of courageous citizens who fulfilled a basic responsibility of citizenship—jury service.

The years have not brought any member riches, but they have brought strengthened conviction that the verdict was in complete accord with the consciences and the evidence—and that it was just. [15]

——————A BOX in the *Standard-Times'* jury story contained the following item:——————

'NO COMMENT'

"I have never commented publicly on the Sacco-Vanzetti case and have no intention of doing so now," said Frederick G. Katzmann of Hyde Park, who as Norfolk County District Attorney in 1921, headed the prosecution staff in the celebrated murder trial. Mr. Katzmann is president of a savings bank and still practices law. [13]

————THE PRECEDING selection from the New Bedford (Mass.) *Standard-Times* makes some important charges against *The Legacy of Sacco and Vanzetti* by G. Louis Joughin and Edmund M. Morgan (New York: Harcourt, Brace and Company, 1948). For this reason a selection from that book discussing the jury is reprinted below.[3]————

Alien, craftsman, agitator, and Red—Sacco. Alien, shiftless laborer or peddler, agitator, and Red—Vanzetti. These reputations must have been known to the thousands of Norfolk citizens, the hundreds of the jury panel, and the twelve men chosen to determine the guilt or innocence of the accused. Now the problem with which we are here engaged is this: To what degree did this knowledge of the men influence the judgment of the jury? Apart from what we might like to believe, is there any proof of deep-seated class aversion having played a part in the finding of a verdict of guilty of murder in the first degree?

If an answer is sought in the form of specific evidence, there is the affidavit against jury-foreman Ripley who is said to have used the expression, "Damn them, they ought to hang them anyway." Neither Judge Thayer's failure to comment on these words nor the pompous sophistries of the Supreme Judicial Court and the Advisory Committee clear Ripley; he stands undefended against the charge of being malicious and unfit to judge another human being. Nevertheless, it is extremely important to remember that only one juror is discredited. We have no right without further proof to assume that any other individual among his eleven fellow jurors was a hateful man given to vulgar and profane prejudgment. Sacco and Vanzetti may well have been found guilty by eleven men as good, true, and decent as could be found in Norfolk county.

When one turns to an examination of the circumstantial evidence, the situation is appallingly different. There is a vast quantity and variety of proof to the effect that nowhere in America, and nowhere in Massachusetts, could any jury have been assem- [203] bled by any ordinary means whose majority would have been free from superstitious fears, irrational hatred, and incapacitating prejudices. Here is the heart of the whole jury problem. Charges against the Sacco-Vanzetti jury

---

[3] Quotation from Louis Joughin and Edmund M. Morgan, *The Legacy of Sacco and Vanzetti*, is by special permission of the authors.

are unprovable; but the incompetence of *any* jury, confronted with an issue of the sort tried at Dedham in 1921, can be proved up to the hilt.

The case of Sacco and Vanzetti against "the jury system" rests, in the first place, upon the reasonable presumption that the opinions and habits of thought which prevail in society at large will have about the same force in any representative selection from the larger group. The thinking of Massachusetts on the crime at Pearl Harbor was like that of America as a whole, and seven or eight hundred Massachusetts men—call them a jury list if you will—could speak for their State. And no doubt twelve men, previously qualified as to average intelligence and sanity, would hold the same general opinions about the Japanese attack. This presumption is fundamentally unassailable; it is the essence of our jury system and makes us all more or less willing to submit to the judgment of our fellows when we stand accused. The "law" of the plaintiffs, as they present it before the court of historical judgment, is simple but sound.

On the whole, this is a fairly effective principle. When a jury assesses damages against a man who has through carelessness burned down his neighbor's house, the verdict probably approximates the opinion which most men would hold on the significance of that accident. Once in a while there will be a man on the jury who long ago has had *his* house burned down—shall we say his name is Ripley? —but after all he is in a minority.

But suppose that the entire nation stands fear-struck before the threat of epidemic disease; and suppose that although the defendant in court is charged with nothing more than carelessness, it is generally known that in another place he has cultivated a horrible virus which may bring death to thousands. In all honesty, what chance has he before a jury of a million, a thousand, or twelve?

There, in all its grim simplicity, lies the substance of the charge against the jury system as it operated in the Sacco-Vanzetti case. The defendants were tried before a jury drawn from a community and a people whose social mind was unfit to deal with any issue involving its hysterical passions.

As far as the jury is concerned, it was inevitable that the qual- [204] ity of the verdict should be tainted. A sick society makes sick decisions. [205]

————THE FOLLOWING letter appeared in the *St. Louis Post-Dispatch*, August 23, 1957.————

To the Editor of the *Post-Dispatch:*

Three decades have passed since the execution of Sacco and Vanzetti in the first few minutes of Aug. 23, 1927.

Those still living of the multitudes of individuals around the world, noted and unknown, who had become convinced at that time the electrocution of the two Italians was a miscarriage of justice, do not need to be reminded of this thirtieth anniversary.

That event in Charlestown Prison close by Boston Common and Charles Bullfinch's Massachusetts State House was an experience for them they have always kept vivid in their consciousness. Ask any one of them what he was doing the night of the execution. He'll invariably respond instantly and in detail, no matter how many thousands of miles he was away from Boston.

*   *   *

This complete memory recall is a phenomenon born of the personal anguish of those days over the imminent fate of Sacco and Vanzetti and what it meant. Not since that time has there been another effort by so many people in so many places to bring about what they conceived to be justice in a particular case.

Questions present themselves insistently when one reflects on the deep-seated personal commitments engendered by that case on so far-flung a front among people of all kinds and conditions.

Could similar commitments be again evoked on such a scale by another case embodying factors and elements like those in the Sacco-Vanzetti case? Or have three decades so altered human circumstances that a comparable evocation would be impossible?

There is value for the community in attempts to answer such questions. The potential role in this regard that the two men's tragedy might play was foreseen by Vanzetti. In one of his final letters from the prison death cell he wrote:

"What I wish more than all else in this last hour of agony is that our case and our fate be understood in their real being and serve as a tremendous lesson to the forces of freedom so that our suffering and death will not have been in vain."

Gutzon Borglum cast that sentence prominently on his large bas-relief of the two men. A standing offer of the sculpture was made 10 years ago, on the twentieth anniversary, to the Governor of Massachusetts and the Mayor of Boston by a committee of prominent citizens which included Albert Einstein, CIO President Philip Murray and Mrs. Franklin D. Roosevelt.

* * *

From his Princeton home on that occasion Einstein said: "Everything should be done to keep alive the tragic affair of Sacco and Vanzetti in the conscience of mankind. They remind us of the fact that even the most perfectly planned democratic institutions are no better than the people whose instruments they are. . . .

"At that time (during the Sacco-Vanzetti case) the desire for justice was as yet more powerful than it is today, although it did not triumph. Too many horrors have since dulled the human conscience. Therefore the fight for the dignity of man is particularly urgent today. May Sacco and Vanzetti continue to live as symbols in all those who strive for a better morality in public affairs."

We share the faith and hope expressed by Einstein and his associates. We sign this letter on the thirtieth anniversary of Sacco's and Vanzetti's execution because we believe that special periodic re-evaluation of notable past experience in the search for justice helps to revitalize that search from generation to generation.

ROGER N. BALDWIN
GARDNER JACKSON
ALDINO FELICANI
JOHN R. CHAMBERLAIN
HOWARD LINDSAY
EUGENE V. ROSTOW
ARTHUR M. SCHLESINGER
JOHN DOS PASSOS
EUGENE LYONS
NORMAN THOMAS
GERALD W. JOHNSON

New York City. [2B]

BIBLIOGRAPHY

The following works are some of those consulted in the preparation of this book. Many but not all of them are referred to or quoted in the text. The most complete Sacco-Vanzetti bibliography will be found in *The Legacy of Sacco and Vanzetti*, pp. 557-580.

BOOKS

Anderson, Maxwell, and Harold Hickerson. *Gods of the Lightning,* [and] *Outside Looking In.* New York: Longmans, 1928.

Broun, Heywood. *Collected Edition of Heywood Broun.* Ed. H. H. Broun. New York: Harcourt, 1941. Contains the powerful but inflammatory columns Broun wrote on the Sacco-Vanzetti case in August, 1927, in *The World* as well as Ralph Pulitzer's letter explaining why he ordered Broun to stop writing about the case.

De Voto, Bernard. *We Accept With Pleasure.* Boston: Little, Brown, 1934. A novel in which the Sacco-Vanzetti case figures importantly.

Dictionary of American Biography. New York: Scribner's, 1935. The Sacco-Vanzetti article is at 16:279-80. "S.G." is Silvester Gates.

Dos Passos, John. *The Big Money.* New York: Harcourt, 1936.

———. *U.S.A.* New York: Harcourt, 1937. *The Big Money* is the last third of this trilogy.

———. *Facing the Chair; Story of the Americanization of Two Foreign-born Workmen.* Boston: Sacco-Vanzetti Defense Committee, 1927. A booklet that anticipates Dos Passos' later more implicit analysis of the case.

Ehrmann, Herbert B. *The Untried Case: The Sacco-Vanzetti Case and the Morelli Gang.* New York: Vanguard, 1933. The fascinating story of the search precipitated by the Medeiros confession as told by a man who was one of the defense lawyers during the last year of the case.

Fraenkel, Osmond K. *The Sacco-Vanzetti Case.* In the *American Trials* series. New York: Knopf, 1931. The longest and most complete analysis of the legal aspects of the case.

Frankfurter, Felix. *The Case of Sacco and Vanzetti: A Critical Analysis for Lawyers and Laymen.* Boston: Little, Brown, March, 1927. The most provocative, widely discussed book about the case.

Grabill, Ethelbert V. *Sacco and Vanzetti in the Scales of Justice.* Boston: The Fort Hill Press, 1927. This relatively rare book is among the very few written in support of the prosecution.

Joughin, G. Louis, and Edmund M. Morgan. *The Legacy of Sacco and Vanzetti*. New York: Harcourt, Brace, 1948. A superb study of the legacy of the case to law and literature written by a professor of law and a professor of literature.

Musmanno, Michael A. *After Twelve Years*. New York, London: Knopf, 1939. A review of the last weeks of the case by the attorney who was most active in getting the case into the Federal courts.

Sacco, Nicola, and Bartolomeo Vanzetti. *The Letters of Sacco and Vanzetti*. Ed. Marion Denman Frankfurter and Gardner Jackson. New York: Viking, 1928.

The Sacco-Vanzetti Case; Transcript of the Record of the Trial of Nicola Sacco and Bartolomeo Vanzetti in the Courts of Massachusetts and Subsequent Proceedings, 1920-7. 5 vols. With a supplemental volume on the Bridgewater case. New York: Holt, 1928-29.

Sinclair, Upton. *Boston*. Pasadena, Calif.: Upton Sinclair, 1928.

Thurber, James, and Elliott Nugent. *The Male Animal*. New York: French, 1941.

Wells, Herbert G. *Mr. Blettsworthy on Rampole Island*. New York: Doubleday, 1928. A fantasy based on the Sacco-Vanzetti case.

MAGAZINE ARTICLES

Beffel, John N. "Eels and the Electric Chair." *New Republic*, 25:127-29 (December 29, 1920). Possibly the earliest article in a national periodical to deal with the case.

Cowley, Malcolm. "Echoes of a Crime." *New Republic*, 134:79 (August 28, 1935).

Dewey, John. "Psychology and Justice." *New Republic*, 53:9-12 (November 23, 1927).

Frankfurter, Felix. "Case of Sacco and Vanzetti." *Atlantic Monthly*, 139: 409-32 (March, 1927).

"Radicals." *Time*, 10:9-10 (August 29, 1927).

"Reaffirming the Sacco-Vanzetti Verdict." *Literary Digest*, 94:5-7 (August 20, 1927).

Thompson, William G. "Vanzetti's Last Statement." *Atlantic Monthly*, 141: 254-57 (February, 1928). One of Vanzetti's last lawyers reports on his final interview with his client the day of his execution.

[It should be emphasized that the above bibliography contains only a small portion of the materials available on the case.]

EXERCISES

Four kinds of topics are presented below. For each chapter there are discussion questions which can be used in class, topics for library research, and topics for short documented essays ranging from 250 to 1,000 words. Following the exercises for Chapter 7 is a list of major topics for longer documented essays.

The topics for library research are designed to acquaint the student with some of the basic reference sources, *e.g.*, *Readers' Guide to Periodical Literature*, *New York Times Index*, *Book Review Digest*, *Encyclopedia Britannica*, and *Dictionary of American Biography*.

Many of the topics for shorter papers have been designed to provide the student with practice in a variety of the basic rhetorical forms, for example, *definition, comparison, characterization, process analysis, argument, evaluation*, and *classification*.

Chapter 1. *SETTING THE STAGE:* 1919-1921

1. Consult the *Dictionary of American Biography* for information on Sacco and Vanzetti and the case. Write a brief report of your findings.
2. Do the newspaper articles and editorials in this chapter prove that any jury impanelled in 1921 would have been hostile to aliens, radicals, and draft dodgers? Would it be easier to select an unprejudiced jury today?
3. Write a documented analysis of several pages in length of *The New York Times'* handling of the Red Scare of 1919-1921.
4. State the case for suppression—or control—of alien radicals and the case against it as they are presented in the materials found in this chapter. Document your paper.

Chapter 2. *THE TRIAL*

A. *The Case for the Commonwealth*

1. Write a short documented paper defining one of the following terms: circumstantial evidence, hearsay, murder, or reasonable doubt. Consult not only the material in this chapter but also a law dictionary.
2. What do you learn about Sacco, Katzmann, and Judge Thayer from Katzmann's lengthy cross-examination of Sacco?
3. Write several pages of documented comparison of the openings by

Williams and Callahan. Speculate on the effect of each of them on the jury. Which is more effective? Why?

4. Write several pages analyzing the handling of the identification issue by the prosecution.

5. Write a comparison of the credibility of Splaine and Bostock.

B. *The Case for the Defense*

1. Is it possible that Sacco and Vanzetti, as aliens, were not subject to the draft? Vanzetti hints at this in his direct examination. Consult the World War I "Selective Service Act" in *The United States Code*.

2. Vanzetti wrote in a letter after the trial that if William Thompson had represented him and Sacco, they would have been acquitted. Do you agree that another lawyer might have achieved what the McAnarney brothers and Moore could not?

3. Write a critique of the handling of the issue of consciousness of guilt by the defense. What did they do and what might they have done?

4. Write a critical discussion of the alibi evidence.

C. *Summations*

1. One legal authority has commented that an opinion as to whether Sacco and Vanzetti had a fair trial might almost be reached by studying only the closing speeches by the defense and prosecution. Discuss this or write an analysis of the two sets of speeches.

2. Re-write some phase of the closing argument for either defense or prosecution as you think it should have been written. Preface your paper with a brief explanation of the defects you are attempting to correct.

D. *Charge to the Jury*

1. Consult both the trial record and a law dictionary for a definition of the term "consciousness of guilt."

2. Write an analysis of Judge Thayer's charge to the jury to support the conclusion that he was a) partial, or b) impartial.

3. Is Judge Thayer's handling of the issue of identification fair or distorted?

Chapter 3. *SHOULD THERE BE A NEW TRIAL?*

1. Explain the difference between the type of material that the Supreme Judicial Court could review and could not.

2. Use *New York Times Index* to check on the facts cited in the Dearborn (Mich.) *Independent* editorial.

3. Discuss the logic of Judge Thayer's lengthy denial of the Proctor and Gould motions.

4. Use the *Readers' Guide to Periodical Literature* to write a short report on the number and type of magazine articles published on the Sacco-

Vanzetti case from 1921 to 1927. Characterize the magazines that published most of the articles.

5. In denying the motions for a new trial, the Supreme Judicial Court ruled that Judge Thayer had exercised "judicial discretion." This term has been defined as follows: ". . . the calmness of a cool mind, free from partiality, not swayed by sympathy nor warped by prejudice nor moved by any kind of influence save alone the overwhelming passion to do that which is just." (*Davis* v. *Boston Elevated Railroad*, 235 Massachusetts 482, 496-7.) Using this definition, or one of your own, write a documented discussion of Judge Thayer's conduct in which you attack or defend the Supreme Judicial Court's ruling.

Chapter 4. *THE SENTENCE*

1. Consult a copy of a newspaper or magazine carrying a news story describing the sentencing of Sacco and Vanzetti. Write a brief report commenting on the accuracy of the story (as compared to the materials in this book taken from the *Transcript*) and the absence or presence of editorializing.

2. To what extent do Sacco's and Vanzetti's speeches to the court before sentencing reveal the characters of the two men and the differences between them?

Chapter 5. *LAST EFFORTS*: April 10-August 22, 1927

1. After consulting the *Book Review Digest*, write a brief documented report on the critical reception of *The Letters of Sacco and Vanzetti*.

2. Compare Philip Stong's version of Vanzetti's statement, "If it were not for these thing . . .," to the version quoted by Dos Passos in *U.S.A.* (See Chapter 7.) What are the differences? Which version is a) more likely Vanzetti's, b) more effective?

3. In its Report, the Advisory Committee stated that "the District Attorney was not in any way guilty of unprofessional behavior." One legal definition of the proper behavior of a district attorney is contained in a Supreme Court decision which states that he is ". . . the representative not of an ordinary party to a controversy, but of a sovereignty whose obligation to govern impartially is as compelling as its obligation to govern at all; and whose interest, therefore, in a criminal prosecution is not that it shall win a case, but that justice shall be done." (*Berger* v. *United States*) (Note also what Mr. Williams' opening statement says about the district attorney's duty.) Would you say that the prosecution in this case operated within the above stated limits?

4. Write a character sketch of either Sacco or Vanzetti based on material from the letters.

5. Analyze, step by step, the legal process through which the defendants passed from the moment of their arrest on the streetcar to their execution in Charlestown Jail seven years later.

6. Write a brief comparison of the appellate procedure in Massachusetts in 1920-27 and today.

Chapter 6. *THE EXECUTION*

1. Compare *The New York Times'* story on the execution to the Associated Press story. Is it apparent that the AP story was written by a first-hand observer? Does either story reveal any bias? (To obtain the AP story, consult the newspaper files of your library.)

2. Compare the story of the execution of Sacco and Vanzetti in *Time* magazine to the story in the same magazine of the execution of the two atomic spies, Julius and Ethel Rosenberg. Write a brief report discussing the differences in the way in which the two events are written up. Are the articles equally objective?

Chapter 7. *THE REPERCUSSIONS*

1. "The more the evidence is examined, the less heroic and the less odious do the leading actors become. The case was not a battle between good and evil, and such a view simplifies it to meaninglessness." Does this comment on the Dreyfus case apply also to the Sacco-Vanzetti case?

2. Compare the articles on the Sacco-Vanzetti case in the current *Encyclopedia Britannica* and *Encyclopedia Americana*. Write a short discussion of the more striking and significant differences between these two articles. What conclusions about the case and about encyclopedias does your comparison lead you to?

3. How do you account for the opinions expressed by the jurors in 1950?

4. Does the New Bedford *Standard-Times* reporter accurately represent what *The Legacy of Sacco and Vanzetti* says about the jury?

5. Many letters were written to *Outlook* commenting on "Fear," the Edna St. Vincent Millay article. The editors of the magazine turned over a group of these to an eminent psychologist, Dr. Joseph Jastrow, who wrote an analysis of them in the following issue of *Outlook*. Read the letters and his analysis of them; then write a short documented essay supporting or attacking his views.

6. Compare the Millay poem, "Justice Denied in Massachusetts," to "Fear." Which is more effective? Why? (The poem can be found in *Buck in the Snow* by Edna St. Vincent Millay or in the *Collected Poems* of that author.)

7. Consult a dictionary of quotations to see if either of the defendants is quoted in it. Can you justify the inclusion of the material? Can you suggest material from the case that would be more deserving of inclusion?

TOPICS FOR LONGER PAPERS

1. Using the Sacco-Vanzetti case as a source of illustrative evidence, write an essay on the strengths and weaknesses of our adversary system of justice.

2. Answer the question: Did justice prevail in the Sacco-Vanzetti case? In working out your definition of justice, consult Judge Thayer's advice in his charge to the jury, "Let your eyes be blinded to every ray of sympathy." Contrast this advice to the following statement: "Justice entails understanding; and the most direct way to understand men is to approach them with sympathy." (Piero Calamandrei, *Procedural Democracy*, N.Y.U. Press, 1956, p. 51.)

3. Discuss the problems raised by expert testimony, using the Sacco-Vanzetti case as a source of examples. Judge Learned Hand has said that the objections to expert testimony are that ". . . the expert becomes a hired champion of one side; second, that he is the subject of . . . contradictions by other experts." ("Historical and Practical Considerations Regarding Expert Testimony," 15 *Harvard Law Review*, 40, 1901.) Should experts be barred from the courtroom? Should they be controlled? How?

4. Write a documented essay contrasting Sacco and Vanzetti. Do not attempt to show one was innocent, the other guilty. Instead, use their testimony, letters, and reactions to arrest and conviction to point up their differences and similarities.

5. Write a comparison between the Sacco-Vanzetti case and some other famous case, e.g., Dreyfus case, Mooney case, Salem witchcraft trials, Haymarket affair, or the Gastonia case [199 No. Car. 278, 298 (1930)].

6. Make a study of the coverage of the Sacco-Vanzetti case by one newspaper or a study comparing the coverage of two newspapers, preferably one liberal and one conservative, e.g., *St. Louis Post-Dispatch* and *Boston Evening Transcript*.

7. Write a documented analysis of the role played in the case by one of the following: Judge Thayer, Prosecutor Katzmann, or counsel for the defense.

8. Judge Thayer thought that "consciousness of guilt" was what convicted Sacco and Vanzetti. Write an analysis of this important issue in the trial.

9. Identification occupied a major part of the testimony heard at the trial. Describe the various problems of identification in this case and the tactics used by the prosecution and the defense in attempting to cope with them.

10. Vanzetti in his petition for clemency described himself as an anarchist and referred Governor Fuller (who said he did not know what the term meant) to the Kropotkin article on anarchism in the 14th edition of the *Encyclopedia Britannica*. Read the article and in the light of it discuss Vanzetti's anarchism as it is revealed in his testimony and letters.

11. Read *U.S.A.* (or the last third of it, *The Big Money*), *Boston*, *Winterset*, *Gods of the Lightning*, or *The Male Animal*, and write a discussion of its effectiveness as a commentary on the Sacco-Vanzetti case.

12. Use the *Readers' Guide to Periodical Literature* to select two or more major articles dealing with the Sacco-Vanzetti case; read the articles and write a critical analysis of them.

13. Examine a half dozen different periodicals published during August, 1927. Write a documented essay classifying their responses to the Sacco-Vanzetti case. Some suggested sources: *Literary Digest, Outlook, New Republic, Time, The New York Times, Spectator* (London), and a newspaper from your city or state if one is available in the library.

14. Write a full-page editorial similar to the one reprinted from *The World* of August 19, 1927, or to the Pulitzer-Prize-winning editorial in the Boston *Herald* of October 25, 1926. Sum up the principal evidence and arguments on one phase of the case and vigorously defend your position.

15. Write an analysis of some aspect of the defense attempts to secure a new trial, for example, Medeiros and the Morelli gang, efforts to enter the Federal courts, the Proctor motion, etc.

16. On Dec. 24, 1919, two bandits attempted to rob the $35,000 payroll of the L. Q. White Shoe Co. as it was being transported in a truck through the streets of Bridgewater, Mass. One of the bandits fired a shotgun at the truck, but the men guarding the truck fired back and drove on, successfully evading the bandits. On June 11, 1920, Vanzetti was charged with being the bandit who fired the shotgun in the Bridgewater assault. He was tried in Plymouth before Judge Thayer with Frederick G. Katzmann representing the Commonwealth. On July 1, 1920, a jury found Vanzetti guilty of assault with intent to rob and murder. Judge Thayer sentenced him to the State Prison for from twelve to fifteen years.

Although the record of the Bridgewater case is not complete, it bears a significant relationship to the Sacco-Vanzetti case. Two of Vanzetti's lawyers, William G. Thompson and Herbert Ehrmann, called it, ". . . a crude dress rehearsal of the tragedy later enacted at Dedham." Read the stenographic minutes of the Bridgewater case (it occupies 299 pages of a supplemental volume of the *Transcript*), and write an analysis of that trial. Emphasize the parallels between the two trials as well as the value of the Bridgewater case in increasing our understanding of the later case.

17. Write a critical analysis of this book. Your aim might be to discover how objectively and effectively the editor has presented the case. This would require you to compare the primary source materials available

to the editor, or some segment of them, to the selections from them in this collection. You could select a given time period of the trial and compare the complete stenographic minutes to the selections taken from them; you could compare the treatment accorded a given episode in the *Transcript* and this book; or, you could examine part of the large body of material from which the editor selected letters, editorials, and articles. You might, for example, read all of the collected letters of Sacco and Vanzetti.

INDEX